Black Marquette

In Their Own Words

Black Marquette

In Their Own Words

Overcoming Obstacles and Achieving Success

Edited by Valerie Wilson Reed
with George Lowery

©2021
Marquette University Press
Milwaukee WI 53201-3141
Founded 1916

Library of Congress Cataloging-in-Publication Data

Names: Reed, Valerie Wilson, 1957- editor. | Lowery, George, 1946- editor.
Title: Black Marquette in their own words : "overcoming obstacles and
  achieving success" / edited by Valerie Wilson Reed with George Lowery.
Description: Milwaukee : Marquette University Press, 2021. | Summary:
  "Black Marquette in Their Own Words: "Overcoming Obstacles & Achieving
  Success" is a collection of essays from or about African American alumni
  of Marquette University and how their college experiences influenced
  their successes. The years span from the 1920's to the 2000's"--
  Provided by publisher.
Identifiers: LCCN 2020047114 | ISBN 9781626000582 (hardcover)
Subjects: LCSH: Marquette University--Alumni and alumnae--Biography. |
  African American college graduates--Wisconsin--Marquette--Biography.
Classification: LCC LD3231.M5419 B53 2021 | DDC 378.1/982077595--dc23
LC record available at https://lccn.loc.gov/2020047114

The gratitude of the editors is extended to Marquette University
for their support of this project

Book and cover design by Shawn Biner

First printing March 2021
Manufactured in the United States of America

ASSOCIATION
of UNIVERSITY
PRESSES

DEDICATION

To ALL parents, who worked extremely hard to provide the education,
love and support that brought us to and through Marquette; the university
that has become such an integral part of our lives including my parents,
the late Charles F. Wilson and Evelyn Jones Wilson.

Table of Contents

The Golden Eagle Years

(1994 – Current)

Photographs |

Acknowledgements

A PROFOUND THANK YOU to all those who took time out of their very busy lives to provide their essays for this ambitious project.

Extreme gratitude is given to Provost Kimo Ah Yun for enthusiastically embracing this project and providing his unwavering support. His encouragement and the backup of the Office of the Provost was invaluable. Many thanks to the Marquette Press, the Klingler College of Arts & Sciences, former interim Dean Heather Hathaway, Associate Dean James South, and Maureen Kondrick for giving their blessings and support to bring this project to fruition.

A sincere debt of gratitude must be extended to Dr. Arnold Mitchem, the founding director of Marquette University's Educational Opportunity Program (EOP) in 1969. Dr. Mitchem's efforts made it possible for more than 10,000 students of color, some of whom submitted essays for the Black Marquette Book Project, to receive a college degree.

George Lowery, former head of the Upward Bound Program at Marquette University and Professor Emeritus at Roosevelt University, who was the first Marquette person I approached about the idea of writing the book. His interest and support was the impetus I needed to push forward.

Of special assistance was Rachelle Shurn, Engagement Officer at Marquette, who provided enthusiastic support with research of Black Alumni as well as accompanied me on a very special interview.

A special mention goes to Douglas Kelley. Douglas, the dedicated Black alumni, spent decades securing the sanctioning of the Ethnic Alumni Association (EAA), and becoming the organization's first president. Douglas went on to be elected as the first Black President of Marquette University's National Alumni Association. He was pivotal in providing names and contact information for this project. Also lending their contact and follow-up support was Robert Simpson and Nkozi "Jay" Knight, the current President of the Black Alumni Association (BAA), formally known as the Ethnic Alumni Association (EAA).

Sande Robinson (former Director of EOP), Rose Richard (former Assistant Dean of the College of Communications) and Howard Fuller (Director, Institute for the Transformation of Learning at MU) are legends among the Black students at Marquette, spending many years recruiting, nurturing, mentoring and supporting them. They were an invaluable resource in providing sources and information for this book project.

A special acknowledgement to Don Wycliff, former editorial page editor of the *Chicago Tribune* and editor of *Black Domers*, the book of Black Alumni at Notre Dame University for his invaluable information regarding the process of his book's conception.

Relatives of several deceased alumni from the fifties provided us with their stories and photographs. They are Joy Bennett, a Marquette Legacy and daughter of Gloria Sylvester Bennett, and Phyllis Stone, daughter of Betty Marie (Johnson) Washington.

Ralph H. Metcalfe, Sr., is undoubtedly one of Marquette's most accomplished and earliest Black alumni. He was an exceptional student, defiant track star & medalist in the 1936 Olympics in Hitler's Germany, a congressman from Chicago, and co-founder of the Congressional Black Congress. It is befitting that the proceeds from this book will be donated to the Ralph H. Metcalfe, Sr., Scholarship Fund, which provides much needed financial support to African American students through the Black Alumni Association of Marquette University.

Finally, I would be remiss if I didn't acknowledge my husband, Reginald Reed, who patiently endured the numerous and sometimes ungodly hours I spent involved with this project. And, Cathy Stamps Covington, the first friend I met at Marquette and still best friends to this day, who listened to me almost every day and provided her support.

Valerie Wilson Reed

Preface

THE "BLACK MARQUETTE BOOK" was an idea I had been considering for over eight years. I had the pleasure to serve as a founding member and past president of the Ethnic Alumni Association (EAA) followed by my years serving on Marquette University's Alumni Association's National Board of Directors and MUAA's Past President. I attended numerous MU events, meeting Marquette alumni throughout the country. But where were our Black alumni? What are they doing now? I knew thousands existed. Many graduated with the support of the Educational Opportunity Program (EOP). It was as though many of MU's Black alumni were living in the shadows of the university — keeping their successes under wraps. A few perhaps feeling the misconceived notion that MU did not care. Therefore, I asked Marquette and they decided it was time. Time for them to share their essays "in their own words" and stories of "Overcoming Obstacles and Achieving Success." Time for all of Marquette to know about their success and pride in being a Marquette Alumni.

But who would have predicted that in the beginning of this book project, we would be hit hard by a global pandemic with over 360,000 deaths to date in the United States alone in less than one year. And in the midst of this, the killings of African American men and women like Breonna Taylor, Ahmaud Arbery and of George Floyd, an unarmed Black man killed by rogue white police officers in Minneapolis, Minnesota. Floyd's death sparking worldwide Black Lives Matter rallies and protests; opening the eyes of all races, ages, genders, social and economic backgrounds to the long history of racism resulting from slavery in the United States. The banding together for a change in systematic racism towards Black lives in the areas of health, education, employment, voting rights, and police brutality. All of these events making this Black Marquette Book project even more relevant and timely by highlighting the successes of African American alumni in the area of education, media, medicine, engineering, government, entertainment, business and sports.

Historically, Marquette admitted its first female undergraduates on June 28, 1909, making Marquette the first Catholic university in the world to accept women. However, many Marquette Alumni are not aware that Marquette University accepted its first known Black students in the 1920s and '30s. The exact date is not documented regarding the first Black student since records were not available noting race. It is possible that several black students "passed" as white, as they were able to easily assimilate among their white counterparts because of their fair skin. They did not reveal their race at the time in order for them to receive an education. We do know of Mabel Rainey, the first African American woman to attend Marquette's Law School in the late 1920s, passing the Wisconsin Bar Association and becoming an attorney in the Milwaukee area.

A good number are familiar with some notable and famous MU African American alumni such as actor and comedienne Rondell Sheridan, Congresswoman Gwen Moore (D-Wisconsin) and famous athletes including Dwayne Wade, Jimmy Butler and Jae Crowder. But in the 1930s there was Ralph H. Metcalfe, Sr., the first well-known Black student to attend MU, who graduated cum laude from Marquette in 1936. He helped put Marquette on the world stage with his medal winning participation in the 1932 Olympics in Germany. He went on to a career in politics and service during the Civil Rights movement in Chicago. Metcalfe is undoubtedly one of Marquette's most accomplished alumni. It is fitting that the proceeds from this book benefit the Black Alumni Association's Ralph H. Metcalfe, Sr., Scholarship Fund in his honor.

It was a struggle for some Black alumni to complete their essay. A few of those participating described it as "peeling off a band-aid" to reveal some of the memories. There were tears shed. But those tears washed away the negative and turned to tears of joy. Joy for the lifelong friendships they made. Appreciation for the Jesuit education they received and for the professors and administrators who made a positive difference in their lives. Fond memories of the activities they participated in that helped them make it through those college years.

This book is a labor of love—a love of Marquette and the love of the students who proudly attended the university. Though the book highlights the lives, struggles and successes of Black students over the years, it is a reminder to all students that you can overcome any obstacles and achieve success.

This book is about MARQUETTE PRIDE. The pride of the all African American alumni of Marquette University of whom many of their successes have gone unnoticed and overlooked. Many of the accomplishments hidden in the shadows to now be celebrated in the light by all of Marquette alumni.

This book is just the BEGINNING. Over 150 requests for essays were sent out to a group of MU Black alumni. The selections in this book are a small sampling of the Black Alumni that have passed through the doors of Marquette Hall, and walked the campus blocks of Wisconsin Avenue and Wells Streets in search of an education; finding out who they are and who they strive to be. These are their stories in their own words. There are many more stories left to be told. It is my hope that this Black Marquette Book will continue to be updated in the years to come. This book only scratched the surface of our many accomplishments. But the ultimate goal is that there will come a time where a specific book highlighting the successes of Black alumni will be included in Marquette's overall successes because WE ARE MARQUETTE!

Valerie Wilson Reed

Foreword

Michael R. Lovell, President

THROUGHOUT MY UNIVERSITY CAREER, a constant has been how education flows both ways. Yes, faculty, staff and administrators all have a significant role to play in educating our students. Yet students, whether they know it or not, are constantly educating us, too. That doesn't stop when students graduate. Our alumni continue to show us the way on how the world is being made better by how they are applying their Marquette University experience to the world around them.

This book further illuminates this reality, with the stories being brought together by an individual who has lived and breathed the Marquette experience since first arriving here as a student in the 1970s. Valerie Wilson Reed has an advantage over me in that she came under the mentorship of one of my most distinguished predecessors, Rev. John P. Raynor, SJ, Marquette's president 1965–1990 and then its chancellor 1991–1997. Father Raynor's many accomplishments included leading Marquette's response to the social unrest of the 1960s, which included the creation of the Education Opportunity Program. Marquette's EOP became a national model for educating first-generation and low-income students, and just celebrated its 50th anniversary.

She stayed in touch with Fr. Raynor, even sharing with him the shortcomings of alumni events she attended years after graduation. The solution was straightforward, he replied, if you don't see ethnic diversity in alumni activities, help us lead the change. She did and we did and, again, our students-turned-alumni were educating us.

Another of my outstanding predecessors, Rev. Robert A. Wild, SJ, came to learn from and appreciate Valerie's continued support of Marquette when she helped lead creation of the Marquette Ethnic Alumni Association and fundraising for the association's Ralph Metcalfe, Sr., Scholarship during his tenure as president. She's gone on to further serve on Diederich College of Communication and Marquette University–wide committees and boards.

On top of all that, Valerie is one of our most dedicated alumni fans of Marquette Athletics. I don't recall being to a single Chicago-area basketball game during my tenure as president that didn't include her among our most passionate fans.

As might be expected from someone with such a wide range of experiences, Valerie made a lot of connections. It's from such relationships that a book like this one becomes possible. That's because for Black alumni to tell their Marquette stories honestly, there's going to be good and, unfortunately, some bad.

I know because even now, in the Fall 2020 academic semester, Black students are rightly continuing to demand that everyone should feel welcomed and supported at Marquette, regardless of skin color. It's an issue that students, staff and faculty have been working on for years. I believe that some progress has been made. I also know that change has neither been as fast, nor as thorough, as everyone wants. I have gained a healthy appreciation for those who succeed and want to tell their stories. I know the reader will learn from their stories, too. We will all also be thanking Valerie for bringing these stories together in this book. Clearly, she continues to hear Fr. Raynor's encouragement from so many years ago: get involved and help make changes happen.

Reflections

Robert A. Wild, SJ, Past President

As I LOOK BACK over my sixteen years as Marquette's president, one of things I am most proud of is the success of the Ethnic Alumni Association, now the Black Alumni Association. I started as president in 1996 and knew right from the start that one of the things I would really need to do would be to go around to our various alumni gatherings and meet many of the men and women who had graduated from MU and begin to get to know them. That was something I really enjoyed doing, but as time passed and I visited more and more groups, I couldn't help but notice a considerable disparity between the rather sizeable number of African-American graduates that I knew we had in our records and the small number of such men and women that I actually was meeting at these gatherings. Some very splendid alums to be sure, but not very many of them in attendance.

Our National Alumni Board, it turned out, was also aware of this problem, and there was a proposal on the table with them for the creation of a new alumni chapter that would be open to all but respond especially to the interests and needs of our Black graduates. The Board discussed this proposal at length, but when it came to a vote, they found themselves split right down the middle, some thinking this type of alumni group would really be worth a try, others worried about the separateness and possible divisiveness of it. The next year, after I asked the Board to reconsider the whole matter, the same thing happened. I said to them, "Look, what we are doing now isn't working, that's for sure. So let me as president break this deadlock and say we should go ahead with the new proposal." Which we did —and am I glad, so very glad, that we did so!

I still vividly remember our first meeting of the Ethnic Alumni Association. It was down in Chicago on one of the upper floors of the Sears Tower. What a wonderful gathering that meeting was! A great turnout, about sixty or seventy people, not only people from Chicago and Milwaukee, but also from Indianapolis and even one couple who came all the way from Atlanta.

The energy and excitement among the group? Electric! Just so much excitement! It was clear—with the EAA we had a winner. We went from the success of that first gathering and never looked back.

Reports of that first meeting and its splendid success spread rapidly among MU's Black alumni, and the membership list of the new EAA/BAA alumni chapter steadily grew. We at Marquette encourage all our alumni chapters to increase their numbers, to encourage family members and friends who are looking at colleges to think Marquette and to raise money for scholarships, and the EAA membership responded enthusiastically and generously.

But what was of most importance to me were the repeated opportunities to meet numerous MU Black alums from around the country and hear from them the gratitude they had for their Marquette experience and for the opportunity now to gather as proud Black members of the MU alumni association. Not that all their experiences back then as students and even now as graduates were always what they should have been. But they recognized that Marquette was steadily working to make things better in that regard. And as members of a large and important alumni chapter, they would now have a larger voice in university affairs.

It is well worth mentioning, as Valerie Reed reminded me, that this present book of reflections on the Black experience at Marquette would never have been possible without the existence and success of this alumni chapter, the Black Alumni Association of Marquette. We would not even have known who to ask to provide such reflections. That sixty-one of you proved willing to do so offers just by itself powerful testimony to the value of the BAA.

For my part, I found it an honor and a privilege to get to know many of the members of this impressive group of alumni. May the God of us all bless and be with the BAA and all the men and women who belong to it, whether living or deceased. Again, thank you for your involvement with and care for our Marquette University.

Dr. Kimo Ah Yun, Provost

ANY PERSON OF COLOR who has attended college in the United States likely knows well the obstacles—many of them built into our systems—to success. From gaining admission to securing funding to graduating, the college experience for people of color is frequently marked by struggle, four and often more years of financial insecurity and frequent bouts of self-doubt.

It also means that crossing that stage at graduation is even more gratifying.

That is why this collection of essays from Black Marquette alumni is so important. In *Overcoming Obstacles and Achieving Success*, Valerie Wilson Reed has captured in raw, first-person detail the struggles and the triumphs of Black students at Marquette University.

Struggles punctuated by triumph were certainly my experiences as a first generation undergraduate student of color at California State University, Sacramento, and later at Kansas State University and Michigan State University where I respectively earned my master's and doctoral degrees. Each step of my journey was difficult, but each success fueled and motivated me to reach the next milestone. Education changed the trajectory of my life and I am so grateful to the many people who pushed me to get better each and every day.

When I was named provost at Marquette University, I had no moment of "I've made it." Rather, it gave me pause; it was a moment of deep reflection that I learned to appreciate more than I ever thought would be possible through the many Jesuits I am fortunate to spend time with at Marquette. As the first person of color to lead the university's academic enterprise, I understood what that meant to the institution. I had to reconcile what it could and should mean to me.

While it meant a lot of things, many of them deeply personal, one thing was clear: I was duty bound to improve the campus climate for students of color at Marquette. I am proud to play a small part in the strides the university has made in the areas of diversity, equity and inclusion. We have more faculty of color than ever before and we recently welcomed our most diverse incoming class. But there is more to do.

If we are to truly live out our Catholic, Jesuit mission and remain committed to the vision Archbishop Henni laid out 140 years ago, we have to work hard every day and make tough decisions. Diversity is not a goal to be achieved or a box to be checked—it is an evolving pursuit to make Marquette more reflective of the world around us.

Overcoming Obstacles and Achieving Success threads that evolution together through personal, poignant reflections. Though the alumni essays are candid and unvarnished, taken together they are not an indictment of the university's shortcomings or failures. Instead, the book celebrates those strong young Black women and men whose lived experience at Marquette made it a better place.

My great hope is that *Overcoming Obstacles and Achieving Success* becomes standard reading for incoming Marquette students, particularly our students of color. I hope the words of those who came before them provide solace and inspiration, a clear message that our struggles are worth the sweetness of our triumphs.

Dr. William C. Welburn,
Vice President for Inclusive Excellence

"THERE IS THE DEFINITE DESIRE and determination to have a history, well documented … and administered as a stimulating and inspiring tradition for the coming generations." —Arturo Schomburg, *The Negro Digs Up His Past*

It is an honor as someone who is not an alumnus of Marquette University to be able to add a brief reflection to this remarkable volume. This work is long over-due for several reasons; however, the most salient among many that might be given is absence. Absence of a narrative that is so central to the history of Marquette and to Jesuit higher education in the United States, a history of the manner in which Black students sought and achieved their aspirations over generations and in ways that mirror the changes that we have borne witness to in our society.

As with colleges and universities across America, the late 1960s were a de-fining moment for Marquette and its relationship to access and equity for new generations of students spurred on by two decades of mass mobilization around Civil Rights. A succession of actions in the courts and in the streets of America defined education as a fundamental civil right for children left out of opportunity due to institutionalized racism. Education had become a necessary ingredient for social progress, and it followed that access to higher learning would frame social mobility. In 1967 Father Pedro Arrupe, then Superior General of the Society of Jesus, sat down with National Urban League president Whitney Young for a series of conversations leading to issuance of the "Interracial Apostolate." Through this groundbreaking document, Father Arrupe called on Jesuit colleges and universi-ties to turn their attention to respond to the "gravity of the current racial crisis in the United States" with a cogent plan of action, among them to "make increased efforts to encourage the enrollment of qualified Negroes, and the establishment of special programs to assist disadvantaged Negroes to meet admission standards; special scholarship funds and other financial assistance should be solicited for this purpose." ("Interracial Apostolate," 1967) By April of the following year, Mar-tin Luther King had been assassinated; protests at colleges and universities across America ensued. At Marquette, Black students would withdraw from the univer-sity, citing institutional racism and demanding change, and in 1969 the univer-sity took a crucial step to address equity and access for Black students and other students of color by opening the Educational Opportunity Program under the direction of Arnold Mitchem.

Recounting this history at this instant is crucial because Marquette, like many institutions of higher education, confronted a moment of fundamental transformation. It was a moment of Ignatian indifference, staying engaged in what helps one to serve God. It was a moment of realization that the obstacles to a Marquette education for Black students harmed the whole community. With great anticipation, the university invested in hopes and opportunities for a community eager to embrace higher learning.

Another reality should also be noted. It would be an ungrounded narrative for Marquette to begin its story of African American access in 1968. This volume creates an opening to a much longer, deeper, history of African Americans who attended Marquette University over a span of more than one hundred years. Provisional profiles of Eugene Scott, Horace Scurry, and Mabel Watson Raimey, all students in the Marquette Law School in the early decades of the 20th century, demonstrate a contradiction between the presence of documentary evidence about their existence and their relative anonymity from the official historical record.

The practice of repairing the narrative of history of Marquette University is one of inclusion. Rather than the addition of names and places, it is imperative to show patterns of interrelationships, of interconnections and connectedness between Marquette and all its students who share a common cause for higher learning through a Jesuit lens and whose contributions are framed by sharing in God's redemptive work throughout our community and our society.

Interracial Apostolate, Pedro Arrupe (1967). The Portal to Jesuit Studies (https://jesuitportal. bc.edu/research/documents/1967_arrupeinterracial/ last accessed 10/5/2020)

Marina McCoy, Ignatian Indifference. IgnatianSpirituality.com (last accessed 10/5/2020)

Comments

Dr. Howard Fuller, Emeritus,
Distinguished Professor of Education

ARNOLD MITCHEM LITERALLY SAVED MY LIFE by giving me the opportunity to work for the Educational Opportunity Program (EOP). That job put me in touch with students who had enormous potential, but for so many of them they had not received the quality education they deserved prior to coming to Marquette. EOP allowed us to look past grade point averages and consider the heart of the young people coming into the program. So, many of them were not supposed to "make it." But, because of Mitch's vision and the willingness of Marquette to support such a program, there are hundreds of people making contributions to our society today.

Our job was fairly straightforward—give the students who were accepted into the program the financial, academic and counselling support they needed to successfully matriculate through Marquette University. I always viewed it as a blessing to be able to work with such fine young people. There were of course some very intense conversations at times (lol). But, I think the vast majority of the students understood we were there to help them be successful. The point I made over and over again was—you were accepted into Marquette through EOP. But, you will not graduate from EOP, you will graduate from Marquette University. You will have to meet the same requirements for graduation as any other student, and they DID!!!

Dr. Robert Shuter,
Professor Emeritus, Communication Studies

IT WAS 1973. I WAS JUST 27 YEARS OLD with a newly minted PhD from Northwestern University in the field of communication. Dean Sokolniski and Assistant Dean Michael Price met me my first day at Marquette University and warned me that my age and particularly youthful looks would be distracting for me in the classroom. Little did I know they were right. And that my teaching style added to the problem by circling the chairs in the room—all 30 of them—for the purpose of increasing the empathy between students and in interpersonal communication, the name of the class I was to teach for four months. My Black students and white students were excited by the material and my teaching style.

My age and my style were an instant success with the students of Marquette University. Many of them saw me as a peer and I liked it. Val (Wilson) Reed, James Austin, Felicia Mabuza-Suttle and Rondell Sheridan were just a small number of those students who seem to enjoy me and wanted to get to know me personally. I taught many Black students during the 46 years I was at Marquette University and, for some reason, they gravitated to me. I genuinely cared about their future.

For example, James Austin was at Marquette in the early '90s. He was not majoring in communications and was taking my class as an elective. I became instantly attracted to him and he to me. He had a strong interest in jazz music, a favorite of mine, and he played the piano. I went to see him perform when he was an undergraduate, and I was thoroughly impressed. Black students tend to have an outgoing personality compatible to mine, and that led to all sorts of interesting opportunities to share our compatible interests.

Consider Rondell Sheridan, a freshman at Marquette University. We became friends for the four years he was at Marquette. He was serious about becoming an actor, and I utilized his talents in a few of my Black-white simulations for class. He loved participating in them. Rondell left Marquette after four years and joined Circle in the Square, a theater group in New York City that he and I talked about during his time at Marquette. The rest is history. He eventually took the role of father on the NBC hit show *That's So Raven* and became a working actor in Los Angeles.

Then there was Val (Wilson) Reed, a loyal entrepreneur with a grand personality, who I watched develop over the years. And there was Felicia Mabuza-Suttle, a graduate student of mine in the '90s, who later became the "Oprah Winfrey of South Africa," with a string of award-winning television shows and documentaries.

It's clear from my experience at Marquette that mentorship is a dual role. That is, the student must be attracted to the teacher, and the teacher must be attracted to him or her. It takes two to tango, and in my view, mentorship requires reciprocal understanding, attraction and chemistry between two or more people. Hopefully, this was achieved in my communication with students at Marquette University.

Sande Robinson, Former Director, Educational Opportunity Program

I BEGAN MY PROFESSIONAL CAREER as a kindergarten teacher. My undergraduate major at Kent State University was Early Childhood Education. I intentionally chose to become a kindergarten teacher because I wanted to be at the very beginning of the formal educational experience. As such, I witnessed the joy and trauma of children as they took their first steps into the world of school. I witnessed the sense of pride and hopefulness on the faces of their parents.

I am sometimes asked "How did you go from being a kindergarten teacher to working with college students?" My reply, the transition was easy. After five years of teaching, I returned to Kent State University, where I earned a Master of Education Degree in College Student Personnel. This degree opened the door for me to become a college administrator, and I walked right in.

During my 36-year tenure (1974–2010) as Associate Director and Director of the Educational Opportunity Program at Marquette University, I had the privilege to meet, know and serve several thousands of young students. I saw the same joy and trauma on the faces of the students as they moved into McCormick and Cobeen Halls at the beginning of the EOP Summer Program. I saw the same sense of pride and hopefulness on the faces of their parents. I was at another beginning—a life passage.

When I reflect on the Black students at MU during my tenure, I think of the Nina Simone song "To Be Young, Gifted and Black." The Black students entering Marquette encountered many new social and educational challenges. They learned to adjust to the independence and responsibility that came with campus life. They learned the time and discipline that academic rigor requires. They learned the academic jargon and expectations of their respective discipline. They learned to survive being "the only Black" in the class. They learned that with every obstacle, difficulty and setback, that resiliency and persistence mattered. They graduated! I am grateful to have been a part of their journey.

It was Dr. Mitchem's goal that our Black alumni would become the future leaders of the Milwaukee Community. Today that goal is being manifested. Our Black alumni are recognized as the emerging leaders of the community. They have been elected, appointed and employed in the full spectrum of the civic life of Milwaukee and beyond. Their voices are being sought after and listened to as they are needed now more than ever.

Rose Richard, Former Assistant Dean, College of Communications

IN MY NEARLY 30 YEARS as the only person of color in a leadership position in the Diederich College of Communication, I wanted African American students to know that Marquette University and all that it had to offer was there for them. If I saw students in the hallways, I said "hello" and told them to stop by my office. Most of them did. I may not have been their assigned adviser, but my door was always open. Sometimes, students came from other colleges on campus. I never turned them away. I offered guidance and support to all African American students while also getting to know them as people, not just students. Most students were willing to be guided. They listened carefully and succeeded. If my interactions were rewarding for them, they were doubly rewarding for me when they succeeded.

Over the years, students have thanked me in many ways, including the support for the National Conference of Editorial Writers Barry Bingham, Sr. Award (2003), an award that recognized my efforts to get African American students into journalism.

The Hilltopper Years

1916 – 1954

Mabel Watson Raimey

Law, Class of 1927

Not much is known about the first Black students to attend Marquette University. We can, however, trace one of the earliest African Americans to attend Marquette—Mabel Watson Raimey, the first African American woman to attend Marquette University Law School. Prior to her arrival, the law school had previously accepted a small number of African American males.

Her parents were descendants of freed slaves, and the Raimey family settled in Milwaukee in the 1840s. Born in Milwaukee on December 12, 1895, Ms. Raimey graduated from West Division High School at age 14. She went on to study English in college and in 1918, became the first African American woman to obtain a bachelor's degree from the University of Wisconsin–Madison. The fair-skinned graduate was hired to teach in the Milwaukee public school district but was fired after only three days when they discovered she was Black. Following her dismissal, she worked as a legal secretary while attending night class at Marquette University Law School. She was admitted to the Wisconsin Bar in 1927. Unfortunately, there were few employment opportunities for her, so she continued to work as a legal secretary until she had the opportunity to open her own law practice.

It is important to note that she did not graduate from Marquette Law School. She had enrolled in the law school's evening program in 1924, the year those classes were eliminated. However, the decision was made that those enrolled that year were permitted to finish the evening course without any additional students to be admitted. Evening classes were not revived in the Marquette Law School until 1997.

Furthermore, evening students of her era were not eligible to receive law degrees. Therefore, she was technically not a graduate. In order to qualify for the bar exam in that era and become a member of the Wisconsin Bar, one had to just

2

prove they had studied law for three years, whether full time or part-time. She met those requirements. The privilege to receive diplomas was not extended to Marquette Law students until 1934.

Mabel Raimey was an original member of the Milwaukee Urban League. She was a founder of the Northside YWCA (now called the Vel Phillips Center) and the Epsilon Kappa Omega Chapter of the Alpha Kappa Alpha Sorority. She was a trustee of the West Allis Tabernacle Baptist Church and a member of the Milwaukee Chapter of the National Association of Black Women Attorneys.

A single workaholic, she retired in 1972 after suffering a stroke and passed away in 1986. In 1984, the North Central Region of the National Association of Black Women Attorneys named its chapter the Mabel Raimey Chapter.

(Sources: https://law.marquette.edu/facultyblog/2011/08/mabel-watson-raimey/, https://emke. uwm.edu/entry/mabel-raimey/, https://en.wikipedia.org/wiki/Mabel_Watson_Raimey, https:// core.ac.uk/download/pdf/148689008.pdf)

Ralph H. Metcalfe, Sr.

Class of 1936
Ralph H. Metcalfe, Sr., Scholarship

Born in Atlanta on May 30, 1910, and raised in Chicago, Ralph Harold Metcalfe became a national interscholastic sprint champion in high school. He later attended Marquette University in Milwaukee on a track scholarship. At Marquette, he served as class president and captain of the track squad. Ralph dominated collegiate sprinting while at Marquette. During the 1930s, he broke or tied several world records and qualified for the 1932 US Olympic track team, resulting in silver and bronze medals in the Los Angeles Games and being regarded as "the world's fastest human."

After graduating cum laude from Marquette in 1936 with a degree in physical education and a minor in sociology, it was politics that ultimately occupied the balance of his life. He taught at Xavier University in New Orleans from 1936 to 1942, served honorably in the US Army and eventually became an influential leader in Chicago long before the rise of the Civil Rights movement. He served as alderman from 1955 to 1970, and as president of the Chicago City Council before being elected to Congress in 1970.

Among his many achievements, Ralph Metcalfe, Sr., co-founded the Congressional Black Caucus. He also introduced a resolution in Congress officially designating Black History Month in 1976. He was seeking a fifth term in Chicago's First Congressional District when he died in 1978. Posthumous honors include the naming of elementary schools, parks and the Federal Buildings in Chicago and Milwaukee, where an entire neighborhood, Metcalfe Park, bears his name.

The Black Alumni Association is an organization that focuses its efforts on the needs of students and alumni of color from Marquette University. It achieves this through promoting networking opportunities for alumni, recruiting, mentoring, and fundraising for scholarships on behalf of matriculating minority students. Contributions may be mailed to: Black Alumni Association, Marquette University Alumni Engagement & Outreach, 1250 W. Wisconsin Avenue, P.O. Box 1881, Milwaukee, WI 53201-1881.

(Source: https://alumni.marquette.edu/baa-about-metcalfe-scholarship)

The Bennett Family

Gloria Sylvester Bennett
Journalism, Class of 1953

Joy T. Bennett
Journalism, Class of 1979

Constance J. Bennett
Class of 1980

Courtney J. Bennett
Class of 1980

By Joy T. Bennett

The Bennetts have a long and storied connection to Marquette University (MU), sparked by the dedication of our mother, Gloria Sylvester Bennett. Born into a family who traced its Catholic roots to the late 19th century and taught as a child by the Dominican sisters, Mom was encouraged by them to apply to Marquette. The nuns and priests who taught Black children in the segregated schools of the South impressed Mom. She shared their social justice mission. I can't imagine the bravery of a young Black girl from Whistler, Alabama, making the long trek north by herself to a predominately white university in the late 1940s. The Jim Crow trains and buses made travel daunting AND dangerous.

Her Marquette experience began in the fall of 1949 at Merritt Hall on the Marquette campus. Her lifelong MU friend Peg Fennig told me that for Mom to be a Black woman on the MU campus then was to give the word MINORITY a new meaning!! There were some obstacles—initially no one wanted to room with the Black girl. MU solved that by giving Mom—as a freshman—the only single room in a crowded dormitory!

Peg said that Mom melted barriers with her personality and smile, and that by her sophomore year so many girls wanted to room with her that she herself didn't make the cut!

At Marquette, Mom joined the Interracial Club where she was very involved. One of those activities was a prize-winning speech highlighted with her singing "Were you there when they crucified my Lord?" Mom was a serious student and worked on assignments for the *Tribune* and the yearbook. During summers she worked in Chicago as an intern at Johnson Publishing Company and joined *JET Magazine* as an associate editor after graduation. As a young journalist she located the elusive writer Zora Neale Hurston and was involved in the legendary *JET Magazine* coverage of the murder of young Emmet Till, which many say along with the Montgomery Bus Boycott helped start the modern Civil Rights movement. Through her work, she met and married my dad, Lerone Bennett, Jr., who for many years was executive editor of *Ebony Magazine*. My parents were actively involved in the Civil Rights movement, in Chicago and nationally. I remember our family home often used as a rest stop for exhausted civil rights workers who would arrive bloodied from civil rights demonstrations down South and would sleep on the living room couch for 48 hours straight!

In the 1960s, Mom established a friendship with Trappist monk Thomas Merton. Scholars often cite their correspondence, which is preserved in the Merton archives. She also gave generously of her time to children's causes. In addition to her serving on the board of the Chicago Child Care Society for 27 years, she was a Girl Scout leader, a Den Mother for the Boy Scouts and a Little League sponsor.

Mom stayed connected to Marquette throughout her life. She was invited to join the President's Women's Council. She also drew my dad into the MU family as well. It was a proud family moment when Marquette awarded him an honorary degree at *MY* college graduation in 1979. He also served on the college's Board of Trustees, where he was frustrated at what he saw as the slow pace of minority hiring at Marquette. His parting rebuke to the board was memorable—saying that our esteemed Catholic institution should be ashamed that *Playboy Magazine* was doing a better job in minority hiring!

My sisters and I all attended and graduated from Marquette. It was an exhilarating time on campus and in the world. In 1977 Marquette won its first ever NCAA championship. My sisters were cheerleaders for that team and have their own stories of the legendary coach Al Maguire and his players. Dad used to joke that when he was serving on Marquette's board all anyone wanted to talk about was the basketball championship!

At the same time as the university's hoop dreams were being realized, I was involved in journalism at the college and in Milwaukee, writing pieces for both the city's Black newspapers and *Sentinel*. I started a campus Black newspaper—*Counterpoint*, which university administrators tried to censure. To their everlasting credit, my professors and dean backed me up in my assertions of freedom of the press. My journalism dean, George Reedy, had been the press secretary for former President Lyndon Johnson. I learned a great deal from my experienced professors. I was also involved in the student advisory councils and the Black Student Union, where we worked with Milwaukee-area public schools, sponsoring Halloween and Christmas parties for the students.

Black social life was blooming during my time at Marquette with all of the Black sororities and fraternities starting charter chapters on campus. I wanted to pledge freshmen year, but my grades weren't up to par. When I wrote home for money to pledge, my Dad wrote back with a quip—"You need to pledge Books Phi Books!"

I was a Resident Advisor (RA) in O'Donnell Hall working with a smart and rambunctious group of young women! A searing event for me during my RA year was the suicide of a young Black man, Wally Spence. He jumped from McCormick Hall on a very rainy night. His girlfriend was one of my girls, and I promised myself that I would never forget his name.

Following my graduation in 1979, I immediately started work as a general assignment reporter for the *Battle Creek Michigan Enquirer and News*. The summer I graduated, the journalism business changed from hand-editing to computers. I learned the new computer system while on deadline in the newsroom!

Since then I have worked in newspapers and in politics as an appointee of Detroit's first Black mayor, Coleman A. Young. During my Michigan stint I earned a master's degree in business journalism from Michigan State University. After having covered too many police brutality and child murders as a general assignment reporter, I decided to switch to covering companies who were bleeding red ink—and not blood. I worked for *Crain's Detroit Business* and finally came back to Chicago as Senior Editor of *Ebony Magazine*, where my dad was my final boss! It took me more than a decade to accept Mr. Johnson's first job offer in 1979. I told him then that I was going to go about my career backward! I was going to let the establishment press train me—and then come to Johnson Publishing!

And through it all the Marquette experience has been the backdrop and forefront of my life. In 2007, the School of Journalism awarded me its By-Line Award. I was very proud that my parents lived to see that day.

Mom passed in 2009, and not only was a Jesuit priest from Marquette on the altar for her funeral mass, but there was also a floral tribute in the shape of a "J" from her MU J-school classmates. She had stayed in touch with her large coterie of MU friends for 50-plus years. And that's why the slogan, "We Are Marquette!" is not just a hollow chant. Because: We. Are. Marquette.

The Warrior Years

1954 – 1993

Betty Marie Washington

1956

When she died in 1994, Betty Marie Washington's journalism colleagues at the *Milwaukee Journal Sentinel* described her in a written tribute to her using these words: "quiet power," "beautiful inside and out," "soul sister," "compassionate," "a wonderful storyteller," "a lyrical writer supported with detailed reporting," "a great sense of humor [*which she may have gotten from her father—see letter excerpt below*] along with the ability to laugh at herself," "a presence that made you feel there is goodness in the world," "a kind spirit," "a humble approach," "always sharing her wisdom, or, something even better, asking as though you might possess a little wisdom of your own."

Betty Marie (Johnson) Washington, born in Chicago, Illinois, in 1936, loved learning, reading and writing, and her lifelong passion was journalism. So when she died, her colleagues at the *Milwaukee Journal Sentinel* thought that establishing a scholarship for journalism students in her name would be fitting at Marquette University, where her education as a lifelong professional journalist began. Through the generous contributions from her colleagues at the *Milwaukee Journal Sentinel*, and thanks to the continued giving of so many others, including Betty's family, the Betty M. Washington Scholarship was endowed, and numerous Marquette journalism students have received scholarship funding.

Betty was born to be a writer. She grew up on the South Side of Chicago, the eldest of four children and a student at what used to be Immaculata High School, an all-girls Catholic high school in the Lakeview neighborhood of the city. In her high school days, she wrote for community papers. But she continued her writing education, heading to Marquette to study journalism in the early 1950s. From there her career as a journalist took off and blossomed. Betty actually left Marquette in 1956 to marry another Marquette student, Jonarthur Washington, and together they moved to Germany after Jonarthur joined the US Army. Although she put her education on hold (she completed her undergraduate degree at

Depaul University in 1981), Betty's journalistic endeavors continued and she wrote as a correspondent in Germany for the *Chicago Defender*, one of the most influential Black news publications in the mid-to-late 20th century. Just a few short years after her return to Chicago from Germany, she officially joined the *Defender* in 1964 as a reporter at the height of the Civil Rights movement. She was fortunate to cover historic events such as the March from Selma to Montgomery in 1965 and events in the South following the assassination of Dr. Martin Luther King in 1968. But she also wrote about the passionate race protests and riots happening all over the United States, the plight of families living in poverty in the Chicago slums and the humanistic intent behind the work of the Black Panthers, thought at that time to be domestic terrorists.

The *Chicago Daily News* brought Betty onto their journalist staff following her tenure at the *Chicago Defender*. In fact, Betty became the second Black reporter at the *Daily News*. It was here that she shined a spotlight on the injustices in the Chicago projects, including the lack of healthcare, education and decent housing, and the struggles of Black families to move out of poverty. The *Daily News* also allowed Betty to evolve the focus of her writing to white-collar crime, the rise of the Black middle class, religion, politics and the justice system. When the *Chicago Daily News* folded in 1978, Betty joined the *Chicago Sun Times*, which stretched her writing even further to the federal courts, but she continued to tell the stories of the poor in public housing, unemployment among Black youth, education and religion. She never veered away from the human stories of life's challenges and the goodness of humanity.

Betty ventured into an editorial career upon moving from Chicago to Ft. Wayne, Indiana, joining the staff of the *Journal Gazette* in 1984. While at the *Journal Gazette*, she served as the assistant metro editor, and as an editorial writer and religion page editor. A detour in life in 1987 landed Betty in the position of the director of the Catholic Information Center in Ft. Wayne, which she founded for underserved families in downtown Ft. Wayne, and she remained dedicated to the center for three years. Betty loved children of all shapes, sizes, colors and hues and she felt a need to respond to a call to provide families in the community that needed a safe place for their children to hang out—to do homework, play games and yes, to hone their reading and writing skills—all under adult guidance—until they could return to their homes and their parents in the evening.

But the call back to journalism was strong and she soon left Ft. Wayne to join the *Lexington Herald-Leader* in Lexington, Kentucky, as the assistant metro editor, until Milwaukee came calling again. Betty joined the *Journal Sentinel* as assistant metro editor and a features writer. She had come full circle back to Milwaukee and home to Marquette.

Milwaukee and Marquette were the places she had not only begun her education as a professional journalist, but where she had also dabbled in theater as a student with a singing role in Marquette's production of *Carousel*, met the love of her life, Jonarthur, with whom she had four adoring children through the years, and bonded with friends and roommates for life. Her best friend and roommate, Irene (Yarber) Howard, also from Chicago, became the godmother of Betty's eldest daughter. Another good friend and fellow Marquette student from Chicago was Gloria (Silvester) Bennett. Betty maintained close connections with several of the friends she met at Marquette well into adulthood. In fact Gloria and Betty's children attended elementary school together at St. Francis de Paula (now closed) in Chicago's Grand Crossing section on the South Side. She cherished the time she had spent at Marquette and it was here that she met many of her best lifelong friends.

Betty's life was cut short by a brain tumor just three short years after returning to Milwaukee and to Marquette. She had begun to reconnect with the university and had formed bonds with some of her journalism colleagues she had known through the years from her work in Chicago and her days at Marquette. Over the years that Betty changed cities and newspapers, what never changed was her love for humanity and her deep, deep love for God. These were always reflected in her writing no matter the topic. It was said that her writing through the years put a human spotlight on hard facts and even more harsh realities, but that her readers often found the human story underlying many of these realities.

Betty would have a sense of pride about every journalism student at Marquette today, and she would absolutely gush over the many students who have benefited from the journalism scholarship established in her name. She would be so proud of them. Little do they know that they have a mother-in-spirit in Betty. She no doubt watches over them in spirit, follows their careers, encourages them not to give up, to be their best selves, and most of all she passes along her wisdom, or better still, nudges students to tap into the wisdom they have within themselves. The biggest compliment to her legacy for journalism students at Marquette would be to know that their writings reflect facts and realities, but also tell the human stories in compelling ways of the lives of real people.

She was a true trail blazer in the field of journalism and she loved Marquette through and through. She would say that the spiritual and academic environment at Marquette shaped and molded her to "Be the Difference" in a world full of challenges. She would say that Marquette requires it but that our faith demands it.

— Phyllis Washington Stone
Daughter of Betty Washington

Excerpt of 1953 Letter from Albert Johnson to His Daughter Betty at Marquette

Dear Bets,

So you had a Fab- dress on, were with a Fab- boy-friend, had a Fab- time at the Fab- dance. Also a Fab- gay time at the even more Fab- four room apartment which is the greatest. Kid, Marquette has given you a Fab- vocabulary. Happy that you had such a wonderful time and I am sure that you and (pardon the bad word – Jonarthur) were the Queen and King of the ball. Your mother is happy that you thought your dress nice…Well kid, I will take this time to wish you luck in your finals. What say we get all As? Well for now, so long. Tell all the gang hello for me…

Most- Greatest- Fabulous

Dad

William Coffer, Jr.

Class of 1967

William Coffer completed his basic training at Montford Point Camp in North Carolina in 1948 and became one of the first African Americans to become a service member in the US Marine Corp. He rose to the rank of staff sergeant after only two years of serving in the segregated Marines. He was one of 20,000 African Americans who were recruited from 1942 to 1949. In 2019, he was honored to receive the Congressional Gold Medal for his service by President Obama and Congress. Though unable to attend the ceremony at the White House, he received his Gold Medal from the Montford Point Marine Association in Milwaukee, Wisconsin.

Mr. Coffer received an associate degree from Milwaukee Area Technical College in 1957. That year, he also married his wife, Yvonne, with whom he would share 55 years of marriage. In his desire to continue to advance his career and provide for his family, he enrolled into Marquette University and received his bachelor's degree in business administration in 1967.

In 1971, he became a manager at the Milwaukee Housing Authority, where he oversaw more than 2,500 units. An active member of Greater Galilee Missionary Baptist Church, Mr. Coffer has taught Bible study, Sunday school and served as treasurer of its credit union since 1965.

During a personal interview with Mr. Coffer on February 2, 2020, at age 90, he expressed his continued drive towards education and service to his community and country. An avid Marquette basketball fan, Mr. Coffer has been a season ticket holder to Marquette men's basketball for over 20 years. At the end of the interview, he was asked if he had any parting words. He said he did, and while raising his fist with pride said, "GO MARQUETTE, GO MARQUETTE, GO MARQUETTE!"

Sadly, William Coffer, Jr., passed away during the final preparation of this book, on November 23, 2020.

Cherryl Thomas

Arts, Class of 1968

I wanted to travel out East for College. While perusing a back to school copy of *Seventeen Magazine* I discovered what I thought would be a perfect world for me. There was a photo of three young ladies all dressed in English riding apparel and holding a horse! My young self was enraptured; I loved horses!! Wherever they were in school that is where I should be for the next four years! The Mother Superior at my all-girls preparatory school had other ideas. Needless to say, her plans would override my feeble planning of a horsey academic education.

Marquette University was chosen for me, and I have always given credit to my mother and the nuns for making that decision. In less than a month of being on campus I loved Marquette! The experience may have been different; one, if I had not landed at Alumnae House, two, if I had not had Doctor Hayworth as a chemistry professor and lastly if it had not been the sixties.

No one would have listed Alumnae House as a desired dormitory (the description is an independent treatise worthy of a *New York Times* magazine article). Alumnae House was complete with academic overachievers, scholarship recipients, ladies of wealth (who failed to register early) and ordinary young women. We were white, Black, Hispanic and two from a foreign country. We formed bonds and many of us are friends to this day! We were also the last students to live in A-House; what a time.

I had many noteworthy professors at Marquette. I singled out Doctor Hayworth because I remained in contact with him the longest. The Biology and Chemistry departments gave me a foundation that has served me very well in my professional career. The Jesuits absolutely gave me a love of philosophy. And caused me to question and think and want to learn more. The AD Majorem Dei Gloriam will be with me always. I came to understand exactly what it meant while studying theology and philosophy. I have been Catholic all my life, but there was an awakening while I was at Marquette that provided a different meaning to Catholicism. Practicing your faith is one thing; putting your faith into practice is another! I learned that at Marquette.

On the academic side I had one situation that left a question mark. I had one professor whom I thought did not want me or anyone like me in his class. At the time it was a bit hurtful; however, it was also a life lesson. Not everyone will like you or help you; as long as they cannot stop you, learn to deal with it!!

Ah yes, it was the sixties! As Bob Dylan memorialized in song "the times they are a-changin'." Many young people were looking for new friends, new experiences. Were questioning what they had been taught and what they had not been taught. Many wanted to bridge the cultural and ethnic divide. Do not get me wrong—some, many in fact, did not want change. They were disturbed by what was going on around them. They came to the university to get an education, socialize a little, have some fun to that end. However, they met those who while doing the former also wanted to change the world.

A young Black male student thought Marquette was not doing enough for change. He requested that every Black student withdraw from school as a protest. He thought this would force Marquette to meet a manifesto of demands. This caused a schism in the Black student population. The majority of Black students never gave a moment of thought to withdrawing from school. Marching with Father James Groppi for fair housing, protesting, engaging in verbal confrontations regarding civil rights was all good. Sacrificing an education, no way. During this time there were lost friendships never to be rekindled. Students chose sides, a few left school and a few were simply disenchanted.

My Marquette education, friendships and contacts that I made, as stated prior have served me well. There are a few things I would do differently; however, hindsight is always 20/20. I wish I had taken time to know more of the City of Milwaukee. I never ventured far from campus. Even the protests with Father Groppi were usually downtown, or not far from campus. I did not make friends with many of the commuter students. Friendships were solidified in the dorms or the people you lived with senior year off campus.

Marquette has been a strong part of my career and adult life. Living so close, in Chicago, I meet people almost every week or month with a connection to Marquette. During the early years of my career, the connection opened doors for me. I hope that in giving back, I am utilizing that connection to open doors for others.

When I graduated from Marquette I went to work for the City of Chicago as a research chemist. Attending graduate school while working I received a master's degree in physiology. I took advantage of a program the city had, changed my career path and took a few courses in engineering. Over a period of thirty years I was a chemist, engineer in training (worked in all except two of the infrastructure departments), the Mayor's Deputy Chief of Staff and Building Commissioner. I left city service to become the Chairman of the Railroad Retirement Board in President Clinton's Administration.

In 2003 I started a construction management and engineering firm, Ardmore Associates. I was President and CEO of the firm for fourteen years. In 2017 my partners and I merged the firm with the Roderick Group, a full-service engineering firm. Many Marquette engineering grads worked for Ardmore and still work for Ardmore Roderick.

I served on Marquette's Board of Directors for twelve years. I have witnessed so many changes, positive changes! The campus itself has been a transformation. Remember I mentioned Alumnae House! The diversity in the student body. Of course, there is more work to do in the realm of being inclusive; however, I see a desire to be inclusive.

I have endowed a scholarship for students of color who major in the sciences. I am trying to give back and live the Marquette motto of "be the difference."

I am so proud to be a Marquette Alumna. Would I do it all over again, YES!

Lansen Barrow

Class of 1974

I have been asked to write about my time at Marquette. To say it was a life-changing experience would be an understatement. It's difficult to describe how the decision to attend Marquette has had such a profound impact on my life. How I got to Marquette is a story in itself.

I am a native of New Orleans, Louisiana. Prior to going to Marquette, I had only been out of the state once in my life, and that was a trip to Atlanta, Georgia, my senior year in high school. I really didn't have a grasp of where Marquette was located or what the weather or the culture was like.

My first brush with the university was at a college day at a local Jesuit high school. There were recruiters from multiple universities making presentations about their respective schools and how to apply. I was making my way around to the representatives from the schools in which I had some interest.

As I recall, I was walking down the corridor to my next stop when I saw a guy sitting in a classroom all by himself. I stopped and looked at the sign on the door—it said Marquette University. I went in thinking I would get some literature and move on to the next school. He began talking about Marquette and the more he spoke the more interested I became in applying.

I submitted my application shortly after the meeting along with my application for financial aid. To my pleasant surprise, I received notification that I was accepted into the freshman class. I had been accepted by two other universities, and I had to make a decision on where I wanted to go. Weighing the options I had, including the financial aid offered, I decided to attend Marquette. My decision to attend was further cemented when Marquette won the NIT tournament. I remember sitting at home watching the game on TV and feeling like I was already a member of the Marquette community.

Fast forward to August 1970. I had graduated from high school in May and was counting down the days until I would leave for college. I would be the first one in my family to go away to school. I packed all my belongings, including my "winter clothes," in a suitcase and a trunk. I took a taxi to the airport to travel to a place I had never been and to experience life away from family and friends for the very first time.

I landed at the airport in Milwaukee and was immediately overwhelmed by the size of the place and the strange faces and "accents." I managed to find the taxi stand and took a cab to the campus. I was dropped off at Schroeder Hall, and I checked into my room. My name and the name of my roommate were affixed to the door of our dorm room.

I entered the room and felt somewhat overwhelmed by the fact that I was away from my family and on my own for the first time in my life. Additionally, I would be sharing my living space with a total stranger. When my roommate did arrive, I was in for another "first." I would be living for the next year with someone who did not look like me. My roommate was Caucasian. I had limited experience being around Caucasians in Catholic grade school. That experience was not altogether a positive one.

My roommate introduced himself and his family members to me. We exchanged pleasantries, and I must admit I was less apprehensive as time went on. That first day was to be the beginning of a lifelong friendship.

Schroeder Hall, the dormitory I lived in during my four years at Marquette, was divided into a north wing and a south wing. I lived on 3-North my first two years. There were approximately forty students to each wing. I was the only African American on my floor. But, I never experienced anything I would consider to be racist behavior from anyone on my wing or on my floor. My closet friends were the people who lived on my wing. We played intramural sports together. We went to the basketball games together. We socialized in each other's rooms. I felt at ease in my surroundings. This is not to say that I was immune from the sting of racial animus.

From time to time, I would be confronted by some white student who would ask me what it was like to be in the Educational Opportunity Program (EOP) or was I on the basketball team. This was a not so subtle way of trying to imply that I wasn't qualified to get into Marquette on the strength of my academic credentials, and I was taking a seat away from some deserving white student. I had heard about the EOP program, and I came to know students who were a part of the program. However, I wasn't a part of the program, nor was I on the basketball team. When I responded that I was not acquainted with the particulars of the EOP program nor on the team, I could see the bewildered looks on their faces.

There were other instances that arose from time to time, but overall, my experience was a positive one.

I served as a Resident Advisor in Schroeder Hall my junior and senior years. The friends I made during my two years living on 3-North had moved out of the dorm and were living in various apartment buildings around the campus. I did not get to see them much. I had new responsibilities associated with overseeing the well-being of the forty students who were assigned to my wing of Schroeder Hall. This new assignment allowed me to interact with a different group of students than I had been accustomed to the previous two years. I developed a new group of friends—three African American students who were starting their first year at the school and who lived in my dorm. It was a socially rewarding experience.

One of the highlights of my time at Marquette was the Saturday Midnight Mass with Fr. Naus. It was an experience like none other. It was both a spiritual and a social happening. Fr. Naus met us where we were—students who were looking for spiritual guidance, but in a way that spoke to our age group. When he was not saying Mass, Fr. Naus was someone I could go to if I ever needed guidance or just some reassurance.

My four years seem to fly by. Prior to beginning my senior year, I decided to change my career path and look into the possibility of becoming a lawyer. Until then, I had planned to get my degree in business and seek a job in the advertising world.

I took the Law School Aptitude Test (LSAT) and had my scores submitted to three Louisiana law schools.I was accepted into Loyola University School of Law and returned home to pursue this new career path.

I graduated from law school in 1977 and was admitted into the Louisiana Bar. Since then, I have held a number of positions. I worked with the Legal Services Corporation as a staff attorney. I was a Reginald Heber Smith Fellow during my time with the Legal Services Corporation. I left the Legal Services Corporation to work for the Attorney General's Office for the State of Louisiana, rising to the rank of Assistant Attorney General.

For the last 35 years, I have been with the United States Department of Energy where I currently serve as Chief Counsel for the Strategic Petroleum Reserve Project Management Office. This office oversees the government's stockpile of crude oil that can be sold on the open market at the direction of the President of the United States.

Among my professional and civic endeavors, I served as the President of the New Orleans affiliate of the National Bar Association, and I served as the Chair of the Historic District Landmarks Commission for the City of New Orleans. I am a member of Alpha Phi Alpha Fraternity.

Johnny Lee Miller

Class of 1975

My name is Johnny Lee Miller and my humble beginnings started in Tupelo, Mississippi. I was born in a one-room shack by a midwife at midnight on All Saints Day, November 1, 1950.

My dad named me after his favorite blues singer, John Lee Hooker. This famous southern blues singer, who I met later in life at SUMMERFEST. Hey! We became good friends, and he invited me to visit him in California.

My father's name is Troy Lee Miller, and my mother's name is Paris France Miller. We live in a rural farm community in the backwoods of Tupelo, Mississippi, where the primary crops harvested were cotton, sugarcane and soybeans on my grandfather's farm.

My grandfather had a huge influence on my early development and work ethic. He would get me up at 4 in the morning to milk cows, feed pigs and dig ditches. Also, I would pick cotton from sun-up to sun-down in my spare time. Just joking! This was very, very hard work!

My grandfather, Roy Lee Lockridge, was a World War II veteran who was the driver for General Patton in the European front in France and Germany, June,1944. He named my aunt Naples Italy and my mom Paris France for places where he served during the war.

In the early 1950s, my mother and father decided to migrate North to Racine, Wisconsin, for work at J.I. Case company making tractors. They were looking for a better life, education and more opportunity in the North.

Life for us in Racine was going well, and we were living the Black man's American dream. Hood rich, with a nice used car, nice apartment and good food. Shortly after the good times, then came the turbulent times where my father and mother separated and then divorced while I was in the 4th grade.

Now living in a single-family household with a dramatic cut in our income, my mom had to get on welfare in order to make ends meet with three young growing boys. My mother always emphasized that we better go to college and make our lives better than hers. Although she did not graduate from high school, she was an avid/robust reader, a great speller and had a photographic memory. Lastly, she was the hardest worker I've ever known! While on welfare we would work on farms picking crops with migrant workers in Racine, Wisconsin.

While I was in grade school, middle school and in high school, I was a decent athlete and had some scholarship opportunities to play football, basketball and track. However, I was an underachieving student due to being hyperactive and dyslexic. I knew from an early age I was going to have to work twice as hard as the average student. In my freshman year in high school, I was put in the mentally challenged class for kids on the short yellow bus.

I worked very hard to comprehend and understand and master the subject-matter. This required me to study all night and day or whatever it took to get the job done. I was driven by my mother's words!

News bulletins 1969! Dr. Arnold Mitchem came to Washington Park High School in Racine, Wisconsin. He was looking for potential students to attend the Marquette University EOP program for the 1970 academic year.

A miracle happened! While I was in the gym working out on the gymnastics team, I heard over the loudspeaker, "Johnny Miller, please come to the principal's office right away." I thought I was in trouble as usual and it was a serious situation, so I left the gym sweating with no shirt on and went to the principal's office. To my surprise, Dr. Arnold Mitchem was waiting there in the office. He asked me did I want to go on to higher education, possibly Marquette University. Mind you, I had no shirt on and no expectations! I told him I didn't know where I want to go because I had applied to Harvard and MIT. Yes! I set high expectations for myself even though I was not prepared for Marquette, MIT or Harvard.

Back to my mom. She always said to set high goals for yourself. Shoot for the stars, and you may land on the moon! Marquette was my moon, and the EOP program teleported me to great achievements and success throughout life. I met my wife Wanda F. Richards-Miller in the EOP Program, and we had three children who all have college degrees.

"If you see you it, you can achieve it." I had the greatest examples of successful Black educators being my role models. I was capsuled in an intellectual cloud of people who nurtured me, supported me and provided me educational support to build and bridge my deficiencies which made me into a better student.

I graduated in business administration in 1975. I started working for the US Treasury Department, Comptroller of Currency, Bank Examiner and as an auditor for National Banks in the United States.

Next, I worked for the Racine Environmental Committee, which was a Johnson Wax base educational assistance program much like the EOP program. We provided educational assistance and academic support for students who lived in the Racine/Kenosha area that were low-income and disadvantaged students. I worked there for three years.

Finally, I was hired at Northwestern Mutual Life Insurance Company in Milwaukee, Wisconsin. I worked as a project manager/supervisor in various departments. I started in 1978 and retired in 2009, over 30 years.

I'm still living my best life in the Milwaukee area! I volunteer for different causes in the Milwaukee community, such as the Milwaukee Urban League, Voter Education and Chief Inspector for a polling site, work on youth employment and a part-time community activism in order to make our city a better place to live for everyone.

You never stop learning, and you never stop moving forward! Stay awake!

Bobby Rivers

Class of 1975

A child of the Civil Rights era, I grew up in South Central Los Angeles. I graduated from a small yet great high school in Watts. There were about 80 of us in our graduating class. It was an all-boys Catholic school. The student body was predominantly African American followed by Mexican American. There was one white dude in our graduating class. I started my years at Marquette University knowing I wanted a TV career, one that would include elements of film. I was aware of images some white people had of Black people. I was aware that some of those images needed to be shattered. I was also aware that Black folks had to work twice as hard as white folks to get ahead (often for half the money). I was aware that the accomplishments of Black people are subject to being overlooked —if not downright ignored—by White America. Which is why, for one, we have Black History Month. Those things of which I was aware were underscored when I was a student at Marquette University. I went from life in a predominantly Black community in Los Angeles to a predominantly white student body in Milwaukee. During freshman orientation, on our way back to McCormack Hall from a Mass at Gesu Church, a blond guy who lived on my floor and grew up in rural Wisconsin, was fascinated that I could follow the Mass. "Rich," I said, "I was an altar boy. I'm Catholic."

"Oh," he replied. "I thought all you people were Baptists." See what I mean about the images folks had of Black people?

I was passionate about films, especially classic films, before I got to Marquette. In fact, my first ever speaking appearance was on a TV quiz show shot in Hollywood that aired nationally. It was called *The Movie Game*. I was in high school. I became the show's youngest and first Black contestant. It was a classic film trivia quiz show. I was also the show's first Black winner. My classic film passion grew at Marquette thanks to film classes, like the film/journalism courses taught by Professor James Arnold. Those classes were like heaven to me. His lectures, the films he showed in class, the books he assigned—fabulous! I would have written a term paper for him every month of the semester had he required it. I did so well in class that I got an A exemption from having to take the final exam. Professor Arnold, that dear and generous man, went out of his way to get me an interview to be a part-time film critic at a local radio station. That was the first professional broadcast career door opened to me. I was not hired as a film critic there, but I was given another weekly job that led to another job at another station. My broadcast career had started.

Taking film knowledge and insight, much of it learned and inspired by Prof. Arnold, and reviewing films on TV was important to me. Interviewing actors and other filmmakers on TV was important to me. I grew up in Los Angeles where Hollywood was one of the top factories in town. Local TV had no shortage of entertainment reports. The local newspaper had film critics. I never saw one African American face on TV review a new movie or introduce an old movie as a host on TV. There was no Black film critic at a top newspaper. In the field of film journalism on TV, the field of hosts of movie channels and the field of talk show hosts interviewing actors, I never saw a face like mine. I vowed to make a change and some of my MU education would help me do that.

Milwaukee was a racially polarized town, and being a Black student at that time was not always easy. I graduated from high school with a high average, I'm proud to say. However, when I got to Marquette, I felt lost. White kids from high schools that had more privilege as far as scholastic materials and access to financial aid outdistanced me. Being Black at Marquette hit me harder with the reality that America is a tale of the Haves and the Have Nots. My high school in Watts was a humble little school that did the best it could with the budget it had. A few teachers spent money out of their own pockets, not only for materials, but to give us tickets to fine arts events that would benefit us in our college prep courses. It took a while for me to catch up. My broadcast, English literature and film/journalism courses were safe places to fall. In those, I felt my spirit came alive.

My first professional TV job was as a weekly film critic on WISN, Milwaukee's ABC affiliate. That was in the early '80s. I reviewed films for WISN's edition of *PM Magazine* and, later, moved up to celebrity interviews, several of which aired nationally. 1985 brought me a New York local TV job offer. Which I took. In 1988, I went national on VH1 and had my own prime time celebrity interview show. That job took me to London for an exclusive interview of Paul McCartney. In

2000, I pushed to get the entertainment editor spot and review films for a new live ABC News magazine show called *Lifetime Live*. I pushed because white producers had never looked at my resume or bio but sent back the word, "Does he know anything about movies?" I got the job. It was 2000, and I was on national TV doing something Black people were rarely seen doing—film reviews and acting as film historians on weekly television.

For me, reviewing films, giving film history and interviewing artists in the film industry was not just a livelihood. For me, it became an act of rebellion to change racial images and inspire racial inclusion. Perhaps I could open a door the way Professor Arnold had opened a door for me.

Lauree Thomas, MD

Class of 1975

Growing up impoverished in a small rural town in Natchez, Mississippi, at the heyday of the Civil Rights movement, there existed a futile hope for a better life. As the ninth child of thirteen children, I realized the only way was to move north to Milwaukee where my mother had secured a job in environmental protection (housekeeping) at St. Anthony's, a local inner city hospital on the fringes of the booming downtown metropolis. My serendipitous journey to Marquette University began one cold blustery winter night in December 1970 when I met Dr. George Lowery for an interview to attend college. I had been referred by Gerry Corbin who was the Director of the Marquette Home Study Center located about two blocks away from my home in the inner city. Noticing my love for learning and teaching, she said to me, "It seems like you would like to attend college." I responded, "Oh, yes indeed!" Several weeks later, I climbed four flights of stairs to reach the fourth floor of Marquette Hall, the headquarters of the EOP. After an exciting interview with Dr. Lowery, I entered the summer program during 1971 and the rest was history. I attended the Health Careers Summer Program at Harvard University in 1972 and 1973 and completed a BA degree in Biology. After acceptance to several medical schools, I entered UW-Madison School of Medicine and Public Health in 1975, graduated in 1979, and subsequently, joined the Internal Medicine residency program at the Mt. Sinai Medical Center in Milwaukee. I had a deep interest in providing healthcare to the underserved population because we had been imbued with the principles of returning back to our community to serve, to become positive role models, to make a difference in someone's life. Dr. Arnold Mitchem had laid that philosophical foundation—we had no other choice but to succeed while we were at Marquette. So many people were counting on us to do so!

After practicing internal medicine/geriatrics for seven years, I was recruited by the late Dr. Richard A. Cooper, the Dean at the Medical College of Wisconsin in August 1989. As the Assistant Dean for Minority Student Affairs, I was faced with the daunting task of increasing the school's minority enrollment. There were only four African American students who had matriculated the year I joined Dr. Cooper's administrative team. I developed strong recruitment programs, bolstered the scholarship support by creating endowments and NIH research initiatives to help increase the minority enrollment. I recruited African American, Hispanic, and Native American students from across the United States—to make up more than 10% of the class. To insure their successful graduation, I used the same principles that had been handed down to me from Dr. Mitchem: Encouragement, motivation, persistence, perseverance and a determination to succeed was the battle cry!

After eleven successful years, I joined the University of Texas Medical Branch as their Associate Dean for Student Affairs and Admissions in August 2001. After working approximately 12–14 hours each day, it eventually paid off—not only was there a tremendous increase in the recruitment and graduation of students of color, but also scholarships, research endeavors and board passage rates reached an all-time high and exceeded the national norm. Over a 12-year period, I obtained more than $22.4 million dollars in extramural funding for student programmatic development, research, scholarships and medical student education. My ultimate goal was to provide the guidance for the successful matriculation and graduation from medical school, knowing that it was entirely possible based upon my experiences at MU. Thus, for approximately ten years, UTMB earned the outstanding reputation of graduating the most diverse class of students from medical school.

With every return to Marquette, I reminisce and reflect upon my formative years there: the strong sense of EOP belonging although it was a majority Jesuit institution in the heart of downtown Milwaukee. I remember the camaraderie among the minority students—those upperclassmen who took time to mentor us through and around academic challenges. At every turn, we were never given the opportunity to fail, only succeed. We were told that there were too many people counting on us. I remember professors like the late Dr. James Barrett and Dr. Charles Wilke who took time to teach and encourage us—it was with a sense of dedication that they gave so willingly of their time, of themselves.

I vividly recall some of my most memorable experiences at MU—it occurred during a time when there was unrest and turbulence on the campus. Minority students everywhere gathered together to sit in the President's office to demand a greater enrollment of students of color. I remember students streaking through the library and being marched naked through the lobby after being apprehended by police officers. I remember days sitting in the Memorial Union wishing I could play bid whist like the other students, but knowing I could not afford the time because I had to study in order to earn good grades if I were to go on to medical school. Who would ever forget the meetings held by Dr. Mitchem each year to remind us that we had to work hard, earn good grades, that the very essence of the EOP depended upon our success. What an inspiration—at the heart of the matter was the ever-present knowledge that we had been granted a unique opportunity to learn.

As I reflect over the years, through the passage of time, I have felt the overwhelming need to give back, to shepherd students through the unchartered territory of obtaining a professional education from solid walls of support just as it had been provided for me. We are the ultimate beneficiaries of the EOP and the learned wisdom and experiences of Drs. Mitchem and Lowery. From the rural south, to the inner city, to college, to medical school and now in academic administration, I have been blessed with determination, foresight and the intrinsic fortitude to succeed. For this, I remain grateful and humbled by those who taught us and taught us well. I remain grateful for our past accomplishments and those yet to come.

Dr. Charlotte B. Broaden

Class of 1977

The Road to Marquette

My road to Marquette was a bumpy ride. In the fall of 1970, I received a letter that would change my life. It was my acceptance letter to Marquette University. This was particularly exciting as I had only applied to two universities —Macalester College in Minnesota and Marquette. For a poor, Black kid from the projects in Pittsburgh getting accepted to college was a big deal. Marquette was nationally known, so it was an even bigger deal. However, I was not the first in my family to go to college, I was the third. My brother who was three years older than me was already enrolled in Carnegie Mellon University studying to be an engineer. But he was not even the first in the family to go to college. That distinction fell to my grandfather, my father's dad. Grampa Broaden as we referred to him, was one of the first of thirteen black men to attend Harvard University. Yes, I said Harvard! For years when we would go to my grandparent's house, a picture of my granddad and the twelve other men, in their morning coats, hung on the wall of their living room. My grandfather did not finish, but his only wish, as long as I could remember, was for his grandkids to go to college. The bonus in getting accepted to Marquette was that my childhood friend and high school basketball phenom, Maurice Lucas, was also going to be coming.

That acceptance letter meant the pressure was off of me, so I thought. Little did I know the worst and best was yet to come! The elation that I felt when receiving that acceptance letter, soon turned to sorrow. In February 1971 I received information to fill out an application for financial aid. My family had no money, so I needed a full ride. Several weeks later, my heart would be broken when Marquette sent me a letter saying they were revoking my acceptance due to my need for full financial aid. I did not understand, how could they do this? After I cried my eyes out, my mom told me to go see my counselor at school. Mr. Brown was a kind and gentle man. He said, "Let me see what I can do." A few weeks later, he called me to his office and told me he made some calls and someone from Marquette would be calling me. A lady called and she simply said, "Can you hold for Arnold Mitchem"? I said yes, not knowing what in the world this conversation was all about. I do not remember all the details of that call, but I do remember the question that "Mitch" asked me … do you want to come to Marquette? If I thought that first acceptance letter would *change* my life, that phone call from the Educational Opportunity Program (EOP) *saved* my life!

The Early Years

I struggled, academically, my first two years at Marquette. To be honest, it was not about the courses. Life, and particularly college life, was getting in my way. I had no skills in managing the little money that I had, and I found myself without funds a lot of the time. There were days that I did not eat, or I survived on junk food. Today, we would call that being "food insecure," but for me I was just hungry. Around the midterm of my second semester as a freshman, I contracted mononucleosis. I was extremely sick and lonely. I did not have anyone to take care of me. This was the first time in my life I had been on my own, and I could not cope. I ended up withdrawing and went home. I returned for my second year, but nothing in my life had improved. I did not work during the summer, so I returned to school with little money. To compensate for how I was feeling, I spent way too much time socializing, hoping this would help me fit in. I remember skipping class to play bid whist in McCormick Hall. Too many dances at the "Black house" on campus kept me from studying on the weekends. This all caught up to me rather quickly. At the end of the second term, I received a letter from the Provost saying they were putting me on academic probation.

I felt rejected, but that was just the beginning. Mitch called me into his office for "a talk." Now Mitch is one of the kindest, compassionate people that I know, unless you messed up! I was prepared to give Mitch my "I will do better" speech, but before I could say anything, he told me it was best I take a year off. It was not Mitch's words that got to me, it was the look on his face, a look of disappointment. I not only disappointed Mitch, but my family, all the people who had been so proud of me, and most importantly myself. I needed to fix this. This time I did not run back home. I stayed in Milwaukee, worked three jobs, saved just about every penny that I could, and I was determined to come back to Marquette to finish what I started.

The Second Time Around

Life had a purpose now. I was living off campus, by myself, and thanks to my friend Alzire Brown's brother Henry, I had a job as a security guard at the Milwaukee Public Library. This was the best job ever. I got to spend my evenings studying and getting my homework done all while getting paid. More importantly, I finally settled in on a major in interpersonal communication with a minor in human resource management.

I was not sure what I was going to do with my major, but I knew I wanted to work with people somehow. I managed to be one credit short in my major, so my advisor Dr. Robert Shuter had me take a graduate course with him where he was conducting research on "the dap" in the military. I knew nothing about writing a research paper, collecting data or anything about publishing. In March 1979 that paper would be published, and my name appeared on the cover as a researcher on the project. I finished Marquette in May 1977. It was a triumphant year. Not only was I graduating, but Marquette won the NCAA Men's Championship in Basketball. My friends and I celebrated in style.

Life After Marquette

After finishing Marquette, I landed my first professional job as a personnel assistant. I remember that I was paid $10,000. Now that does not sound like much these days, but a five-figure salary in 1977 was a lot.

Even though I had started my corporate career, I did not cut my ties with Marquette. A group of us had been talking about forming an alumni group on campus, and the idea of a Black Alumni Association came up. I believe this was in 1985, and I remember Tucker Jones being a leading force in this process. I was certainly content to just be a member of this organization, but somehow, and I do not remember how, I was elected to be the first president and it was my job to get the organization recognized by the Alumni Association. The night of the induction into the alumni organization I was chatting with Father Raynor, and he was thrilled that a group of Black alums had decided to continue our association with Marquette.

Milwaukee had now become my home. As a result, I spend 20 years working for Milwaukee based corporations, primarily in the field of personnel or as it is commonly known today, human resources. Two of the corporations had extensive international operations. At my last company, Brady Corporation, I took advantage of the opportunity to move to Toronto, Canada, and work with one of our affiliates in France. Life would never be the same again!

The World Had Become My World!

In 1997, twenty years after graduating from Marquette, I made the dramatic decision to go back to school. Just about everyone that I knew thought I was crazy. I had built a stellar career travelling internationally, and many felt I was throwing this all away. But, if I learned anything from my experience at Marquette, it was to have a plan and stick to it. My plan was to get a master's degree in international business. So, I packed my things and moved from Toronto to New Hampshire to attend New Hampshire College. After getting my master's degree, the plan was to go back to the corporate world and probably get a job in China, since that market was beginning to open up. New Hampshire College had become Southern New Hampshire University, and they had just created a doctoral program in international business. So, my dreams of going back to the corporate world were put on hold, and instead, I ended up getting a doctorate in International Business with a specialization in international finance. While in the doctoral program, I got a chance to teach abroad in Athens, Greece, and Dubai, UAE. Prior to completing my doctorate, I was offered a position to teach at Xavier University in New Orleans. Teaching at a HBCU was a game changer for me. I got to know some of the best and brightest African American students who would go on to create amazing careers. My time at Xavier was cut short when Hurricane Katrina hit.

I ended up back at my alma mater, Southern New Hampshire University teaching international business. I've been back for fifteen years, have taken students abroad to learn about international business and entrepreneurship, created experiential learning opportunities for students to sell products made by students in Africa, and the highlight of my career was being named a Fulbright Scholar in 2015–2016. The Fulbright opportunity was in Botswana, and it was the most amazing year of my life. Being a Fulbright scholar opened up many doors for me. I met with government officials, educational and community leaders, entrepreneurs and of course talented students. While there, I was teaching and doing research at the University of Botswana. I had the opportunity to present some of my research at a conference in Kenya. I also took the time to travel across the African continent. My international career, both corporate and academic, has taken me to forty different countries.

In September 2019, I got a chance to return to Marquette's campus and celebrate EOP's 50th Anniversary. Seeing all my friends, I felt like I was transported back in time. We all have moved on to greater things in life, but the bond we created at Marquette will always be there. To be back in the room with the founders of EOP—Arnold Mitchem, George Lowery, Sande Robinson, Maureen Hoyler and many others—was an honor. To be able to let them know that their hard work, compassion, dedication, and inspiration was not done in vain was an awesome feeling. When I look back on my experience, the good and the bad, there are no regrets. As an alum, I will always be proud to say, "We (EOP) are Marquette"!

Maurice "Bo" Ellis

Class of 1977

"We Are A Winning Team"

It was definitely March Madness! A warm Monday night on March 28, 1977, at The Omni in Atlanta, GA, … flashbacks to that night come to mind often. That winning shot by Jerome Whitehead against University of North Carolina; me, as team captain, being hoisted up to the basket to cut my snippet of the net from the basketball hoop; my team wearing the light blue and yellow jerseys I designed for the championship game; the hero's welcome we received when the coaches and team returned to our jubilant university and supporters. We had just won Marquette University's first, and to date only, NCAA Basketball Championship! This was the highlight, but not the only memorable experience of my Marquette journey. And "We Are A Winning Team" is not just the championship team.

I was born in Chicago, Illinois, and raised in Englewood, a neighborhood on the southside of the city where many did not survive the drugs and the violence, let alone graduate from high school. My basketball skills gave me a better chance of survival and an opportunity to be recruited by over 300 top schools in the nation. After graduating from Parker High School, I was recruited to continue playing basketball and chose Purdue University and Marquette as my two final choices. There were many reasons for choosing Marquette, but the most important was that Al McGuire promised my mom that I would graduate with a degree from Marquette. And, in addition to Coach Al's stellar reputation, the university was close to home and my mom would be able to attend my games. After all, she was the first member of Team Ellis. Another person on that team was my college sweetheart, Candy. The two of them provided me the emotional support I needed while attending Marquette.

My college experience was more than just basketball. Coach Hank Raymonds and Coach McGuire were helping me prepare for a of life after the days of college athletics. The love I had for basketball was important, but obtaining my education was priority. It was even more important to keep the promise that was made to my mom. That was the case with all my teammates, and I am proud of the fact that all on the championship team graduated and received their Marquette diplomas.

Prior to my senior year at Marquette, I became interested in clothing design. Specifically, I wanted to design new basketball uniforms for the team. I mentioned this to Coach Al. He was very supportive and assisted me in taking fashion design classes at Marymount College. We made history with the bold light blue and yellow colors and untucked design the team wore for the championship game. Some thought it was distracting; others obviously liked them. They were later banned by the NCAA in 1985, but I honestly believe I was a trailblazer and innovator for the unique uniforms that came after mine. However, in 2014, Danny Pudi, a Marquette alumnus decided to revive my design with his directorial debut of *Untucked*, a documentary that is a part of ESPN Films "30 for 30 Shorts" series. It retold the story of Marquette's most iconic untucked jersey; it signified the power of uniforms and the benefits of a creative atmosphere, which allowed a 1977 championship team to flourish. "30 for 30 Shorts: *Untucked*" was premiered at the Sundance Film Festival.

In 1977, I graduated from Marquette with a degree in art. I was drafted by the Washington Bullets and played with another team, the NBA's Denver Nuggets from 1977 until 1980. Throughout the years, I have been active in sports as either a head coach, assistant coach, NBA scout or in athletics administration.

But, Team Ellis has always been my priority. Shortly after graduation, Cynthia "Candy" officially became part of Team Ellis. We married shortly after I entered into the NBA. Candy later finished with a degree in business administration from Loyola University. We added to Team Ellis with the blessing of our lovely daughters, Nicole and Christina.

Throughout the years, I've maintained a close contact with my championship teammates, coaches and Marquette. I was particularly euphoric when my daughter Nicole, my legacy and part of Team Ellis, graduated in 2000 from Marquette. But sometimes life has other plans for you. In 2003, while she was planning to attend Marquette Law School, our beloved Nicole Shawnte' Ellis died at age 24, due to a rare blood clot disorder of the liver called Budd-Chiari Syndrome. We were devastated. But with our faith in God, we knew He had other plans for us. We knew Nicole would want us to turn this tragedy into something meaningful.

In 2010, Candy and I established the Nicolle Ellis Foundation dedicated to fundraising for the National Liver Foundation and educational funding for youth, including Marquette students and recipients of the Ralph H. Metcalfe, Sr. Scholarship. Every July, Candy, Christina and I (Team Ellis), host the Nicole Ellis Foundation "Warrior Golf Outing" in Lake Geneva, Wisconsin. A large gathering of former Marquette basketball players, alumni and friends of MU participate in golf, dinner and auctions to raise money for the charities. To date we have provided over $260,000 to Marquette students. Education and giving back to my community has always been a priority for me and my family. Nicole would be very proud.

My connection to Marquette continues and will probably be for my lifetime. I am currently the Athletic Ambassador in the Marquette Athletics Department where I am heavily involved with alumni events, speaking engagements and helping to promote Marquette athletics.

Having the support of several teams throughout the years has been beneficial to me. I have been fortunate to be a part of two of the BEST—Team Ellis and Team Marquette!

Felicia Mabuza-Suttle

Journalism, Class of 1977, Graduate 1978

"No one and nothing should stop you from realizing your dream."

My Experience as an African Student at Marquette University

In my first book, *Dare to Dream*, I dedicated a whole chapter to my student years at Marquette University. It is aptly titled, "Pursuing My Dreams in America." I wrote extensively about my academic and social experiences at Marquette as a Black foreign student from South Africa.

I was in awe and had great determination to prove the apartheid government of South Africa wrong. I wanted to show them that if afforded an opportunity, Black people could accomplish anything. I was ready to make my mark.

Here I was, an international Black student from segregated South Africa at a predominately white university in America. I was overwhelmed but determined. It was a bit of a culture shock for most of us as African students. Some of our experiences resembled some of the funny moments in the movie *Coming to America* where two African brothers from a royal family come to America for the first time.

I first came to the United States on an exchange youth program in 1973. While in America, I got interested in studying print and broadcast journalism. I applied to Columbia University in New York, Howard University in Washington DC, and to Syracuse University. A very good friend then, Earl Suttle, who lived in Milwaukee, who I had met at an international event in Minneapolis, urged me to apply to Marquette University as well. He assured me it was a very reputable university with a great journalism program. He explained to me that the Dean of the College of Journalism, George Reedy, was a former Press Secretary to President Lyndon Johnson. I applied to Marquette University as well.

I was accepted by all these institutions but Howard University. I was crushed. I wanted to attend a Black university because I believed I would feel more at home there, being Black and coming from apartheid South Africa.

I had also met a number of influential African-Americans who had visited South Africa in the early '70s who had talked about the influence of Black colleges. I met leaders like: United Nations Ambassador Donald McHenry, Congressman Charles Diggs, Ambassador Andrew Young, tennis legend Arthur Ashe and more. They were such impressive role models, and I wanted to be educated like them. I assumed they went to predominately Black universities, considering my background in the Black township of Soweto.

As a young Black woman, I was mesmerized by Black American women like authors Angela Davis, Maya Angelou and Nikki Giovanni; singers like Nina Simone, Mahalia Jackson, Aretha Franklin; speakers like Congresswomen Barbara Jordan, Maxine Waters and Shirley Chisholm, the list goes on and on. I wanted to be eloquent like them and believed that I could attain that by going to a Black university.

Earl and I had started dating after we met in Minneapolis at the International Fair. There was a warm and caring spirit about him that I had not experienced in many of the people that I had met in America after having been there for close to eight months. He had what we call in South Africa, ubuntu—empathy. I trusted his judgment and his recommendation to attend Marquette University.

We continued a long distance dating relationship and after I was accepted at Marquette, he gave me a head start, and paid for my first semester and air ticket to come back to America to pursue my education. Philanthropist George Soros paid for my entire undergraduate and graduate studies. He encouraged me to help others as well one day. I am proud to say, I did.

Yes, I had met my Prince Charming. Earl and I got married and became proud parents of two girls, Lindiwe and Zanele. I obtained an undergraduate degree in Journalism and a Master's Degree in Broadcast Communication, reportedly making me the first Black South African to obtain a master's in broadcasting in 1979. Television had only been introduced in mid-1975 and went nationwide in 1976. I was a trailblazer according to reports in being among the first to obtain a degree in broadcasting.

Life at Marquette

I remember my first day at Marquette University very well. It was a proud moment for this girl from the dusty streets of Soweto, as I walked into Johnson Hall armed with determination. Everything looked and felt magnificent—a dream was coming true—my journey to prove to the apartheid government that if given an opportunity, Black people can succeed against all odds. I was embarking on a journey to accomplish what Nelson Mandela had told us during his 27 years in prison on Robben Island. He said, "Education is the most powerful weapon which you can use to change the world."

Here I was, sitting in classes and at times the only Black student or lucky if there were two or more Black students in the classes. My first psychology lecture had about 500 students in the Great Hall. That first test was a multiple choice test. I had never seen a test like that before. I was confused but soldiered on and got my first D in a class that carried four credits. I was devastated but not discouraged. I was determined not to give up. I took tutorials on how to take multiple choice tests. I even opted for taking classes with lecturers who offered no multiple choice tests and more essay tests. It was a challenge finding such lecturers.

My favorite classes were with Dr. Robert Shuter. He used to teach interpersonal communications. He happens to have been the only professor who made an impact in my life. I still refer to his lectures in my speeches today. I was honored in 1996 when he invited me to come and address his classes on the subject of "Ubuntu," the art of exhibiting humanity. Ubuntu epitomizes the spirit of forgiveness of togetherness as epitomized by Nelson Mandela.

Being able to contribute to this book about my experiences as a Black student at Marquette University also afforded me the opportunity to connect with Dr. Shuter after 35 years. We talked for over an hour recently reminiscing and sharing stories about the challenges of cultural differences.

He reminded me how I made him understand how as Africans we were brought up not to look at authority in the eye when we are being addressed. It is a sign of disrespect. But how in American or western culture as a whole, not looking authority in the eye when they are talking to you, is a sign of being evasive.

Socializing on Campus

Socializing was a challenge for most of us as Africans on campus, especially with our fellow African American students. Yes, we looked alike but we are socialized so differently. Both Black and white Americans seemed to have been misinformed about Africa by distorted images of our culture and images on television, especially from Tarzan movies.

Communication was also a challenge as our accents differed. I remember one professor once told me, "Americans have a 'lazy' ear or a low tolerance to different accents." We found even simple gestures such as greeting each other became a challenge or misunderstood on our part as African students.

In African society when we greet you for example, it is a time to build a relationship—a rapport. As we say in South Africa, it is our way to show our sense of ubuntu—humanness.

To my surprise, I would say: "Hello! How are you?" This greeting would be returned with a casual "Hi," and nothing further, as the person continues to move ahead. Greetings to us are an opportunity to connect and to get to know each other better.

As African students on campus, we came to start laughing at our experiences in America, especially with our fellow African American brothers and sisters in general. It was mostly about communications—misunderstandings. I remember Ola from Nigeria was upset once and asked, "Why do Black Americans always ask one, 'What's happening?'" Adding, "They never greet you." I corrected him and told him that was their colloquial way of greeting him. This was obviously a misunderstanding in our cultures. We also had our own intra-continent differences as Africans. We come from a continent with 54 countries, with vast differences.

Today, with the influence of television programming in Africa from all over the world including America, we are able to overcome these communication misunderstandings. Many young people, especially now in South Africa, have even adopted the American ways of greeting each other. They say: "What's up?" Then they fist bump.

Another funny instance on campus was when a student from Zimbabwe, Marjorie, asked me: "Why do African American students always end their conversations on the phone by saying, Talk to you later?" Confused she said, "I wait for the call, and they never call you back." I explained it was another colloquial way of saying "Goodbye, we will talk at another time."

There were many funny interactions between Africans and African American students at Marquette but my goal was always aimed at educating Americans— Black and white—about how the media had distorted and misrepresented our rich diverse African culture and its people. I remember writing opinion letters to the *Milwaukee Journal* and holding lectures in the community to eradicate misperception about South Africa, and Africa in general.

Most African students I interviewed for my book shared their stories of how they found themselves accepted more by the white students than by the African American students, who always seemed to denounce their association or affiliation with their African heritage. Movies like *Roots* and *The Color Purple* in my opinion reflected images that were hurtful and in some ways engrained negative stereotypes.

I found the white students to have been more welcoming, but they too were extremely naïve about our culture or our level of sophistication. They would ask ignorant questions like: "Where did you buy your clothes?" "Did you buy them in America?" I would explain, "No, I bought them in South Africa." Or questions like, "Do you really have animals roaming the streets?"

We understood that all this misunderstanding was the result of indoctrination from media images that distorted Africa. I later started a television show in America on The Africa Channel, aimed at changing American negative perceptions about Africa in America.

The images portrayed about Africa in America were about Tarzan and starving African children. The program I hosted, *Conversations with Felicia*, was about showcasing the beauty of Africa, its sophistication, amazing scenery and rich unique music. I interviewed celebrities who had visited South Africa and other countries on the continent.

Dreams Come Through

While at Marquette, one of my dreams was to be an adjunct lecturer. I managed to accomplish that goal. I used to imagine myself standing in front of a class with Black and white students. The apartheid government had never afforded me to dream beyond my neighborhood of Soweto.

I accomplished that dream to become a lecturer. I remember exactly what I was wearing for that first lecture. I wanted to look credible. I had learned from the experts that "First impressions matter." I wanted to make a good first impression on my students. I was wearing a navy blue suit and white blouse. It was a proud moment that I still treasure and will celebrate for the rest of my life. I later taught at the Milwaukee Area Technical College, Edison College in Fort Myers and Broward Community College in Fort Lauderdale.

In the mid '70s, there were a number of demonstrations at Marquette, encouraging the university to divest from South Africa. I remember being skeptical about whether the university would divest or not. I approached the President of Marquette, Father John Raynor, one day during his afternoon walks to consider starting a scholarship program for Black South African students. This was after the June 16, 1976, student unrest in South Africa. He assured me he would consider my request. The South African Students Scholarship Program was established in the early '80s, through the International Students Office. Mr. David Bruey headed the program.

A number of South African students who went through the program have returned to South Africa and hold responsible positions in the private and public sectors. They are entrepreneurs, engineers, chemists, professors, journalists and more.

I will always relish the years I spent at Marquette and being honored with receiving the Marquette University Metcalfe Award and the Marquette University's All University Alumni Merit Award. My education and experience at Marquette resulted in a stellar career in the academic, corporate and media worlds.

During Mandela's historic American tour in 1991, he encouraged South Africans living abroad to come back home to serve and to rebuild a new democratic South Africa. In 1992, I answered that clarion call and went back to start the first talk show aimed at bringing Black and white South Africans together to discuss issues they could never talk about during apartheid South Africa. The show was aimed at alleviating fear among the races after 40 years of living apart.

The *Felicia Show* was a nation builder and healer. In the words of Former South African Ambassador to the United States, Ebrahim Rasool, "The *Felicia Show* was a mass counseling session for South Africans on how to reach out and forgive during our time of transition from apartheid to democracy." The show ran for 13 years and was featured on various networks in the US, UK and Europe. Thanks to Marquette.

In one of the youth surveys by CASE in South Africa, youth voted me among the three most admired South Africans with Nelson Mandela. In another survey by the South African Broadcasting Corporation, I was listed among 100 Great South Africans. I credit these and all other awards and accolades to a great education at Marquette University.

I am happy now that I did not go to Columbia University, Syracuse University or Howard University. As I say in my second book, *Live Your Dream*: "No one and nothing should stop you from realizing your dream."

Gary P. Nunn, MD

Class of 1977

I arrived in Milwaukee Wisconsin from Little Rock, Arkansas, after completing my sophomore year of high school. I was joining my brother Joseph and sister-in-law Myrtle. My brother had moved to his wife's home state a year earlier after completing his undergraduate business degree at the University of Arkansas –Little Rock. My brother Joseph was preparing to undertake an MBA degree at Marquette University. I enrolled at nearby West Division High School. At West Division High School my existence truly sweetened when I learned that Marquette University had interest in students who previously in the past for economic concerns would not be realistic candidates for admission. From this point forward I personally hand delivered every single piece of application document to the fourth floor of Marquette Hall Educational Opportunity Program, EOP.

I must admit that Marquette life penetrated my entire existence, prior to enrollment. It immediately began filling space created by the sudden death of my father three years prior. Lucky for me I was left with a loving mother who continued to provide a safe and constructive environment. Empathetic to my plight, my mother agreed to this "big brother, little brother arrangement." In retrospect, I am not certain that I would have allowed a 16-year-old to join a 24-year-old based on feeling "incomplete." Who feels complete at 16 years of age? Later she would swell with pride stating, "I have two Marquette Men."

By the time I arrived on Marquette University's campus, I expected that the attainment of a college degree was contingent on a simple contract. This contract was dry, black and white and without compromise. Earn 134 credit hours in the proper fashion and category, goodbye, adios, you are a Marquette graduate.

Strange and unexpected happens when you find yourself in deep waters, thin air and dark forest. My new EOP family and some pretty special Marquette University faculty taught me to look for campfires in the dark, see footsteps and read current waves on the horizon. Marquette University had planted a garden in the form of the EOP which continues to nourish me today, 48 years later. I was blessed, being guided by individuals who possessed passion and purpose. I soon acquired a belief that if I respected this opportunity any and all contracts could be satisfied. Marquette University and its agencies allowed me to discover buried interests and passions. Like many students, I arrived on campus changed by puberty, adolescence and family tragedy. During my journey at MU, I was always treated as an individual. I am lucky today to look hence at challenging periods and personal moments of sure joy with the same ownership.

I recently swelled with pride when reading an archaeology periodical. I stumbled upon a letter to the editor by Dr. Alice Kehoe, a favorite MU professor. My pulse also quickens when I hear of my fellow students changing the lives of Wisconsinites, the nation and the world.

I recently received a letter from Michael Masterson, whom I met on the first night of his freshman year. I am certain that I was the first African American Michael had ever known. Michael Masterson, "class of 1971," introduced me to a group of high school classmates who also entered MU in 1971 from Glenview, Illinois. This pack of ladies and gentlemen without question broadened my vision.

At Marquette I was introduced to "Letter from Birmingham Jail," by Martin Luther King Jr. I was also impacted by an EOP educator whom I shall call "Lady from Birmingham." During one of our many conversations, she suggested that I and other students who were going to become doctors write a grant to fund a storefront site whose purpose was to screen inner city residents for blood pressure elevation and diabetes. This vision in retrospect was so profound. Remember this is circa 1975. Unfortunately, I did not understand the possibilities of such an endeavor. I did not follow through. I believe after 34 years of practicing internal medicine that I am in my finest hour when identifying blood pressure elevation and diabetes as early as possible in my community. Think of the lives that could have been served with early intervention in many cases. Screening remains a very powerful tool today.

It should be obvious by now that I am eternally grateful for all the support given to me by Marquette University. I would like to share the reward that I also received when I was given the opportunity to impact lives of high school students who participated in the Marquette Upward Bound program. I worked as a tutor counselor for Upward Bound students. I know I grew as much from this experience as they did. It was amazing to discover what you personally gain when you endeavor to help others.

I returned to my hometown 34 years ago. I practice medicine as a physician in an underserved community, which happened to be the section of town where my family lived. My everlasting bond to MU has never fatigued. Over the past 44 years with regularity I have shared meals, christenings, camping trips, golf outings, fishing excursions, family gains and family losses with individuals who I first thought were only in place to oversee the "contract."

By the way, I received my undergraduate degree from Marquette University. My brother received his MBA and was a member of the faculty for a short period of time. My sister-in-law Myrtle Nunn received her bachelor's degree from the MU School of Nursing. I would say we are Marquette People!

Cathy Stamps Covington

Class of 1978

As a child of the '60s growing up in Chicago, my life was influenced by the political and social events of the era. My parents grew up in the Jim Crow era of Mississippi with all the limitations that it represented. They always believed that if you work hard and get an education, you can achieve the American Dream. My neighborhood was a working class neighborhood on the South Side of Chicago where everybody had a mother and father at home and everyone had a job. My brother and I were latch-key kids and I was the youngest. But, because I was so responsible, I was given the key to lock and unlock our home.

I have always known that I would go to college. I would be the first generation to become a college graduate in my family, so failure was not an option. (Although to this day, I dream about going to my graduation ceremony at Marquette and my diploma was absent. What a nightmare!)

I attended St. Carthage grade school and Aquinas Dominican High School in Chicago, Illinois. During those days, you had to be Catholic to attend Catholic schools, so I grew up proudly in the ways of Catholicism. The nuns and priests, along with my parents, instilled in me honesty, hard work, self-sacrifice and love for God. The top award in grade school was the 3-C pin, which stood for courtesy, cooperation and courage (I never won). These attributes have taken me a long way in life, but have also dealt me some of my biggest disappointments.

One day while watching an episode of *MASH*, I decided that my profession would be a nurse like "Hot Lips Houlihan," committed to helping people in need or people who can't help themselves. The college that I would attend had to have a nursing program. My counselor at Aquinas High School naturally invited me to apply to religious schools like Marquette, DePaul and Loyola. I wanted to attend UCLA or USC, but my parents would not let me go too far from home. My dad said that I made my decision on which College to attend based on a physical game of basketball that I saw on TV featuring Maurice Lucas. I applied to Marquette and was accepted into their nursing program. Guess what, while walking to the book store my first year, I had a chance to meet Maurice Lucas, who subsequently left school to pursue a professional basketball career. He was one of biggest men I had ever seen and the nicest too. My roommate would be a fellow Aquinas high schooler by the name of Babette Honore. She and I were roommates for two years.

My freshmen year found me in Cobeen Hall, with a Black RA by the name of Jan Barber. I am so thankful to have had someone to help me navigate this dorm and who shared some of the same ethnic experiences. I lived in a quad with four of us—two white females, Babette and myself. The two white females were awesome! They invited me to their homes, baked me cookies and gave me the best birthday present ever—Chicago concert tickets. We enjoyed each other and shared a mutual respect, but we never went out together on campus, or ate dinner in the cafeteria together. The cafeteria seemed to be broken up into the Black side or the white side. After my freshman year, I never spoke to them again or ever saw them on campus, I don't know why other than my college days never included any friends who were not Black.

My experiences at Marquette reminds me of the novel by Charles Dickens, *A Tale of Two Cities*. "It was the best of times and the worst of times." My freshman year was hard. I was unprepared for the rigorous classes, which included chemistry, biology, etc. and constant study. In addition, I had to navigate the indifference that I felt from the large white population. This was the first time I was ever called the N-word. Many white students thought that Black students received a free ride; therefore, I felt some resentment from them. Free was so far from the truth. My parents took out loans to pay for my education, which stills make me laugh when waiting in line at the bursar office. Yes, I was still a paying student there. The classes were huge, lecture style and some professors with heavy accents.

Not all was school work, I remember the basketball games and camping out for tickets. I remember the agony of defeat, and I remember the 1977 Championship when the campus exploded and we all ran down to the lake front. I remember Al McGuire. I remember the basketball players and how tall they were. I remember how nice and how smart they all were. I remember dancing and sweating so hard at the Black Student Union. I remember going to Greebies bakery for late night snacks, the Gym bar, Angelo's and their fish sandwiches. I remember the Blue Bagel. I remember how cold Milwaukee was. I remember the different people and their backgrounds. I remember....

Nursing did not work out for me. But one day, while in a communications class, I met a professor by the name of Robert Shuter. He was a young New Yorker who inspired me to pursue my dreams and let my voice be heard. He talked about critical thinking and to always keep in mind that people are the products of their upbringing. I excelled in oral communications and found my niche in sociology. Oh yes, this career was my calling, as it allowed me to help others and those who did not have a voice. I finally was able to find myself.

After graduating, I worked in Milwaukee at the Blood Center of Southeastern Wisconsin. I was a recruiter and interacted with many different people and organizations. I used my communication skills to excel and made my mark with one of the highest blood donor days ever. But, I always knew Milwaukee was not going to be my home. While visiting a friend in Tampa, I was asked to interview with Johnson and Johnson as a sales person, and before I arrived back home, I was offered the job.

The next few years were all about sales, consumer and pharmaceutical. The same hard work and independence that marked my days at Marquette was needed for the organizational and quick thinking in this field. After a few years in Tampa, I moved to Atlanta where I met my husband and lived for 30 years.

Marquette has a special place in my heart, so much so that my nephew is named after the school. I have returned to Marquette on many occasions—too many to count! I am often reminded of the great people that I've met. So many people have enriched my life, and it's so hard to believe that these years have gone by so fast. One of my greatest achievements was being one of the founding members of the Ethnic Alumni Association. With the support of Father Wild, a group of us alumni ventured out to Chicago the same month of the Twin Towers disaster. My mom asked me if I was afraid to fly in these turbulent times. I told her what better place to be than with a Jesuit priest at my side. Since that time, I have seen the Ethnic Alumni Association morph into what it is today, offering scholarships to outstanding students. One scholarship that is presented to students of color is the Marquette Black Alumni Association's Ralph H. Metcalfe, Sr. Scholarship, awarded annually based on academic performance and promoting diversity within Marquette and the community.

Would I choose Marquette if I had it to do it over again? Absolutely, because it was there that I have made some of my best and dearest friends. They are my family now, and we have endured 40 plus years of marriages, births, deaths, successes and failures, but most of all, we LOVE each other. If I had not gone to Marquette, they would not be in my life.

Alfred G. Davis, PhD

Class of 1978

I grew up in Milwaukee, Wisconsin, my first 12 years in the city, the rest in Brown Deer, Wisconsin. During my junior year in high school, I started exploring different colleges. Because of an illness that kept me home during half of my junior year, my parents encouraged me to look at schools close to home. Although I received interest from several colleges & universities around the country, my choice came down to U of Wisconsin-Madison or Marquette. At the time (1974), Marquette was making a run for the NCAA championship, losing to North Carolina State in the finals. The team was going to be great again the following year, so seeing how bad the UW teams were, and how much fun Marquette looked like, I decided to go to Marquette (Go Warriors)! Soon after I arrived, I found myself isolated from the college experience. I didn't realize that 95% of Marquette students lived on or around Marquette's campus. I was a commuter. I felt deprived, disconnected from the college experience. After a semester, I told my parents I wanted to move to campus. Their response was "We will pay your tuition, but if you move out of the house, you are on your own for rent." Undaunted (and working part time at a local hospital), I found an efficiency apartment on 15th Street. This and joining a fraternity helped me feel closer to the college community.

However, I still did not feel like a full part of the campus. I started looking at outside organizations. A friend of mine from high school invited me to go to the fraternity open houses with him. I recall there was a Black sorority but no Black fraternities at Marquette during that time. After attending the fraternity open houses, we both ended up pledging the local chapter of ZBT. I still remember discovering towards the end of pledge period the fraternity was predominantly Jewish on other campuses. (To alleviate my concerns, the chapter president, said, don't worry, we all are minorities here). I enjoyed my experience and felt closer to the University. However, I must admit, there was no lifelong connection/brotherhood as I see with Black fraternities.

Marquette being a Catholic institution did not enter into my decision. My background was Baptist and Lutheran, so I figured religion wasn't going to impact me. After all, they all believe in God and Jesus Christ as our Savior. I did not realize that I would need to take theology and philosophy courses to graduate. As much as I disliked it then, the classes have significantly helped me in my career and strengthening my faith. They taught me critical thinking and to better understand the historical and spiritual aspects of religion. For that I am thankful for going to Marquette and a Jesuit institution.

As a freshman, seeing few Blacks on campus did not intimidate me. I was used to being the only or one of few Blacks in a class. My high school had 200 seniors with five Blacks. What did surprise me was when several professors asked if I was an EOP student. Why are they asking this? I soon realized that most EOP students were Black and the assumption (by my first year professors) was that the only way you would be at Marquette was through EOP (or an athlete). I was more intimidated by the size of the classes. I still remember when I attended my first history class at the Varsity Theater on Wisconsin Avenue. Six hundred in a class? I was shocked.

I also had to take a foreign language. I took German in high school and tested into accelerated German at Marquette. If I could survive the semester, I would complete the degree requirement. It was my worst experience at Marquette! I knew how to read German but did not learn to speak it well. To my dismay, the class was taught in German! I would ask other students what the assignment was after class. I would embarrass myself when called upon to speak. My professor, Father Joda, had mercy on my soul. I met with him towards the end of the semester, and he said if I promised not to take another foreign language class, he would pass me. He did, and I owe my first-year sanity to him!

Throughout my years at Marquette, I did not interact with many Black organizations, or students. I'm basically an introvert. Even though I had moved to an apartment, working part time and being pre-med kept me busy. I mostly interacted with Blacks and other minorities who were pre-med with me. We had our clique, but I did not really branch out to meet other Blacks on campus.

Pre-med at Marquette was a challenge. Biology and organic chemistry were the weeding out courses. I survived until physics. I had a foreign professor who I found difficult to understand. After struggling with a C, I took a step back and wondered, did I really want to become a doctor. I realized my heart was not in it. I wanted the money and prestige, not the grind. Knowing that, I decided to re-evaluate my college career. I really liked business but did not want to go the extra year to graduate. My second love was psychology. So, I spent my last 1-1/2 years taking psychology classes. I found myself gravitating to social and the pop psychology (at that time) areas such as environmental, marketing and industrial/organizational psychology. I knew that I would need a graduate degree to get a job in those areas, but was not sure I could make enough money with the graduate degree to justify going to school that long. My life changed when I met with the professor who taught the industrial psychology class. I told him of my interest in psychology and business and wanting to be a consultant. He said I could satisfy both interests with a degree in industrial/organizational psychology. However, I would need to get a graduate degree, preferably a PhD in order to do the consulting work. At the time he told me there were less than 5,000 in the field worldwide and he doubted if there were ten Blacks with I/O psychology degrees. I was hooked. I started investigating I/O psychology programs and found a new I/O PhD program at University of South Florida in Tampa, started by famed personnel researcher, Dr Herb Meyer former head of personnel research at General Electric. Milwaukee was so cold (to me) during that time that Tampa sounded like a great place to extend my education! Furthermore, the only feelers I was getting from companies were in insurance and retail, not my personality. Corporate America may not appreciate a liberal arts degree (my business and engineering graduates got the good paying jobs out of school), but I certainly am a supporter of its benefits. I also knew that if I went to a terminal masters program, I may not complete the PhD.

What is interesting is one of my dearest friends, Valerie (Wilson) Reed, is from Tampa. We never met during our time at Marquette. (An example of the challenges of meeting people when being a commuter, then living outside campus vs. starting life in a dorm). I met her family through her grandmother, whose name was given to me as a person who could help me familiarize myself with Tampa and Florida (I had never been there before). Through her I met the Wilson family and discovered that Valerie was at Marquette, and her brother graduated from that other Catholic University (Notre Dame). What a small world! I did get my PhD and am happily retired after 30 years in corporate America.

Alas, I have two daughters who applied to Marquette, but took early decision at schools in the Northeast. Marquette is not a well-known school where I live. Students who want to go to Catholic schools gravitate to those they know in this part of the country. However, every time I am in Milwaukee with my daughters I stop by campus and reminisce to them about the school, Real Chili, the bars, basketball team, Al McGuire, etc. They both have Marquette jerseys.

In conclusion, Marquette was very good to me! It has been a foundation for my career. As much as I did not appreciate the liberal arts curriculum at the time, I admit, I found myself using the skills taught to me in graduate school, business and my personal life. I enjoyed interacting and learning from the professors and priests I met. And have a deep appreciation for the commitment and dedication the Jesuits have made to ensure graduates are prepared to "Be the Difference"!

Hayward Jones

Class of 1978

"Living the Good Life"

Walking past Brooks Union, headed back to my dorm (Schroeder Hall), it's snowing heavily and by dinner there is more snow on the ground than I had ever seen in my life. I settle into a night of studying and relaxing because, being from Virginia, I knew school would be closed for several days. Much to my surprise at about 7 a.m., I hear all this activity outside my door. I ask my roommate Mack, who was from Chicago, why people were not chilling on a snow day. He laughed and said, "look out the window." Looking out and to my surprise the streets were totally clear and people were moving about as if this was normal. I realized as time passed it was for Milwaukee.

At Marquette I had the privilege of an amazing education that started out with the grading of my first English paper in which the professor didn't give me a grade but a comment, "Did you read the same book as everyone else." This quickly made me realize the academic challenges of college and led me to a study group that helped me survive the lyceum of higher learning.

Concerts by trumpeter Chuck Mangione, flutist Bobbi Humphrey, lectures by Nikki Giovanni and Amiri Baraka exposed me to experiences I could not imagine growing up in the rural south. Of course, there was the NCAA basketball championship of 1977 or just a good old throw down at "The Center."

The greatest blessing of attending MU was the people. People who impacted my life and helped me become the man that I am today. Brothers like Sam, Easy, Big C, Freddy, Redman, Rene, Bruce, Romeo and Billy along with myself formed a social club, "The Midwest Express." Together we supported, partied and loved each other along with our fellow African American classmates.

By participating in a student internship between Marquette and the City of Milwaukee and graduating with a BA in Political Science/Public Administration, I was hired by the city as a planner. I continued to work with City of Milwaukee until 1980. Now weary of the Milwaukee winters and wanting something different, I applied and was accepted to the Southern University School of Law in Baton Rouge, Louisiana. Unfortunately, due to financial issues, I was unable to return after my first year.

Spending the next two years in New Orleans on a so-called mission to find myself and now entering my late 20s, I thought it best to get my act together. I returned to my hometown and found that after years of living in the city, small town living was refreshing. I was hired by the City of Martinsville as a tax assessor and would eventually rise to the position of Deputy Commissioner of the Revenue. In the early '90s my father, who was a mortician and owned a funeral home in North Carolina, became ill. I left the City of Martinsville to help run my father's business. I quickly realized that I did not have the personality for this occupation. I turned to substances to help deal with the depressive state of this reality.

By the mid '90s my Father passed, the family sold the business and I entered my "Dark Period." By the grace of the Most High, therapy and a loving family I recovered. I returned to school, got certified in addiction counseling and for the last 20 years I have been working for State Department for Mental Health and Substances Abuse Services as a counselor. I married a wonderful woman, Emily, and raised a daughter, Miranda, who is in nursing school. I am looking forward to retirement in 2021 and as my friend and classmate Bert says, "Living the Good Life."

The experiences and relationships I was blessed with at Marquette University helped shape the person I have become and make me proud to have been, still am and forever will be a "Warrior."

Francis Richards, PhD

Class of 1978

E yes full of amazement, walking on this well-manicured campus that appeared to expand from one end of the city to the other is a memory that will be cemented in the heart and mind of this "Hollywood Swinger," a nickname given to me after pledging Alpha Kappa Alpha Sorority. This impressionable girl from the inner city of Milwaukee, Wisconsin, was eager to learn, open for exploration and ready to experience a new life. A young, innocent and vulnerable 16-year-old whose mind was filled with dreams and desires and who had no idea of who, how, when or what would transpire in the years to come.

To understand my life at Marquette, you must go back down memory lane to a family of seven that included a mom, dad and four additional siblings. Where did this MU graduate fit into this family? She is the second to the last of five children, but the first to graduate from college. During her tenure in school, she had a knack for learning and instead of being named Hollywood Swinger, she should have been named "Miss Motivated" as her claim to fame was dancing, books and conquering everything that she started.

Her parents knew she was special, the neighbors thought she was exceptional and her friends knew her as the girl next door doing what girls do: pageants, double dutch, playing jacks, running track and field, and being an overachiever. Her ability to skip grades going from the fourth to the sixth and then the tenth to the twelve was just part of her plan.

So, ending up at Marquette was not a coincidence; it was her journey which led her to an unforgettable career in broadcasting working for CBS, NBC and *PM Magazine*. In addition to authoring a children's book that was received and acknowledged by Prince Harry and the Duchess of Sussex, Meghan Markel. Fifteen years in higher education coaching and mentoring adult learners allowed her to self-discover her true passion as a podcast host and Food Relationship Eating Expert (F.R.E.E.). One could say that her life was like a well-written script with many acts, much action, some drama and a great ending.

When you think of a foundation, you think of an underlying basis or principle. MU was the foundation and the building block for how all the other pieces of her life would fit together. Of course, you get some basics in elementary school, high school and life in general, but her true foundation came from MU. Her life at MU centered on some profound and distinct lessons.

You are only as strong as your foundation, **lesson one**. After entering Marquette and struggling academically during my freshman year, it only took me two and a half years to succumb to switching my major. Although I finished at the top of my class, I soon realized my high school foundation was not strong enough to allow me to maintain and sustain the rigorous demands of the college of engineering.

This leads me to **lesson two**, "You don't know what you don't know," and obstacles are only opportunities to make you better and stronger. The Educational Opportunity Program (EOP) was amazing and obtaining my degree could have been nonexistent without the support and guidance of Dr. Arnold L. Mitchem, Sande Robinson and the staff. Yes, I was in the program, yet as a teenager I was void of understanding, wisdom and knowledge. My awareness of the puzzle pieces and how they fit together was incomprehensible at that time. So, I did the best that I could do, failing some courses, passing some courses and eventually crossing the finish line. It was about that time that I started to understand the people in my life, their purpose and how to take advantage of the opportunities that were right before me and leading me to the next lesson.

Lesson three, your network determines your net worth. It was not until years later that I realized my greatest network was the people that I met at MU. College friends and professors are your best references as you travel through the terrains of life. Yet my parents and siblings were not college graduates; therefore, they could not tell me how to be present in my academic experience or most importantly how my future net worth would be determined by my network.

Lesson four, failure is feedback, and in my life from the early days at MU to present, I have had many personal feedback journals. One of the greatest lessons I have learned over the years: when you are not successful, look for feedback in the failure. Failure is a part of life, and it is definitely a part of business. From Oprah

Winfrey, to Vera Wang to Thomas Edison, we can all learn that failure is a part of life, and a part of business and it will give you some valuable feedback.

Lesson five, NO simply means the Next Option. Before college I never really had anyone tell me no; I only heard this word from my parents during my upbringing. So, after graduating from MU with my degree in hand, I was ready to make my mark on television. I was on top of the world until I arrived in Las Vegas and had several doors slammed in my pretty little face. What … this happening to a recent college graduate believing the hype about a college degree and my ability to write my ticket, this was my welcome to the professional world, and I now had to face a reality that I had not met before!

With bags packed and the NO word circling in my head, which I renamed to mean Next Option, I moved to the City by the Bay, San Francisco. The move was another great life decision. I thought just what the doctor ordered, right … not quite!

The next days, months and years would be extremely difficult and trying. I never had so many doors shut in my face, coupled with insurmountable obstacles to land a job, any job, now that my funds were low. At first, my focus was on landing a job in broadcasting, but after six months of being unemployed, it quickly caused me to pivot and focus on getting any job regardless that my career would not start in the field that I loved. That experience was a turning point in my life and that "just get any job" mentality parlayed into years, then decades of taking any job to survive. This goes back to **lesson three**; I had not developed a network that would play a part in me getting a high paying job or where anyone in my circle would help me start a "career."

Lesson six, nothing is impossible, and don't ever give up when things get tough, you have to stay the course. Over the years I developed this never give up attitude, and I believe it all started at MU. No matter how difficult I thought something was, I always knew there was a solution because critical thinking and problem-solving skills were developed in those philosophy classes that I once thought were a waste of brain cells. When you start asking the right questions you will eventually get the best answer, which led me to become a professional coach. I believe the answer is within us and if we continue to push and focus, we can finish what we start no matter how many U-turns we make in our life.

Lesson seven, the journey through life is never a straight path and there are many roads to your destination. From humble beginnings as a receptionist; to playing in the big league as an associate producer in television; to coaching hundreds of adult learners in obtaining their degree; to organically growing Black Entrepreneur Experience podcast to 40K active listeners; to publishing a children's book that ended up at Buckingham Palace—the road was never straight. Yet, that strong foundation at MU gave me the perseverance and reinforced my motto: "Don't YOU ever give up, don't YOU ever quit."

Lesson eight is knowing winners never quit and quitters never win. My dad finished sixth grade, and my mother and youngest sister graduated high school in the same year. Education was important to our family and my parents taught us the value and benefit of getting a college degree. There were so many opportunities for me to throw in the towel, from the numerous jobs to the failed attempts of climbing the proverbial ladder to break the glass ceiling to feeling the impact of my backside sliding down the ladder. I remember telling a friend that my degrees did not pay off for me, and her words: "Frances, you have never been without a degree, so you can't say that your degrees did not add any value." The statement was made at a time in my life when things were lean and not going according to plan. I refocused and remembered my motto, "Don't YOU ever give up, don't YOU ever quit." Over the years, I also discovered "your attitude determines your altitude."

Lesson nine is all about your D.A.N.C.E. In life, you should want to D.A.N.C.E. like everyone's watching and keep dancing like nobody's watching. Oh, do I remember those campus parties, and jamming all night at Bump City. I will never forget dancing from dark to dawn and then hanging out talking with friends until the wee hours of the morning. One of my favorite pastimes is dancing. Even to this day, I love to dance, and one of my 100 dreams is to learn the Argentine tango in the suburbs of Buenos Aires. I have coined an acronym that **D.A.N.C.E.** means **D**etermined **A**ction **N**ow **C**reates **E**nergy. This is what I tell my coaching clients; you want to dance in life because life is a dance. I can see why I was given the nickname "Hollywood Swinger."

The final **lesson, ten,** which is the summation of all the lessons, is to always walk in love and forgiveness. Faith and Jesus Christ are a big part of who I am and what I believe. Catholicism or that Marquette was a Jesuit University was not the reason for my choice of school though; during my tenure at Marquette I attended St. Mark's AME Church. The fact that you could study religion and openly talk about your faith on campus made it an easier adjustment and a peaceful environment.

In closing, I can still remember that young innocent 16-year-old girl that entered the campus of Marquette and finished with a BA in speech to this now seasoned professional, known around the world as a creator and host of Black Entrepreneur Experience podcast, holding an MBA and PhD in business, author, mother, wife and Glam-Ma to three gorgeous beautiful grandchildren. I will always be indebted to Marquette, the staff at EOP, Dr. Arnold L. Mitchem, Sande Robinson and the many friends, Sorors, and professors that become a part of my amazing life journey that seemingly started with this impressionable teenage girl attending MU.

—Dr. Frances Richards (Agnew), Speech 1978, BA

Michael Byrd

Journalism, Class of 1979

First let me say that I am very proud to contribute to this project *Black Marquette: In Their Own Words*. Whatever success I have had in my life up to this point I owe to the experiences gained from my time at Marquette University and the EOP program. I didn't really choose Marquette … Marquette chose me. I remember like it was yesterday when George Lowery (dear friend/former head of the Upward Bound program) came to my parent's home in Milwaukee and convinced my dad/mom to allow me to join EOP in the summer of '75. I was 17 at the time, and George felt I had untapped potential and could be a valuable asset to the program. My father, who had ultimate control over any decision making in the Byrd household, surprisingly said yes, and off to McCormick Hall I went. My father, like most Black fathers, was an extremely hardworking man who "pushed steel for a living" at the American Motors auto body plant on the East Side. Putting it mildly, his vision for his son's future and George's dream were completely different! The Upward Bound program and later the Educational Opportunity Program provided the foundation for future success. Religion was NOT a factor in the decision making; money and my parent's acceptance of George and the program were the chief factors in the choices that were made.

I was a basketball guy growing up. I played on the high school team, played on the playgrounds and watched the game every chance I could. Marquette at the time was a national power at the college level. Mostly everyone I knew, and hung around with, loved Marquette, the coach, the players, the uniforms, everything. I never thought about the racial composition of the academic university until I actually arrived on campus during that summer of '75. I did know however that Marquette was a "cool" place to be at the time, and if I was lucky enough to be accepted it was a great place to land. To be honest, even when arriving at Marquette, the racial component was very seldom a factor because I was insulated by the EOP program. I spent literally ALL of my time with the "family." The fourth floor of Marquette Hall became my second home and my parents were Arnold Mitchem, George Lowery, Sandi Robinson and Howard Fuller. My uncles and aunts were the many counselors and tutors, and my brother and sisters were my fellow students and peers. I had many girlfriends during my days at Marquette but it wasn't until many years later that I met my wife Annette, who I have been married to for 32 years. We have one lovely daughter, Kristy, and three grandchildren, Jaylin, Jordan and Demetrius. They are the loves of my life!!

I spent most of my time on campus at McCormick Hall, and I can say that without a doubt that experience changed me dramatically. Being on my own for the first time, having a roommate, developing a schedule, being independent and accountable, creating habits (bad/good) forge qualities that last a lifetime. To be clear some didn't make it—drug habits, women, not attending class and the almost constant encroachment of the "street element" can make the strong weak in an environment where constant supervision is not the norm. I became a man at McCormick and honed my adult skills when moving on to Tower as a sophomore. I always felt like I fit in because I was always with my "family." To me, and many others, the folks that were NOT in the EOP program were the outsiders, NOT ME. I always knew who my family was … seven days a week. The fact that I spent so much time with my campus family, and not the general student body (Black/white) might have been a weakness to some, but not to me. The EOP program and the people that built it, students and faculty alike, all came from the same tree, people of color, poor families, tough backgrounds. That was our bond, our common thread. For the most part it's what made us different from the general student body. Our connection with each other, our common ground was, and is, the foundation for success. I didn't really have much connection with any of my professors; to be honest, time has dulled my memory on who they were and what they taught.

I looked at every class as a hurdle to jump over only to get to the next hurdle, and continue the process. That process wasn't always easy; in fact it never was, not even in my major, which was broadcast communication. When I did stumble and fall, EOP was always there to pick me up and center my path. I always felt there was some resentment toward the EOP students (myself included) though I don't have definitive proof of this assertion. But I always felt there was some underlying "We're better than you" attitude. I think most of the EOP students felt throughout their career that there were two separate Marquettes. Usually the gen pop never crossed our path, and we didn't cross their path. Same for the professors!

Most of the time I didn't have room for any on campus activities (other than the occasional party at the Multi-Cultural Center) because I was on the air as a radio personality. First at WNOV, and then later at WLUM. I started my radio career earlier than most in my field (sophomore year), and by the time I got to my senior year I not only had a job on the air but I also moonlighted as a promoter at a dance club in downtown Milwaukee. So, in essence, my work life started LONG before graduation. I look back very fondly on those years. For the most part it was the best time of my life, and I enjoyed every aspect of it. These experiences and my campus life thoroughly groomed me for life outside the academic bubble of the university. I always thought my broadcasting classes were the most beneficial to me at my time at Marquette. I had the chance to meet many people in my chosen field (many who had connections or family with ties to broadcasting), but it also gave me the opportunity to "talk the talk" with people who, like myself, wanted to be in the field. It proved to be a valuable experience that was priceless!!!

I always attend the five-year reunion of the Marquette Upward Bound/EOP functions, largely because it gives me a chance to stop the clock for a weekend, and relive those precious memories once again with friends of the past. I DO NOT attend the general reunions because other than being a Marquette alumni, I don't feel I have anything in common with students who were NOT a part of the EOP experience. Much as I enjoy the five-year EOP reunions, I can't say that I will attend any more. I see fewer and fewer of my old friends every five years. Many are sick, can't travel, or sadly, dead. I enjoy seeing the changes on campus, the EOP faculty, and reliving the experiences with those who are there, but for me there is a void that is difficult to replace. Who knows though, maybe I will reconsider in five years and go despite my trepidation.

The first and the last experiences at Marquette were the most memorable. The first experience was the first scheduled meeting of all the EOP students on the third floor of Marquette Hall, in an enormous room with stadium seating. It was at that meeting that Dr. Arnold Mitchem addressed the students for the first time and gave a fire and brimstone speech about the expectations of every student in attendance. Expletives echoed throughout the room with great regularity. It was at that moment I realized "we weren't in Kansas anymore." My parents couldn't save me, I wanted independence and a degree … this was the cost. The second most memorable experience was the last … receiving my degree. Words can't express looking out over the crowd in a sea of blue and gold and receiving my sheepskin.

The race was won!!! Despite all odds. There is NO DOUBT that if I had to do it all over again, Marquette would be my choice, I wouldn't change a single thing about my experience. ZERO.

My greatest achievement is my marriage to my wife Annette, and raising a family which includes my daughter Kristy. No man could ask for more. Second to my marriage, having built a successful business (multimedia/sports) from the ground up, and keeping the dream alive for 18 years and counting, is certainly an accomplishment. As I tell anyone who cares to listen, any success I have had, I owe to Marquette University, EOP and the man who nervously but with conviction came to my parents' home in the spring of 1975, Mr. George Lowery. Thank you all for giving me the blueprint to become the man I am today. I am truly grateful.

Andrida McCall Hosey

Class of 1979

I remember August 1975 as vividly as the Florida sunsets I now experience. I was excited to be part of the freshman class at Marquette University. I had just finished 12 years of Catholic school in my hometown of Pittsburgh, Pennsylvania, and I was ready to spread my wings by joining one of the most revered Jesuit colleges in the country. Marquette was magical.

I formed my most enduring friendships there. Friendships that have carried me through life's ups, downs and curves. I remember fondly getting to know basketball greats from the 1977 national championship team, like Ulice Payne and Jerome Whitehead. My best friends, Sharon Irving and Sheena Carey, no doubt are writing their own Marquette stories. We shared in triumphs and challenges. We were strong Black females navigating a predominantly white institution during the post-Civil Rights era.

My journey at Marquette started at O'Donnell Hall, the freshman dorm. My roommate, Lajaynes Harris, and I were the only two Blacks on our floor. One girl's mom came and removed her, because she did not want her daughter living near Black students. All we had done was say hello. That was the first sting of racial prejudice, and it rose up to dull the sheen of an otherwise pleasant experience. But I did not let this get me down. I just prayed for her and her family. I continued to be excited by all the new experiences, such as making it onto the debate team. I traveled all over the state of Wisconsin, and I am honored to say I received several first-place awards, as well as a third-place award in oral interpretation of literature. I gained tremendous respect for my team.

Several times, traveling back from tournaments, we stopped to eat, and the restaurants would not serve me because I was Black. One time, a restaurant was bold enough to say that it wouldn't even let team members buy food for me. My team always ate together, searching until we found a place that would serve all of us!

Originally, I enrolled in the College of Speech, studying speech audiology, but I quickly realized that this was not what I really wanted. So, I changed majors. The theater had been my link to oral interpretation all through high school, and I realized that my passion would be fulfilled in the Marquette University Theatre program.

Once enrolled, I discovered I was the only Black student. Yet I was determined to press on. I loved most of my classes. Dr. Leo Jones was my first instructor, an intellectual who taught me how to portray your character on stage. He gave me insight into techniques and history. Mr. Jay Glerum, my tech teacher for three years, was the best. He was fair, and his textbook went on to be used throughout the country.

I'm convinced that my movement teacher was prejudiced. She tried to humiliate me—the only Black student—during every class. She gave me a low grade and told me I could not move, as if I didn't have rhythm! To this day, I shake my head, wondering where all of that came from. Understand, I had been in dance for five years before Marquette, trained in jazz, modern, ballet and African dance by some of the most influential instructors in the Pittsburgh area. I could move and take on anything she gave me. In fact, I believe she took my moves and coined them as her own! Oddly, she helped me build confidence. I learned to stand up for myself, to move past her insults and disrespect. I was not going to let her run me away from the class or the program. After Dr. Hepburn took over the movement class, things got much better. He challenged us with stage combat and fencing. His class was fantastic. He even had the students over for dinner a few times. Dr. Andrew Hepburn was my shining light.

The discrimination in the theater department was mostly subtle. I never got cast in any major roles, even when I was a senior. They always cast seniors in major parts. I began to see everything in black and white and grew very angry at times. My chairman gave me the wrong counseling and told me I was not going to graduate from the program. He said he forgot to let me know about required coursework, and I'd need to take 24 credits in one semester. Thankfully my mother booked a flight after I told her everything that was going on. She went directly to his office, where a heated discussion ensued! After that, I got the right assignments, and I graduated that December in 1979. I was the first Black student to graduate from the theater program. Some people had told me I wouldn't make it through, but proving them wrong, getting past all those obstacles, instilled in me a fierce determination.

The Multi-Cultural Center run by Ms. Ford was a saving grace. We could go and vent, as well as develop strategies to combat racism. We also had great social gatherings. I belonged to a group called the Party Freaks, which was an organization for students of color. We sponsored events that were always fun. I also served, for two years, on the student advisory panel for dorms. The experience inspired me to help change and influence policies.

After graduating, I became a cast member of the notable Hansberry Sands Theater Company. I received rave reviews for several roles, including the lead in Nights Alone. Early in my career, I did a fair amount of stage work, TV commercials and industrial films. Later, as an educator, I taught and led theatrical productions of many genres. For more than 20 years, I've been a theater teacher for a magnet arts middle school in St. Petersburg, Florida. I've drawn on my Marquette experience to prepare my students for the challenging world they, too, are facing.

My Marquette journey was worthy and notable. And I'm grateful.

Douglas D. Kelley

Class of 1979

W hen I decided to go to college, I wanted to go to a university that had a diverse culture, since I had gone to predominantly Black schools. Marquette University became my choice.

Upon entering college, I immediate became active in student government/politics. I was appointed freshman representative of the New Student Orientation Steering Board and was protesting on campus for minorities and women rights, the year 1975.

Sophomore year I became youngest Director of the New Student Orientation Steering Board, changing the whole optics of the organization. I was appointed Media Commissioner of ASMU and started having blockbuster movies in the varsity theater. I also became one of the co-founders for the Black Student Council.

In my junior year, I became President of the Black Student Council, which primarily occupied most of my time considering the state of the campus environment and had to give some time to my academics. However, a good friend, Robin Flowers, had been elected to the Vice President of ASMU. Our goal was that he would run for President and I, Vice President; it never happened. He was ousted out of his position and was not allowed to come back to Marquette, a great political move.

The highlight of my senior year was that a group of ten students were selected first for season tickets to Marquette basketball games; they were great seats that year.

My experience at Marquette really taught me a lot. I learned how to dance, found out what true friendship was and what real love felt like. However, it wasn't all peaches and cream. I also got a BIG taste of racism, discrimination and hatred. Regardless of the good, the bad and the ugly, my education and experience was PRICELESS.

Upon graduation my career went into a lot of directions, but for now I want to concentrate on how Marquette has stayed in my life.

I always felt that as an African American who graduated from such a prestigious university, that those who have come before me and those after needed to come together to be able to assist others. As an alum, I believed it was important to give back to the university regardless of your past experience.

From 1979 to 1995, I tried to start an alumni organization for Marquette's African American graduates. The first time in the early eighties lasted maybe a year. The second time in the early nineties, it lasted just a few months. But by early 1995, I answered a call to become a mentor at Marquette, then it all changed.

After becoming a mentor, Jody Sneed, Valerie Ricks, Regina Wilkinson, Keith Reid and myself decided that we wanted to start an alumni organization for Blacks. In the fall of 1995, two dozen individuals from all over the country convened in Milwaukee to discuss what we were going to do. After eight hours, the Ethnic Alumni Association of Marquette University was born.

In August 1996 our first event was held on Summerfest grounds during Afro fest. It was a well-attended event, and we were moving forward. Over the next few years, we held parties, seminars and cultural events to create an opportunity for ethnic alumni to network. During this period of time, the Advancement Office at Marquette was very supportive in allowing us to have space on campus for our different events. But it was time for EAA to get a seat on the National Board of Directors, but others had a different opinion.

In 2000, I had to make a presentation to the National Board of Alumni Association Directors on why the Ethnic Alumni Association desired a seat on the National Board. The vote came down 12 to 11 "no," and we would not be given a seat on the national board. Yes, we were extremely disappointed about their decision. It was like we were living the things that happened on campus into the real world, but the fight had just begun. We continued doing events over the next year. But in April 2001 a miracle happened!

I received a phone call and was requested to attend a meeting at the university alumni office. I was informed that the then President of the university, Father

Robert Wild, was going to make a presidential decision to grant the Ethnic Alumni Association of Marquette University a seat on the national board. WOW! The first time in the university's history that this has been done. But I had to keep it a secret for two weeks until the press release went out. Just imagine, I had a board meeting a few days later where we were preparing to make this great presentation to the national board again, but I could not tell them there will be no need. Finally, we could celebrate that we had a seat on the National Board of Directors.

Since Father Wild had given us a gift, the board decided we were going to give a gift back to the university by becoming the first alumni organization to endow our scholarship within twelve months. We had to raise $25,000 by June 30, 2002. We were off and running. Believe it or not we did it! We raised the money to be endowed within twelve months as our gift back to the university.

Let's briefly talk about the Alumni Board of Directors, I held the seat first since I was the current President of EAA. Well let me tell you, those bad things that I learned on campus as a student came full circle again; however, the impact was much different. They could show their true colors; I just had to figure out how to deal with it. After my second year on the national board, I ran for President and lost. Yes, I wanted to win, but really did not think it would happen. A lot of my peers said Douglas, immediately announce that you are going to run again. After a few months I did and became the first African American elected to that position. Well, I made a lot of headway in different capacities while I was on the board. But the one thing I did not see coming is when the second African American (and first Black female) was elected to that position, Valerie Wilson Reed.

The one thing that I am pleased to see is the name changed from the Ethnic Alumni Association to the Black Alumni Association of Marquette University in 2019. That was our original goal. But remember, those two dozen individuals that came into Milwaukee in 1995 chose a different path for us to be all-inclusive.

Finally, being the first in my family to graduate from college was just beyond my belief. My career has taken a lot of turns over the years. Currently I am blessed to have a dual career. I have been a real estate consultant with First Weber Inc. for 17 years and vice president of sales for Courier Communications for seven years. I truly know that my life experiences and career opportunities have been because of my education from Marquette.

Mascelia Miranda

Class of 1979

It was a night like any other school night. Dinner was finished, the kitchen was spotless, and the children were in their rooms doing homework while the parents watched television in the family room. Suddenly, Mascelia popped into the family room and announced to her parents that she would be attending Marquette University. Her mother responded, "Marquette is a really expensive school." Mascelia replied, "I know. I'll work hard to get a scholarship." At 12 years old, time was on her side.

When Mascelia was nine years old, she and her two younger sisters—Florida natives—spent summers with their aunt who worked for the medical school at Marquette (now the Medical College of Wisconsin). Mascelia enjoyed talking with doctors and medical technicians about their work, exploring cells and other findings under microscopes, looking at the developmental stages of babies (1–9 months) stored in formaldehyde, observing pictures of cancerous lung tissue, and just watching out for the unexpected. When roaming the halls of the medical school, you never knew what you were going to stumble upon. You could find medical students in the middle of dissecting any body part of a cadaver. Mascelia was comfortable on the campus. The facilities were state of the art. She figured if the professors of the other colleges were like the ones that she met at the medical school, then she would get an excellent education. Its reputation for excellence in education, its environment and the quality of its people were key factors that drew Mascelia to Marquette.

By the age of 16, Mascelia was well positioned as a candidate to attend Marquette and was competitive for scholarship dollars. During the summer before her senior year in high school, she visited the admissions office. An admissions counselor provided a timeline of items needed for admissions. Although attending Marquette had been her goal for many years, Historically Black Colleges and

Universities and one Ivy League school also were in pursuit of Mascelia; Marquette, however, did not lose its luster.

Mascelia's mother and aunt settled her into a single room at O'Donnell Hall. During a floor meeting, she met many of the women who would become lifelong friends. They registered for classes together, shared meals in the dining hall and in some cases worshipped/prayed together.

Mascelia bonded with two sets of friends (white and African American). For Mascelia, there was a high need to connect with people who were from the same or similar background. She valued getting to know African Americans from Chicago, New York, Philadelphia, Milwaukee and Florida. One of her best memories was of the soul food meal events. They were open to all and were an opportunity to have a different experience with white friends. It was a joy to see their faces when they tasted foods for the first time or tasted a known food that was prepared differently from their custom.

Who could forget the evening Marquette won the NCAA basketball championship in 1977? It was exciting and a great time to be at the university. This win created a ripple effect for Mascelia's youngest sister, who became popular at her junior high school because big sis went to Marquette. Another memorable moment was the Blizzard of 1978. The university closed for the first time in its history. The drifts were up to the fourth floor of McCormick Hall. It was a great play day in the snow for all.

Mascelia and many of her friends were biology majors their freshmen year. It was a challenging curriculum. At the end of her freshmen year, she asked herself, "Is this the right major for me?" She reevaluated her goals and decided to change her major to business administration with a specialization in marketing. The associate dean of the business school took an interest in her progression. He provided counsel and checked in with her from time to time, both motivating and encouraging her. In addition to the associate dean, she had a market research and a statistics professor who genuinely cared about her as a person and student. Unfortunately, there also was a management professor who invited her to his office to recommend that she quit business school and enroll in secretarial school because she would never be more than that. Some minority students, including some of Mascelia's closest friends who left Marquette after hearing similar messages, were discouraged by such professors in a variety of ways. Mascelia, however, decided that some people never would have her best interests at heart; they were biased and or racist, but that was *their* problem—Mascelia would not allow their issues to become *her* problem. She remained focused on her path and kept working hard toward graduation.

Changing her major from biology to business administration required one extra semester to meet graduation requirements. To cover the extra costs, Mascelia applied for on-campus employment, but was less competitive than a gentleman who had better typing skills than she. She landed an internship with the City of Milwaukee instead, and ended up marrying the man who edged her out of the campus job. They are still married and have two adult children. She also applied for an Educational Opportunity Program (EOP) grant to cover the tuition for her final semester. The program was a godsend. The semester was fully funded by the grant and her part-time job, which eliminated a need for an educational loan to cover books, food, housing and transportation costs.

Mascelia's interests were varied. She pledged Delta Sigma Theta Sorority, sat first chair flute in the symphonic band, sang in the gospel choir, and joined ROTC in her junior year. Mascelia completed the US Army Airborne School while at Marquette and was pinned a US Army Second Lieutenant upon graduation. As a side note, the colonel of the ROTC department was Mascelia's freshman advisor. Whenever she went to see him for course approval, he recruited for the Army. After taking elective military courses for two years, she signed a contract to join the Army.

Following graduation, Mascelia became a US Army officer, Field Artillery, Pershing Missile specialty. She was stationed at Fort Sill, Oklahoma, where she served as the brigade logistics officer for the US Army Field Artillery School. After three years of active duty service and earning two Army Commendation Medals, she transitioned to civilian life. She moved to Dallas, Texas, and was employed by Texas Instruments, where she worked in the quality engineering division with emphasis on software quality. After spending a few years moving up to supervisory levels, she transitioned to the training organization. She traveled the globe teaching engineers in the disciplines of project management, failure modes and effects analysis, and quality function deployment. She also completed a Master of Science degree in organizational development and change management, which enabled her to create partnerships with senior management levels, where she and colleagues could influence major change agendas. She won an Exception Award at TI for delivering excellent consultation to engineering and project management leaders for delivery of missile systems.

Mascelia was eventually recruited away from TI by Eli Lilly and Company in Indianapolis, Indiana, where she continued change management work for about five more years. She then moved into a line human resources role, where she provided consultation to supervisors and directors in the areas of employee relations and investigations. She won a human resources team award for her participation in an organizational restructuring immediately before a Christmas break where the team worked tirelessly to retain as many employees as possible. Mascelia retired from Eli Lilly in December of 2017.

Outside of work and raising a family, Mascelia was involved in her congregation(s); she taught Sunday School, was a youth group leader and served on the church board in a variety of positions, including the office of president. She served as president of the board of the Housing Crisis Center of Dallas. Mascelia was the first African American woman to serve as president of the Business and Professional Women's Club of Dallas, where she was recognized by the national organization's president as the most outstanding local organization president in the United States. For ten years she was a volunteer flute teacher for an after-school program for underserved children in Indianapolis. She has continued service with Delta Sigma Theta with a focus on scholarship activities.

At the end of the day, did Marquette provide a good education for Mascelia? Her answer: It was one of the finest money could buy and well rounded. The purpose of college is to teach one to think and analyze problems/situations/data, determine alternatives/options, and select/execute the best solution. Mascelia asserts that Marquette provided an excellent foundation to start a fruitful career. Whenever she tells others that she attended Marquette, the response is often, "Great school. That's in Michigan, right?" Recognition as a great school is apparent, but work might be needed in helping the general public know the university's location.

Valerie Wilson Reed

Class of 1979

O ctober 31, 1975, I was a freshman at Marquette University in Milwaukee, Wisconsin, slowly getting acclimated to my new dorm, Cobeen Hall. It was miles away and a totally different environment from my home of Tampa, Florida. FLORIDA! What have I done? How did I get here? I was peering out my dorm window, slightly alarmed at these strange white particles floating from the sky. "What is that?!" The person standing next to me laughed and said, "Uh … SNOW!" Yes, it was the first time this native-born Floridian had ever witnessed snow! My alarm quickly changed to amazement and thus began my learning experience, not just in higher education, but life.

My choice to attend Marquette was an easy one. I had attended Catholic schools from first grade through high school. My high school, the Academy of the Holy Names in Tampa, Florida, was an all-girls, private Catholic, boarding school (I did not board), where I was always only one of two African Americans in my class. My late father was an attorney and mother, a realtor while she also worked in the mayor's office in Tampa, Florida. Both stressed education as a major priority. College was expected. Though my mother wanted me to attend an HBCU, I wanted to continue my education at a Catholic university. My father said it was my decision, but one that once made, I had to stick with. He stated I could go as far away as my older brother. He attended Notre Dame University and Notre Dame Law School and would be there close by during my four years at Marquette. I then took a map, ruler and that thick, green book of listings of colleges and universities throughout the country (there wasn't internet back then), measured the distance between Tampa and South Bend, added about an inch and landed on Milwaukee, Wisconsin. I applied, was accepted and off I went to blaze my new trail from an extremely sheltered lifestyle to a campus, site unseen.

I originally enrolled into Marquette with a focus on dentistry. Marquette had a dental school, which made my discussion with my parents to attend Marquette more compelling. Honestly, I had no desire to be a dentist, but I figured it was a career they would approve and allow me to move so far away. I happened to take an interpersonal communications course my first semester with Dr. Robert Shuter. It was a new major in the College of Speech and drew me in with enthusiasm. I changed my major to interpersonal communications with an interdisciplinary major in marketing. Though my parents were not pleased with my change in career paths, I promised them I would make it worth the tuition they were paying for my education. They both worked extremely hard to provide for me and my brother, and I am extremely appreciative. It could not have been easy for the paying for both my college education and my brother's undergraduate and law school degree at the same time. (My brother graduated from Notre Dame Law School on the same day I graduated from Marquette in 1979.)

Before arriving at Marquette, I had attended an all-girls, private, Catholic high school where I had experienced quite a bit of racism. But I give thanks for the wisdom of my parents who were both active in Civil Rights and always stressed to be open to all people regardless of race, gender, religion or economic background. At Marquette, I made friends with everyone who wanted to be friends with me.

I was active in numerous on-campus activities and internships. I served as Senator for Associated Students of Marquette University (ASMU). Honestly, one of the main reasons I joined was to be in charge of basketball ticket sales. At that that time, you had to camp outside in tents in order to get student tickets. I had camped out once and swore I would never go through that experience again. How fortuitous! The 1977 Marquette Warriors men's basketball team won the National Championship and I had front row seats, right behind the bench that year. I participated in several internships, one of which was the first Student Sports Information Director for the Marquette women's basketball team. It was the first time their stats, personal information and photos were compiled into a program book. I felt at that time (and still do) that the women's team should be recognized just as much as the men's team and so attempted to increase student attendance at their games.

My freshman year, I lived in a quad on the eighth floor of Cobeen Hall. My roommates were great! We got along well but lost contact after that year. The following sophomore and junior years were in Carpenter Tower. The roommate I had my sophomore year didn't last long. The minute she said the N-word and handed me her laundry to clean was the last day she would be my roommate. She was asked to leave the dorm immediately for that as well as other dorm infractions. No more roommates for me. Junior year, I had a single room and moved into the Abottsford Apartments my senior year.

One of the first friends I made on campus was Ellen Raynor. We met my freshman year in Cobeen Hall. Her uncle was none other than the president of Marquette, Fr. John P. Raynor, SJ. I was a frequent guest for dinners with them. From that time on, Fr. Raynor's door was always open to me. He became my mentor throughout my life up until his death.

In one of my many discussions with Fr. Raynor, I discussed my displeasure at how Marquette was not addressing the needs nor acknowledging the many students and alumni of color. We were not being recognized in ads, marketing materials nor the *Marquette Magazine*. His advice to me was, "Come back and volunteer at Marquette and change it!" I took his advice to heart once I married and moved to Chicago in 1990. In 2000, I became even more involved with Marquette when I was approached by my fellow MU classmate and friend, Douglas Kelley, to help establish the Ethnic Alumni Association (now the Black Alumni Association) of Marquette. He had been trying for many years to receive sanctioning by the Board of Trustees. President Fr. Robert Wild, SJ, interceded, and the EAA became a fully sanctioned association with a seat on the National Board. I became EAA's third president from 2004–2006. From 2011 to 2012, I served on the MU Alumni Association's National Board of Directors. I was proud to be elected President of the national MUAA (the first Black female) and served my term in 2011. It was during my term as president that I traveled all throughout the country to meet my fellow alumni (of ALL backgrounds) and encouraged them to become more engaged with our alma mater. I have served on the College of Communications Board, the Mentoring Program, and many Marquette University committees.

During my 20 years of volunteering at Marquette, I've recruited many Black students. So many, I've actually lost count, but somewhere close to 15 (one currently attending MU, Class of '23). All the students I recruited, graduated! I am so proud of the young, productive adults they have become.

I am also a proud mom of a Marquette Legacy, my daughter, Francesca (Reed) Cianciolo, class of 2014. Francesca also graduated from the College of Communications. While at MU, she became station manager and general manager of the MU Television (MUTV). She was also the recipient of two College Emmys from the National Academy of Television Arts and Sciences (Chicago Midwest Chapter). I am extremely proud of my legacy.

My first 15 years after graduation were spent building a successful career in sales & marketing with Pabst Brewing Company, Hershey Chocolate Company and in national accounts with G. Heileman Brewing Company. In 1990, I married and became a homemaker, mom, volunteer and entrepreneur. My past businesses include: "He'll Lift You Up" Gospel Music Video for Kids (the first gospel music video for kids); Valcooks Designer Hostess Aprons, which featured on the Home Shopping Network (HSN); Valcooks Coffee and currently Valcooks Kitchen, which features my self-produced, cooking videos on American Legacy Network TV, a national African American news & entertainment streaming service.

I have truly been blessed. Most of the friends I made at Marquette remain my dearest friends to this day. Who I am and still am becoming I owe to my supportive family and my volunteer life at Marquette. In 2018, I was humbled and honored to receive the All University–Service to Marquette Award. I will treasure that moment for the rest of my life! I also view the compilation of the *Black Marquette* book as a gift to my alumni "family" who have been always been supportive and a major part of my life. WE ALL ARE MARQUETTE!

Honorable James A. Wynn, Jr.

Law, Class of 1979

I am, and have always been, a North Carolinian. I grew up on my family's farm in the eastern part of the state—not far from the coastal waters of the Atlantic Ocean. Unsurprisingly, therefore, of the many questions I get regarding my days at Marquette, the most common is, "Why did you choose to leave North Carolina and attend law school in Milwaukee, Wisconsin?"

Truthfully, for many years, I too questioned why it was that I chose to replace, even for a time, the familiar environs of North Carolina—its temperate climate, its beaches and red clay soil, its boiled peanuts and barbeque—with the harsh winters of Milwaukee.

I now know that it was God's will. With all my heart, I believe that the success I have found in the legal profession arose from my formative experiences at Marquette. Those experiences taught me the value of perseverance and self-belief in the face of unrelenting scrutiny. Along the way I gained lifelong friends and an abiding appreciation for the Jesuit principles underlying Marquette's vision.

The '60s and '70s in the South were activist years, bent on forging a new world beyond *Brown v. Board of Education*, the Vietnam War and the Civil Rights movement. Historically, African American students in the South had attended one of the region's many Black Colleges and Universities. But in the early '70s, a cadre of students, like me, decided to contribute to Dr. Martin Luther King's dream by attending major universities that were predominately white. I chose the University of North Carolina at Chapel Hill, where I graduated after three years. My degree in journalism would, in the years to come, serve me well as I chose to become a lawyer.

I'm not quite sure how, but Marquette University Law School came to my attention. It may have been during the gap year I took after graduating from UNC, which I spent serving as a supervisor of a VISTA program in Greenville, North Carolina. My faith has always been Baptist, but I was intrigued by the religious commitment and traditions of the Jesuits. So, when Marquette Law accepted me with an offer of financial support, I decided it was time to leave North Carolina for a while and experience life in another part of the country.

On the long drive from Raleigh to Milwaukee in the fall of 1976, I realized that I did not know a soul in my new hometown. My father had promised to call a lifelong family friend who had moved there some years before. But Dad hadn't seen that friend for decades, and in all honesty, the call I placed on arrival was made only out of obligation. To my pleasant surprise, the friend's wife answered, "Jim, we have been waiting for you with dinner prepared and your bedroom ready. Come on over." I will never, ever forget those words—my welcome to Milwaukee.

The three years I spent at Marquette seemed long at the time. The winters were characteristically extended and brutal. But as with all temporal matters, retrospectively, those years flew by. I had no debt after graduation because most of my time there I lived at a boarding house that cost $50 per month, including utilities. And I worked as a law library assistant—which the Dean said would ensure I was studying. We were a particularly close class with intense study groups punctuated by many trips to Haggerty's Bar, located a block from the school. I spent one summer as an intern at the Milwaukee Corporation Counsel's Office and another interning at Schlitz Brewing Company. The latter made me a popular source for beer among my classmates.

Milwaukee then had distinctly identifiable ethnic areas. While the first African American law student appears to have attended Marquette in the 1890s, only four African Americans started in my class and just two of us graduated with the Class of 1979. Though de jure segregation had not historically been a part of Milwaukee, it sure appeared to me that de facto segregation was alive and well in at least parts of the city. In fact, I had before never seen the type of living conditions that existed for some, which I then saw firsthand as I served as a trustee at a church in the inner city. But, I had never spent much time in a major city. In any case, I found much warmth from many of the people I encountered in those areas, and I enjoyed basement parties, backyard grilling and well-informed conversations with them. As a Southerner, I felt at home, since many of them were only a generation or two removed from the Great Migration out of Alabama, Mississippi and Arkansas.

Within the school, the Black Law Student Association was a major activity for me. I served as its President during my senior year and was on the moot court team that won the best brief award in the national Frederick Douglass Moot Court Competition. We sponsored legal clinics in the inner city and traveled to undergraduate colleges, primarily in the South, seeking to recruit minority students for Marquette Law School.

Of all the excellent professors and deans at Marquette Law School, Dean Robert Boden was my most supportive mentor and inspiration. He acknowledged and promoted my writing talents and encouraged me to start my career in the Judge Advocate General's Corps of the Navy, which proved to be another game-changer for me. That level of support from Marquette Law has been consistent over the years, culminating with current Dean Joe Kearney enthusiastically recommending me for the University's Board of Trustees.

So, who knew that a young man who grew up in the tobacco fields of eastern North Carolina would someday sit on one of the highest courts in the land—the United States Court of Appeals for the Fourth Circuit? No one—certainly not me. But what I do know is, Marquette University helped me get there. And for that, I will always be thankful.

Todd Beamon

Journalism, Class of 1980

I was 13 when I knew I wanted to become a journalist. I was fortunate to have a supportive mother, Mrs. Lena A. Triplett, and teachers who nurtured my talent.

At Washington High School in Milwaukee, I took my first journalism class junior year and joined the student paper, *The Purgold Press.* I became editor-in-chief the next year.

But the year before, my newspaper adviser, now Mrs. Lynne McCready Baumgardt, introduced me to Echo Writer's Workshop, which taught writing and business skills to inner-city students. Its founder was Mrs. Virginia W. Williams, a retired Milwaukee Public Schools teacher.

One Sunday morning in March of my senior year, Mrs. Williams woke me up with a call that she had arranged an interview at the Marquette University College of Journalism and with Dr. Arthur Mayberry of the Educational Opportunity Program (EOP).

The EOP session conflicted with the city-wide cross-country meet—and that's where I planned to be. My mother, however, had other plans. She surprised me by taking off work, accompanying me to Marquette Hall and waiting in EOP office's lobby during my interview. I was accepted on the spot.

I entered Marquette in the fall of 1976, assigned to Room 826 in McCormick Hall. I had a full view of campus, downtown Milwaukee and Lake Michigan.

My first roommate, who was of color, and I did not get along: "You have to move. I'm not giving up this view."

My next roommate was from a farm in River Falls, near the Minnesota border. It was a goofy, serious, daffy relationship: He'd play my Roy Ayers and Sinatra—and I didn't mind Hank Williams.

Freshman year was tough, though. I came from an inner-city high school, but I knew I could handle the writing curriculum and received my first A in a core class that inaugural semester.

Other classes were harder—and I learned study skills from other students. The best was reading Shakespeare to records borrowed from the Milwaukee Public Library. *The Tempest* remains my favorite.

That second semester, I took Philosophy of Man—and in the first class, an African American classmate put his head down. I soon did likewise.

But after class, the Rev. Robert Maloney called me over. "Never put your head down," he advised.

His words defined my class participation for eight more semesters. I actively engaged, but never said a word. Nods, winces, smiles, frowns. Non-verbal communication at its finest.

Father Maloney also began class with prayer. I didn't know what it was. I told my roommate. "Todd, that's 'The Lord's Prayer.'" I asked him to teach it to me. We then stood in our room, holding hands and reciting "The Lord's Prayer."

The highlight of freshman year was Marquette's climb to the 1977 NCAA Championship. I didn't camp out for tickets; I won a season pass in the lottery. First row, under the home-team basket, behind the cheerleaders. No complaints.

But the night Marquette won in Atlanta, I was studying for a political science test. I was dismayed at missing the party on a rainy Wisconsin Avenue. I was furious the next morning when the test was postponed. Only seven other students showed up.

Before my first year ended, a McCormick Resident Advisor, Robin Flowers, approached me about a minority-student newspaper that he had envisioned.

Counterpoint grew from a four-page newsletter my sophomore year to an eight-page newspaper chronicling Marquette minority-student life. I was managing editor my junior year, serving under seniors Joy Bennett and David Boyd. Allen S. Jones and Cecile Pereyra also were editors.

The newspaper was financed by the Multi-Cultural Center (MCC), but funding was cut—and the death knell came when the Journalism College recruited me as city editor of *The Marquette Tribune*.

My *Tribune* experience was tenuous, at best. I resigned after an interview with Milwaukee Police Chief Harold A. Breier—he called to respond directly to a story I had assigned—was buried in a front-page corner. "Well, there goes our experiment in tokenism," the editor-in-chief lamented, I later learned, once I left the office the very last time.

My toughest year was as a sophomore. Two extensive writing courses each semester, Spanish classes—rougher than usual, since I did not take them seriously—and 18-credit loads proved difficult.

I nearly had a nervous breakdown. My EOP counselor, Dr. Howard Fuller, advised me against leaving for a year, arguing that I likely would not return—and we added another semester to my program.

He also told my mother. *"Are you NUTS???!!!???"*

Regarding grades, I challenged instructors when I perceived that I was not marked fairly. Most didn't like it, particularly teaching assistants.

"I could have done this," one said regarding a sociology quiz grade. "Don't tell me what you could have done," I responded, "tell me why you did what you did."

Most graders were much more attentive afterward.

Outside of class, I got involved in several organizations, particularly Black Student Council (BSC), for which I later served as Legislative Vice President.

The position gave me access to Associated Students of Marquette University (ASMU), which set funding and made programming decisions. I was thankful to help several Black organizations through this opportunity.

I did not pledge any Greek auxiliaries—"I went after the white, racist student newspaper, and that took all my time," I'd later tell my two daughters—but I supported all of Marquette's Black groups.

But one position remains critical to my life: Speakers' Bureau Chairman of Interdenominational Student Church. Under the MCC, it provided a Sunday worship service for Black students.

"I only go to church on Easter—and I haven't been in ten years," I told the director, Greg Moore. "So," he retorted, "you're a good organizer."

We brought in a diversity of speakers—one pastored the Chinese Baptist Church of Milwaukee—but I was most influenced by the Rev. Deborah A. Bent, an associate minister at the storefront Lighthouse Deliverance Church on Milwaukee's North Side.

I was in tears by the time the "Call to Christ" came—and I still don't remember how I got so quickly to the front of the room in the Brooks Memorial Union that Sunday afternoon in October 1980.

I gave my life to Christ that day. Days later, I dedicated my fledgling journalism career to Jesus. I feel blessed that God continues to guide me and helps me to strive for balance, ethics and excellence in all I do.

I regularly dealt with Campus Ministry. In December 1980, Father Rick Abert invited me to read scripture at the Graduation Mass at Gesu Church. I read from the New Testament Letter of James.

Reverend Bent—now Dr. Bent, a retired MPS administrator—and I remain good friends. Dr. Fuller is still a mentor—and Ms. Sande Robinson, my initial EOP counselor, and Dr. Mayberry were always helpful and encouraging.

I received two Marquette service awards: from the MCC and the Office of Student Affairs.

Marquette proved invaluable two other ways: I learned to write my resume in classes taught by Dr. Gail L. Barwis—still use what I learned—and Associate Dean Edward F. Pepan posed a critical question as graduation neared: "Do you want a job, or do you want a career?"

I chose the latter.

I am humbled to have a career approaching its 40th year, bridged nearly every major facet of print journalism—newspapers, magazines, digital—and to have witnessed some of the most significant events of our time.

I started out reporting at the *News-Tribune & Herald* in Duluth, Minnesota, before moving on to local government at *The Richmond News Leader* in Virginia. I was baptized in Richmond in 1983.

Each job had its challenges—subsequent ones, too—but by remaining tenacious, patient and flexible; keeping your facts straight; doing quality work, learning from others, and trusting God, as well as yourself, you will overcome racism—no matter its form.

My father, Willie E. Beamon, who warmed to my being a journalist, provided much strategic advice—gleaned from years as a United Auto Workers' union steward and as the first African American to sit on the statewide leadership board.

I proudly introduced my father to my colleagues at the 2001 convention of the National Association of Black Journalists (NABJ) in Milwaukee.

At *The New York Times*, I was a Business Day copy editor when the Dow Jones Industrial Average plunged 22.6 percent on October 19, 1987—"Black Monday"—throwing the nation into a recession that would last six years. I specialized in the Tokyo Stock Market.

As business editor of the *Philadelphia Daily News*, I shepherded its first computer-assisted reporting effort, on racial bias in bank mortgage-lending, which placed second in a statewide journalism contest.

I then served as senior editor of *BET Weekend Magazine*—interviewing Luther Vandross, Audra McDonald, Chaka Khan and others—and helped create *Savoy* magazine, which also targeted African Americans.

At the Journal Newspapers outside Washington, I slotted all the Maryland reports on the 9/11 attacks. I also was adjunct-teaching, and I saved the Associated Press dispatches for class. "This is how the biggest story of your lives unfolded on the wires."

Moving to Baltimoresun.com, I witnessed digital journalism in its infancy, seeing the genre's potential during the "DC sniper attacks." We first confirmed the third fatality, beating larger competitors and effectively putting the site on the map.

Throughout these years, service remained as important to me as it did at Marquette.

Professionally, I oversaw volunteers who organized hotel and travel accommodations for the 1989 NABJ Convention in New York. Speakers included Army Lt. Gen. Colin Powell and Jamaica Prime Minister Michael Manley. I also negotiated a $250,000 donation for the organization's first technology-based skill workshops. Similar sessions were held in succeeding years.

I have served the community through church—tutoring students, teaching Sunday School—through career panels and workshops, and I worked "turkey duty" three years at the "Christmas Family Feast" in Milwaukee.

I now am editor-in-chief of Digital Privacy News, an independent news website of the nonprofit Magnusson Institute in Reno, Nevada, devoted to coverage of "all things privacy."

We launched on March 30, 2020. By June 3, we had 10,000 Twitter followers.

I manage freelance writers in the US and across the globe—and, at 61, I learn daily as much about myself as I do my writers.

"And we know that all things work together for good to those who love God, to those who are called according to His purpose."

— Romans 8:28 NKJV

Sharon Irving

Nursing, Class of 1980

Finding My Resiliency, Nurturing My Toughness

August 1975—driving to Wisconsin Avenue and 18th Street with my parents in a beige Buick, finding O'Donnell Hall. Me, a 17-year-old Harlem-grown girl, by way of upper New York City and the BRONX—how was I now in Milwaukee, Wisconsin? Well, by way of a New York State Regents scholarship that various circumstances prevented me from using in New York, the need to increase underrepresented minorities in the College of Nursing at Marquette and a persuasive mother telling my father "let her go"—here I was. I was at Marquette! Not at all sure I wanted to be a nurse, but I was going to the College of Nursing at Marquette University, one of the best in the country. I was ready—were they???

"Culture-shock," no other way to describe what I felt as I started at Marquette. I knew the Midwest would be different, I knew that Marquette was low in minority and underrepresented groups in the student population, but I was from New York—I saw and grew up with every race and ethnicity, and now, what was I immersed in? There were NOT enough faces that looked like mine walking around campus. I was not prepared, not ready. I was not ready for the differences, not ready for "pop"—it's soda; I wasn't prepared for pizza cut in squares—what happened to the wedge that you fold in half; mostly, I was not prepared for the cultural differences and blatant dislike I experienced being a Black girl from New York. I wasn't prepared; I wasn't ready.

I quickly realized I needed a community to survive. That was null at the College of Nursing. I made a few friends, Diane, Barbie, Nancy, Patti, Susan and Peg, who were a part of me obtaining a solid nursing education at Marquette, they helped me survive; however, I did not have a sense of belonging. I was tolerated—a little. Inside the College of Nursing was not the place to go for help adapting to this environment so far from home. I, a first-generation college student, a Black girl from New York, I did not find help adjusting to college life from faculty. I learned commuting across town wearing the navy blue dress with white apron was not fun. I learned that the late classes on main campus necessary to meet my elective requirements made me miss campus hall dinner. I learned that being in the top 2% of my high school class did not mean a thing here, as everyone else had been at the top of their high school class too. For the first time ever, I struggled to attain and maintain good grades. The struggle was real. In part, I struggled due to the workload, and traveling across town for nursing classes—I attended and graduated from Marquette before the College of Nursing was on the Wisconsin Avenue campus. In those days school for me was across town (two buses) at St. Joseph's Hospital. In part I struggled to acclimate to life in the Midwest—culturally different than New York; and in part I struggled to adjust to dormitory life. Lots of "parts" adding to my struggle. Too many girls sharing bathrooms, showers, work and eating spaces, just too many, and not enough that looked like me. One of many experiences that was a constant reminder of my struggle at Marquette: my roommate and I (also a Black female) were asked by one of our neighbors in O'Donnell Hall if we could stay away from the dorm for a weekend as her parents would be visiting and she didn't want them to know she lived next door to two Black girls. Yes, I struggled.

Nursing school at Marquette was tough. Nursing education is a combination of science and humanity with hands-on skill development and care delivery, an over-simplification, but nursing education and nursing care crosses race, ethnicity and gender, doesn't it? In the late 1970s at Marquette in the College of Nursing, I was often and openly reminded that I "did not belong," "would not make it" and accused of not exhibiting "seriousness" toward my educational choice. One of my professors, (I wish I could remember her name) who also happened to be my advisor, suggested in one of our advising sessions that I should quit, transfer out of nursing, because "you won't finish, and if you do, you cannot represent Marquette nursing." A blow to my intelligence, my ego and my self-confidence. Was this statement to encourage or discourage me? I wasn't sure. But I learned from my patients (even as a student) and little did I know a foundation and passion for nursing clinical practice was developing. Following the initial shock of a nursing professor advising me to quit nursing school, I found my resilience, my determination. But nursing school is tough. I believe that advisor reminded me of my innate toughness—I was from New York! So, after taking a semester off to ground myself, I embraced my resilience, and even more, my toughness. The educational foundation I received at Marquette, the self-recognition of my resiliency, my inquisitiveness and my toughness, set me on a path for career success that I now enjoy as a nurse practitioner, nurse educator and nurse scientist.

I will forever be grateful to the community that found me and that I found in my early days at Marquette. Ms. Sarah Ford, the "Midwest Express" (who became my big brothers), my roommates Jody in Schroeder Hall and Andrida in our "da bomb" apartment up on Wisconsin Ave and 25th Street, Sheena always encouraging and Cedricka my "big sister." My Milwaukee parents, Mr and Mrs J, the sorors of Delta Sigma Theta Sorority, "Pope" keeping jazz alive and so many others rounded out that community. All are a part of my fabric of resiliency, my determination; they collectively helped me strengthen my innate toughness. Toughness needed to survive the challenges of the culture, the school, and then of course, the weather. Whatever clichés go along with bitterly cold weather—INSERT HERE! The cold was a definite obstacle to be endured, freezing temperatures, lake-effect wind and snow, not a good combination; but I had my community, and I continued to develop my resiliency and toughness. When it is −25 degrees, snow to your knees and classes are not cancelled, a warm coat, hat, gloves, boots and toughness is what you need!

What have I learned, what did I take away from Marquette, a great deal. My undergraduate nursing education while challenging on so many levels and clouded with racial bias and intolerance strengthened my toughness, the foundation of my being, that which my parents proudly gave me and growing up in life in New York solidified. After my early experiences at Marquette I set out to discover what I really wanted to do, I no longer thought it was nursing, but my passion was growing and, I would work as a nurse, while I pursued what I really wanted to do. So, within days of graduation—back to New York!

I never pursued another career; I am still a nurse. My career journey has taken me across the country and back, and for now in Philadelphia. I have been in patient care in some capacity since I left Marquette, feeding my passion. I have been called the lowest of the low and thanked by families and colleagues alike for the fervidness I exhibit in care delivery—all seeded from my education and my Marquette experience. Experiences throughout my career, have put me in situations that were it not for my resiliency, my determination, and my toughness, I may have left nursing. What did I learn at Marquette? I learned not only the science of nursing and hands-on care delivery, I learned resiliency, I learned tolerance, I learned to recognize bias, and I learned to accept differences; taking all these lessons and numerous others, I continue to nurture my toughness, develop my passion of caring, my passion for nursing.

I completed the Bachelor of Science in Nursing (BSN) program in 1980. I left Marquette bitter, and it took 25 years before I would return. At the time of my return for an "Ethnic Alumni Reunion" I was thrilled to revisit with so many from my community and honor those whose memory gives me strength and reminds me of the challenges and obstacles Marquette placed in my path, reminding me of the lessons learned, strengthening my resiliency and my toughness. I have since earned both a Masters and PhD degree in Nursing, so I did graduate—a couple times after leaving Marquette. Disproving the words of my Marquette advisor, telling me: "you won't graduate," I have come full circle—in 2013, I was awarded the Distinguished Alumni in Nursing Service Award from Marquette University College of Nursing. Now, when I think about my days at Marquette, I am not bitter—I have survived. I made lifelong friends there, I nurtured my resiliency there, my passion for nursing burgeoned at Marquette.

Bruce Spann

Civil Engineering, Class of 1980

Growing up in South Bend, Indiana, I did not visit my public high school counselor's office for the first time until early in my senior year. I guess I inherited being good at math from my mother and father, who are both good at math. So, I did decide I wanted to be a math major. One day in senior year I did not want to go to my second hour class (don't recall what class, but it wasn't math) and didn't want to skip school. So, I went to the counselor's office. It so happened there was a recruiter from Marquette University visiting. I asked her if Marquette had an architecture major and she said yes. (I found out the first week at Marquette Freshman Orientation that was not true). Several weeks later, I returned to the counselor's office and he asked if I was the person that visited when Marquette was recruiting, and I said yes. He said they seemed very interested in you, and I think you should apply. I applied to Marquette and Purdue University, and both accepted me. I did not want to stay in Indiana, and Marquette was close enough but far enough from home. So, I accepted their offer to attend and major in architectural engineering.

I did not know anyone personally that had attended Marquette. The closest was a mentor I had from kindergarten through high school graduation named Mr. Archibald Bradford. Mr. Bradford founded the Upward Bound Program at Notre Dame and helped to establish Marquette's Upward Bound Program. Mr. Bradford said Marquette was a good academic choice. And off I went.

The fact that the student body was overwhelmingly white did not play a factor in my decision to enroll at Marquette. I attended Benjamin Franklin Elementary School through sixth grade, which was a predominately minority student body. It was at least 90% African American as I only recall one white male and one female of Pacific Islander descent in my sixth grade class. However, Thomas Jefferson Middle School (7th and 8th grades) and John Adams High School (9th–12th grades) were predominately white student body. I would estimate it was at least

80% white student body. By the time I entered Marquette University, I had adapted to a majority white student body.

Religion was also not a factor in choosing Marquette University. I grew up in the Baptist and Pentecostal religions. Growing up in South Bend, Indiana, I was familiar with Catholicism since I would work on Notre Dame University's campus at the Morris Inn Restaurant as a busboy throughout high school and college.

My freshman year at MU I lived in McCormick Hall, which back then had the nickname "THE ZOO." It did live up to that nickname. I had a roommate from British Honduras who also had the same major. He was a challenge to room with because he would come in the room at 2 or 3 a.m., do pushups, then go back out and study more. This was the rule rather than exception, and he did burn himself out and left the university after one year.

My second year I moved to what was at the time the YMCA. Marquette took over the top nine floors as additional dorm rooms. They later acquired the Y and it is now Straz Hall. A nice advantage to staying at the Y was having our own gym; so during bad weather we could choose to go there rather than the Helfear Recreation Center. The Y is also where I met someone that would become a lifelong friend and a person whom I would have the honor to be the godfather of his first-born child, Charles Williams who hails from Queens, New York. Charles went on to work on Wall Street and was later recruited to Nations Bank in Charlotte, North Carolina. He was recruited by Fr. Robert Wild to serve as a Marquette University Trustee along with Glenn (Doc) Rivers and Ulice Payne.

Overall, my professors were concerned and caring. Freshman orientation was a critical time for deciding whether to stay at Marquette. I grew up wanting to be an architect. I did not know any, but I think it was because it sounded cool and because I watched the Brady Bunch and the father was an architect who wore a suit to work. However, orientation week I found out Marquette did not have architectural angineering, but rather I would be enrolling as a civil engineering student. I was upset and thought I would transfer after my first year to Notre Dame, which I knew had an architectural program (of course there was no guarantee I would be accepted). I did decide to meet with Professor Murphy, who was the chair of the Civil Engineering Department. Professor Murphy pointed out that (1) architects were not being hired at the time, (2) it is a very difficult profession to become successful and to make a good living, (3) civil engineers were in demand at the time and were being hired with good starting salaries, and (4) civil engineers, particularly structural concentrations work, with architects who make the buildings look pretty and structural engineers make sure they don't collapse (well, that was the gist of his argument anyway as I saw it). So, I decided to stay, and that was the right decision.

My most negative experience while a student was also the first year when I met with my advisor just before midterm grades were to be released. My advisor was the Assistant Dean of the College of Engineering, Dr. Ted Dziadulewicz. I was very disappointed that even though grades had not been released, he tried to persuade me to transfer out of engineering. After a few minutes of exchanging pleasantries and talking about how things were going so far, he looked at me and said, "You have very good tonal qualities, have you ever thought about being a speech or journalism major?" Not that there is anything wrong with either major. I thought to myself that he could at lease let me flunk out of COE first, but I was so taken aback that I just replied I had not thought of either major. He followed that I should take it into consideration. I did not.

My favorite professor was Dr. Thomas Wenzel, who taught reinforced concrete and prestressed concrete. Dr. Wenzel was very caring of all his students and wanted all of us to succeed. My senior year I informed him I had accepted employment with Bechtel Power Corporation and was relocating to San Francisco. Dr. Wenzel was very happy for me and thought very highly of my future employer. Several years later I visited the campus and stopped by COE. Dr. Wenzel recognized me right away and asked how I was doing and how were things with Bechtel?

I was not accepted in the EOP program my freshman year. I did not understand how I did not qualify. My parents were divorced, and we lived with my father and he was a construction worker that did not earn a middle-class income, not even close. In fact, he worked two jobs from the age of 16 until retirement. Eventually, I was accepted into the program my last year and that was critically important because I needed the financial assistance to complete my fifth year. My other funding (loans) ran out after four years. Were it not for EOP, I probably would have left Marquette without earning my degree, as I saw happen to other minority students.

While attending MU, I was an active member of the Multi-Cultural Center, and I helped to establish the National Technical Association (NTA) at the COE. NTA was a professional Minority Technical Organization that had student chapters on various campuses around the United States. I also served as the chapter

President for one year. I also played intermural basketball. I did not have an interest in joining a fraternity. My most memorable experience was being selected a 1978 Student of the Year Award Recipient from the National Technical Association at the end of the first year I helped found the Marquette Student Chapter. Close second is Marquette becoming the 1977 Collegiate Basketball National Champions.

My Marquette experience had advantages in four key turning points/milestones in my life. First and foremost was my friendship with Jackie Rogers that led to marrying Vivian Portis. We had a son, Jaryd Michael Spann, a blessing from God. I didn't know when I graduated in 1980 that my future wife would actually be 3,000 miles away from where I began employment upon graduation, and six years after graduation.

The second was with my first employer, Bechtel Power Corporation, which was a 120,000-employee sized company with employees around the world. The corporate headquarters in San Francisco had over 9,000 employees. And out of those 9,000+ employees I would be in their power division where one of the upper managers that was responsible for our salaries and promotions was a Marquette University COE Alum. I do not recall his last name, but his first was Eugene. Maybe being an alum was reason to treat me as fairly as he did; it certainly didn't hurt.

My third advantage and turning point in my life was in April 1993 returning to Milwaukee to work for a small, African American owned startup company called Edwards & Associates, Inc. At the time, I was living in Washington, DC, when a friend, classmate and one of the four African American graduates in my 1980 engineering class, Rick Norris, called me about this job opportunity. He told me it was a guy named Horace Edwards who had started this company two years earlier and was looking for someone to run the Milwaukee office. I told Rick I had no intention of returning to the Midwest and especially not Milwaukee. Well, that was January 1993, and I started with the company April 1993. This is because when I researched more, I remembered that in 1984 when I was visiting Charles Williams in New York, we were wowed by an article in *Ebony Magazine*. It was about a man named Horace Edwards, who at the time was President and CEO of ARCO Pipeline and had been selected as the 1984 Marquette University College of Engineering Distinguished Alumnus of the Year. He was the first African American selected for this award by COE, among his several other firsts. Horace was also the only African American in ROTC at Marquette at the time he attended (probably the first), and Milwaukee white residents would come down to campus on Saturdays when the ROTC cadets were conducting drills on campus to see for themselves if it were true there was one. Horace earned a degree in naval science and returned to campus after World War II and earned a bachelor's degree in mechanical engineering. He may have been the first African American to graduate in engineering from Marquette. He earned these degrees in 1946 and 1948. Anyway, Horace had started Edwards & Associates, Inc. after stepping down as the Secretary of the Department of Transportation for the State of Kansas in 1990. Horace started the company for two reasons: (1) when he left Milwaukee in 1956 he vowed to himself and others that he would return one day to do something positive and meaningful in Milwaukee and (2) because he wanted to offer the opportunity for us to earn the right to purchase his company, leaving behind a legacy. I was responsible for managing the Milwaukee offices, which was his intent because he had no desire to relocate from Topeka, Kansas. And because he always tries to be a person of his word, his goal was for Milwaukee to be the flagship of the company. I accepted the responsibility, and although I was in way over my head, I knew when I accepted that he would be my safety net. The ten years I ran the Milwaukee offices gave me invaluable experience, business connections and understanding of how to run a business and that Cash is both King and Queen to its success. Under his leadership, I gained all this and the confidence to start my own company in 2006.

The fourth way the community helped is when I started Spann & Associates, LLC, among the companies I developed good professional relationships with were Graef, Anhalt, Schloemer & Associates (Now Graef USA) and Kapur & Associates, Inc. John Goetter was a vice president and among the numerous Marquette alums to work for Graef USA. In fact, the founders were all alum. John gave Spann & Associates our first contract. Ramesh Kapur is the President of Kapur & Associates, who came to the United States from India to attend COE Graduate School. Ramesh has also been a key supporter of our company and has given us numerous opportunities to work on the largest public works projects in Wisconsin state history, including the Marquette Interchange, the Zoo Interchange, the Mitchell Interchange and the Interstate 94 Corridor from the Illinois state line north along the reconstruction of 35 miles of interstate.

Over the years, I have remained active with my alma mater. I have been an active member of the Ethnic Alumni Association and a financial supporter of Marquette University, including endowing the Bruce A. Spann Endowment

Scholarship. If I had a chance, I would choose Marquette again for the education and friendships I gained and life experiences. I was the first to attend and graduate from college in my immediate family. And fortunate to have my younger brother Ronnie follow me to Marquette. (Ronnie and I are one year apart.)

My greatest personal achievement has been helping my son Jaryd Michael Spann further his education earning bachelor and master's degrees. He and his lovely wife will be making me a proud grandparent of twins in December 2020. Professionally, it was being awarded the 2014 Marquette University College of Engineering Distinguished Alumnus of the Year Award, 30 years to the month after my business mentor, Horace Edwards.

George Lowery, PhD

Class of 1980

As an undergraduate student I attended Fayetteville State University. It is a small Historically Black College in North Carolina. I also participated in the Civil Rights movement as a community organizer in 1968 with Howard Fuller at the North Carolina Fund. My duties included voter registration and home improvement.

After a short time as a graduate student at Southern Illinois University in the Department of Community Development and as a student counselor, I moved to Milwaukee. I met Arnold Mitchem at Marquette University. He hired me as assistant director in the Educational Opportunity Program. I knew nothing about Marquette University other than its reputation in the Black community as an excellent university with very few Black students, especially from Milwaukee. I had no other knowledge or affiliation with MU. However, the academic reputation of the institution made the employment opportunity very attractive.

As assistant director of the Educational Opportunity Program, I learned a great deal about the quality of MU. My colleagues and I worked closely with the university faculty and staff. As a staff member I had a unique experience of connecting my MU experience with my advocacy for civil rights and social justice. I worked as a peer with the university faculty. I found the university faculty and students willing to work with me on critical issues facing low-income and minority students. They were creative in their thinking, and they were prepared to work hard to help our students to succeed.

I enrolled as a graduate student in 1975. The combination of being on staff and later a student provided me with a chance to understand and appreciate the value of the Marquette collegiate experience. Combining my background in community organizing and education was invaluable. My role as assistant director involved contacting families and students, counseling, persuading and explaining to parents and students the value of a Marquette experience. This was a new, scary idea in Milwaukee's low-income minority, first-generation families.

The faculty and staff had a major impact on my thinking as a professional educator. The faculty worked with me to develop an innovative curriculum for pre-engineering and pre-health science students. This would create a pipeline/cadre of minority students entering fields with low minority representation. MU provided these students a positive learning environment.

Additionally, my experience as a graduate in the College of Education gave me the confidence and leadership skills to pursue higher challenges as an educator and advocate for social change. Without the experience, I may not have chosen to pursue my doctorate at Harvard University Graduate School of Education.

As a former university vice president at the University of Detroit-Mercy, dean at Detroit-Mercy, and Roosevelt University, Chicago, I am pleased to have been influenced by the Marquette experience. If had to do it again, I would not trade my MU experience for anything.

Marquette University had a profound effect on my life, my friendships and various transformations I have had while helping others to achieve equality in a traditional and quality educational setting.

I would like to dedicate my work at MU to my colleagues and faculty that supported me 1970–1980.

Vanessa Ann Brown

Class of 1981

Marquette was not my first choice; however, it was one of the few colleges at that time that offered urban planning as an option in the civil engineering program. My parents were concerned about me being far away from Chicago and not having family nearby. I had an aunt and uncle that lived blocks from the university, so Marquette became my first choice. I was a first-generation student coming from a predominantly Black high school and community.

Upon arriving on campus, I was placed in an upper-class dormitory where there were a handful of minorities. I had expected my roommate to not be a minority; however, it was clear from our first encounter with her and her parents they had not expected her to have a Black roommate. Although she and I shared engineering as a major there was little else we shared. I could use her record player, but I could not play race music although she used my refrigerator and electric skillet. Lights needed to be out by 9 p.m. as she was an early riser. At night she slept with the window open (however, the window she opened was on my side of the room). I felt like the third floor orphan as I spent more time either in the hallway studying or in other students' rooms.

Before I left for college my godfather, who was a Jewish, gay male, and I had talked about embracing diversity. Since I had chosen a predominantly white Catholic university of which I was neither, he told me that I was going to have to be the one to reach out and make my experiences. I began reaching out to fellow dorm mates and found myself a part of the touch football team with women from my floor. I also had the cleanest teeth on campus as most of the women on my floor were dental hygienists and whenever their patients cancelled, I was sitting in a chair. For study breaks women on my floor would just come out in the hallway, and we would engage in horseplay. Weekends were reserved for going out for food, drinks and midnight Mass of which I was included. I had become part of the group so on the evening when things had come to a head with me and my room-mate, the resident advisor found her another room.

I remember walking into General Engineering 101; once again I expected to be a minority with regard to ethnicity, but I did not expect to be a double minority with regard to gender. I had attended a technical high school on Chicago's South Side. There were a number of young men and women who had chosen engineering as their major as they went off to college. There were four women and five Blacks including myself in my engineering freshman class. I will never forget sitting in my engineering dynamics class as the instructor would tell the racist "white man –China man jokes." My engineering statics teacher explained to me that I was taking a position in engineering from another male who would need to support his family. When I complained to the head of the Civil Engineering Department, I was told that I was being too sensitive and that nothing was meant by the jokes or statement. But I had a mother who taught me by example, that when faced with obstacles to keep pressing forward, and I completed both classes. While I was not surprised by the response, it brought me back to my freshman year when I had to take on the English department.

Students come to college not realizing that your best in high school may not be that A or B in college. Freshman English was that reality check for me. As I was handed my first graded freshman English paper with a C, I was trying to understand what went wrong. I made an appointment with the instructor to go over my paper so that I could correct what I did wrong and improve my grade on the next paper. As I entered his office, he said he could see I was not EOP (Educational Opportunity Program) and wondered how I could afford to attend Marquette. Since I did not know what EOP was, I replied that I had scholarships, grants and loans. I then tried to ask about my paper and asked how I could improve. The instructor proceeded to state that a C was a good grade for Blacks since we were not that proficient in grammar. Even after his statement I was still trying to understand where my paper could improve. I don't remember if I ever got anything from him as to how I could. I remember leaving angry and frustrated. When I returned to the dorm, I relayed what happened to some women on my floor, one of which was a journalism major and the other's boyfriend was also a journalism major. Both of them agreed to be a reader on my next paper. I completed my second paper, they both read it and provided feedback, I turned it in and received a D. At that point I spoke with my aunt, who suggested I go to the English Department head.

I did, and the department head scheduled a meeting with both of us. Meanwhile my aunt had asked a professor she knew at University of Wisconsin Milwaukee (UWM) to review both of my papers. The meeting was held, and I presented the department head with both of my papers and comments and statements from the journalism students and UWM professor. It was decided that my next paper would also be reviewed by the English Department head. I received a B and passed the class. I was told the instructor went on a sabbatical for second semester. When I met with my engineering advisor to discuss classes for sophomore year, he told me that I was gaining a reputation as a troublemaker and if I wanted to get through the program I need to not take things so personally.

When I look back at my time at Marquette, I am thankful. Because I attended Marquette, I had an opportunity to meet a powerful Black woman named Sarah Ann Ford. She was the first director of the Multi-Cultural Center. For a number of students that were not part of the EOP program, she provided a listening ear, counseling and encouragement and connected students with resources to navigate through the university's bureaucracy. She showed how to lead and provided opportunities to lead. She helped a group of female students, of which I was one, to charter the first Black Greek undergraduate organization (Delta Sigma Theta Sorority, Lambda Phi Chapter) on Marquette University's campus. I got my engineering internship in Chicago due to my affiliation with the sorority. I had not realized that companies interviewed for internships during Christmas break, so when I came home during spring break, Peoples Gas Light and Coke Company had filled their intern slots for the summer. The human resource recruiter saw my resume and offered me an interview for a summer slot with the ability to become part of the internship program for the following years. Why? His wife was a member of Delta Sigma Theta!

The internship and attending Marquette also got me an interview with Wisconsin Electric Power Company, where I worked in numerous positions for over forty years until my retirement. I can say that my experiences at Marquette added to my tool bag. I learned to appreciate diversity, navigate through racism by not being afraid to speak up and out when you feel things are not just. Not to be afraid to lead even when you are not sure of the path. I have also had the opportunity to give back to the Marquette by serving as a past-president of the Ethnic Alumni Association (EAA) of Marquette University. But most importantly, I credit my attendance at Marquette for the people I met; some of whom have become part of my extended family and many of which I am proud to call friends.

Robert L. Simpson

Class of 1981

I am a Milwaukee native and proud to state that I am the twelfth child of eighteen children. I was raised as a Catholic in a very disciplined household. Neither of my parents attended college. My father, Theron Sr., was the provider and together with my mother, Mary Catherine, took a lot of pride in how we presented ourselves publicly, and education took precedence over everything. Our friends were diverse and regardless of the size of the Simpson family, anyone was welcome to join us for dinner. School, especially advanced education, was neither a priority nor a reality for many of the kids in my neighborhood simply because they deemed the abundant and "great paying" factory jobs more desirable.

I always felt I lived in two worlds. I was raised three miles north of the Marquette University campus in a once proudly integrated community; however, it became a predominantly Black neighborhood shortly after the Civil Rights protests and riots of the late '60s. I attended Marquette University High School (MUHS), thanks to a program that subsidized tuition to foster integration into this highly regarded, private and predominantly white all-boys high school.

As a teen, I recall staying up late to watch telecasts of the then Marquette Warriors basketball games, boasting Black stars such as Jim Chones, Dean "The Dream" Meminger, and Lloyd Walton, and led by one of coolest head coaches, Al McGuire. The late, great Maurice Lucas loved to come to our popular neighborhood soul-food restaurant, George & Eula's. My house, the restaurant and playground were all within a few doorsteps, so Maurice would occasionally stop by the court to watch us play. To top it off, I attended a youth basketball clinic in Prairie du Chen, Wisconsin, and much to my surprise, "The Dream" was one of the clinic coaches. He selected me to play a game of one-on-one. I scored on him and then on my next attempt, he swatted my shot across the gym. I was clearly set up. I always envisioned myself wearing the ever-popular bumblebee jersey, playing for my hometown university. MUHS intently touted the 98% of graduates who went on to pursue college degrees, and I was determined not to become part of the remaining 2%.

I was always inspired by my older siblings who went on to graduate from reputable colleges and universities. They established a legacy that could not be dismissed. Plus, the thought of working in a blue-collar environment was far from appealing to me. Once a select of group of my MUHS Class of '76 friends indicated they planned to make the short trip east on Wisconsin Avenue to attend Marquette University, my choice was clear. But first, two minor hurdles needed to be addressed—1) would I qualify for acceptance, and 2) how would I afford it? Unlike my MUHS classmates, I did not come from such economic means. In fact, my mother affectionately referred to our family as being "upper-class poor."

My high school counselor always had my best interests at heart. He informed me of this incredible program, the Educational Opportunity Program (EOP). I secured an introduction to the executive recruiter, Arthur Mayberry, and thankfully it resulted in a successful interview. Being accepted to Marquette University (Class of 1980) was one of my proudest accomplishments. I decided to attend the School of Speech to pursue my love for sports broadcasting. Immediately, I went to the MU bookstore and bought T-shirts and shorts. I wanted everyone to know!

At the start of my EOP journey, Jimmy Carter was inheriting the White House. By graduation, Ronald Reagan occupied it. I was aware of the significance of this period of history. Therefore, I believed I was part of a special group. A group of first-generation college students. A group that would be judged as different. And maybe to some, afforded "special" privileges to be able to attend a respected university. Unfortunately, and fortunately, that was not unlike my tenure at Marquette High, so, I was prepared. EOP had incredible leaders, such as founder Dr. Arnold Mitchem, Dr. Howard Fuller, and of course, Sande Robinson. They were committed to exhausting every resource to foster our success, and they were always transparent and motivating. I understood they carried a tremendous burden to see us succeed, as well, to ensure the foundation of the program would be sustained when there was no precedent to prove this was a smart investment by the government and MU.

My first year had mixed results. I felt I belonged and had no doubt that this was where I wanted to be. Day one, the history professor made it clear his class was challenging, and he asked the EOP students to identify themselves by raising our hands. He then went on the suggest we get a tutor to ensure success. Although I shared their embarrassment and was led to feel less than equal, I was disappointed that half of the EOP students transferred, instead of working to prove him wrong. I also had a journalism professor advise me to pursue another major because I did not have a chance in this profession. In both cases, the experience was demeaning and severely misaligned with the Jesuit values MU touted.

Although I could walk home, EOP afforded me the privilege of living on campus. I loved this first taste of freedom, as it made me feel like a real college student and it helped my maturation. However, the benefits that came with being an EOP student were not taken as seriously with a few of my classmates, and they eventually were released. I refused to let my family, the leaders of EOP and myself down. I was committed to overcome the home distractions and the naysayers.

If you mentioned Marquette back then and today, the first thing most would say is Warriors. I was fortunate to be there when the team became NCAA Basketball National Champs in '77. I remember that day like it was yesterday. The rain did not stop everyone from running down Wisconsin Avenue, screaming, hugging and passing out beers. The team's success, led primarily by Black athletes, resonated throughout my years. They were "our" guys. They made us proud and somewhat more acceptable to the masses on campus.

Much like Milwaukee communities, MU was very socially segregated. The dorms were integrated, but Black students were heavily scrutinized upon entering buildings or engaging in student activities. The Multi-Cultural Center offered a safe haven to meet others like us, whether EOP student or not. Our campus parties were the best, and other area students wanted to be part of them. While at MU, I remained very active. I was a disc jockey, member of the Alpha Phi Alpha Fraternity (Nu Xi) and a member of the gospel choir, to name a few. The balance of Chicago and Milwaukee area kids made for seamless connecting and sustained relationships, many of which I still enjoy today. We wanted the school to demonstrate we were accepted, but that was not always welcomed. We had each other. For example, to offer diverse engagements to campus, the first minority student president, Douglas Kelley, was met with racist objections to booking an on-campus performance by R&B group Sister Sledge. It was one of my least favorite, though most memorable, days to see white students protesting with signs stating, "Sister Sledge are Whores."

I eventually graduated with the Class of '81. My younger sister, Monica, graduated from the University of Wisconsin that same day. Miraculously, my parents were able to make the commute and attend both ceremonies. This was my second proudest day. I accepted my first job in sales with Milwaukee Headquarters, Miller Brewing Company. I enjoyed fruitful tenures in marketing and sales with a few Fortune 500 firms. Although it was seen favorably with Miller, Marquette did not carry the same cachet outside the Midwest. Being a MU grad did not open doors, but it prepared me for professional life and enabled experiences I only dreamed about growing up on 12th and North Avenue.

I was not the only Simpson that furthered their education at Marquette. My siblings, Douglas and Madeleine, obtained a law degree ('82) and biochem ('90)/ med tech ('04) degrees, respectively.

I remain supportive, especially regarding anything EOP. When possible, I attend Golden Eagles' games in Milwaukee and Chicago. I served an incomplete role as At-large Alumni Board Member. Reminder, money matters. Now a resident of Chicago, I attend select chapter engagements. In 2019, I attended EOP's 50th Anniversary Gala. I could not be any more humbled, honored and inspired to be a part of hundreds of diverse alumni that realized the benefit of EOP to overcome their own personal barriers to reach their full potential. Successful journeys like this have generational and social impact.

Currently, I am a business development executive with a global financial and insurance firm and reside in the greater Chicago market, with my wife of 23 years, India, along with our 21-year old daughter, Taylor; 19-year old son, Alex; and 16-year old son, Christian.

We Are Marquette!

Regina Dixon-Reeves, PhD

Journalism, Class of 1982

I applied to Marquette University because the basketball team had won the 1977 NCAA Championship. I knew nothing of its academic ranking, faculty reputation, cost of attendance or placement rate of graduates. As a first-generation student, the only college advising I received from my Catholic high school was to apply to Jesuit universities. I received admissions offers from six schools including UCLA and Howard University. My mom said that if I went to California, she could only afford to bring me home once a year. As an only child, that seemed unbearable. She vetoed Howard University because my best friend had been accepted there, and she feared we might go to DC and end up flunking out together. Since Marquette was only two hours away and had a championship basketball team, it seemed like the perfect choice.

Once I made my decision, I remembered a postcard inviting me to take a tour of the campus. I caught the Greyhound bus to Milwaukee for the tour. I hadn't known to visit schools before I made my decision. I thought everyone made their selection using the college catalogues. I had no idea how I was going to pay for college, but figured I would find someone there who could tell me about financing school.

While on the campus tour, I happened upon a group of Black students. I was so happy to see them because there were no people of color in my tour group and I had seen almost no people of color in any of the buildings we had toured. One of the students asked if I were a new EOP student. I had never heard of EOP. They explained it was the Educational Opportunity Program, a program for low income, ethnic minority first-generation college students. They suggested I visit Johnston Hall. Sande Robinson was the first person I met. She told me about the program, looked up my record and asked me if I could come back in a couple weeks for the six-week summer pre-college program. EOP became the way I financed my undergraduate education. I am convinced that if I had not had that serendipitous meeting with those students, I would not have attended Marquette.

I arrived at Marquette the summer of 1978 for the pre-college program for entering freshmen. I was proud to be at Marquette on scholarship. I was a first-generation college student and only the third person in my extended family to attempt college. The other two were my mother's youngest siblings whom my mom helped to send to college. I am the first of my cousins (children of my mother's 12 siblings) to graduate from college.

I enjoyed my time at Marquette and loved being part of the EOP family. EOP offered a great mix of academic and social activities designed to support us and make us feel welcome to a campus that was often hostile and indifferent towards us. I will never forget Howard Fuller speaking to us from the fourth floor of Johnston Hall. As we sat surrounded by people who looked like us, he told us to look to the left and the right. He said if we didn't work hard, we could expect that two of us would not be there in a year or two. He said that we should imagine ourselves on a giant waterslide that ran down the steps of Johnston Hall and out onto Wisconsin Ave. I remember thinking he was harsh and the analogy ridiculous, but by my junior year, I was the only one left of my eight-member crew from freshman year.

The first day of fall orientation was a complete culture shock for me. I remember looking out my dorm window at what seemed to be a "sea of whiteness" crossing Wisconsin Ave. I didn't know where all the white people had come from. When I came for the college tour, it had been during spring break—so there weren't many people on campus. When I came for the summer program, we attended classes as a cohort, and in retrospect, I don't think a lot of people attended summer school. I was completely flabbergasted when I went to register for fall classes and saw how few people of color were actually on campus. It was not unusual for me to be the only one or one of a few people of color in my classes. I was from segregated Chicago; I had never been in academic or social spaces with white people. EOP provided me with a comfort zone where I could find students who looked like me and a group of staff, mentors and tutors that I could turn to for respite.

I credit Sande Robinson for my success at Marquette. I earned three D's my first semester and was put on academic probation. I'd never received anything lower than an occasional B during elementary or high school. Sande got in my face and told me that I was much smarter than my grades suggested and that she believed in me. She also insisted that I participate in supervised study. She encouraged me to develop real study habits that I carried with me long after I was no longer required to attend the supervised sessions. Each quarter she would check in with me even though she was not my counselor. It was her consistent belief in my abilities and my unwavering determination not to let my mother down that kept me at Marquette. I was not going to return to Chicago without a college degree.

After digging myself out of academic probation, I had an epiphany while taking a sociology course taught by Dr. Carol Y. Smith She was a full-time administrator and an adjunct professor in the sociology department. She was also the only Black professor that I had during my four years at Marquette. I remember being completely engaged in her class. I don't remember ever having a teacher who was as passionate, animated or knowledgeable. She had to be because she was regularly challenged by the white students in the class. She held her own and it was during that class that I decided I liked Marquette academically not just socially. I received my first A in her class.

Receiving that A changed how I saw myself. The only message I remember hearing from EOP and my mother was that I needed to "keep my scholarship." The GPA requirement for the scholarship was 2.0 so I did just enough to maintain it and keep my very active calendar of extracurricular activities. Getting that A and a couple after that made me realize that I really was as smart as any of my white counterparts. That knowledge was essential when I applied for graduate school. I graduated from Marquette with a 2.34 GPA. Given my grade point average, I should never have gone to graduate school and definitely not to the University of Chicago. But it was that A and Sande's many lectures about how you could turn anything around with hard work that made me think anything was possible.

I enjoyed my time at Marquette. While I did not excel academically, I flourished socially. I joined a sorority my sophomore year, participated in several student clubs and was very active in student government. Much of what I know about student-centered programming, I learned from being such an actively engaged student leader. While I am happy to say I graduated from Marquette in four years, I do have a few regrets that are a direct result of my status as a first-generation student. I regret not studying abroad. I know it would have been a transformative experience. I regret not making use of campus resources like working at the campus radio or television stations or utilizing the career placement center to secure internships or jobs. I regret not making one white friend during my four years at

Marquette. Despite these few regrets, I came of age at Marquette, made lifetime friendships and earned a degree that has served me well over the course of my working career.

I've spent more than 35 years as a practitioner and educator expanding access into higher education and working to improve the experiences of those who are underrepresented and often underserved in those institutions. As an educator, I have a passion for students who are low-income, first-generation and/or immigrants who dream of earning a college degree. I currently serve as Assistant Provost at the University of Chicago but have worked across several industries including philanthropy, social science survey research and educational administration at both the high school and collegiate levels. My liberal arts education from Marquette has allowed me to pursue my passions as opportunities arose. I will forever be grateful to have attended Marquette University. What started with a random and arbitrary decision ended up being the best uninformed decision ever!

Robin Barksdale Ervin

Class of 1982

I remember like yesterday, although it has been over 40 years now, the call that I believe changed everything for me.

I was standing in the kitchen of our home, a ready-to-leave-my-small home-town, 18-year-old delighted that my student number had arrived from the University of Georgia. All I needed was to select a dorm name and food plan. I would be offered an opportunity to compete for a tennis scholarship. I had my student number. Escape was at hand.

And then something far-fetched happened. The phone rang—the yellow hang-on-the-wall kind of back-in-the-day. It was my high school tennis coach saying something crazy about Marquette University was offering me a partial tennis scholarship, and I could attend school there. Marquette University! The same Marquette where Al McGuire and team had just won the National Basketball Championship? THAT Marquette?!

Still, I had that student number from Georgia in an envelope. On cue, I got a call from a Marquette student, calling prospective freshmen. Just to chat. To tell me about the school—to share his own anecdote. Of course, he mentioned the weather, noting that I was "down South." He saw that I was interested in journalism and wanted to tell me what classes I might like. I wasn't just a number. I was a real person—or at least that's how I felt. That's what I recall most from his call. And so with a cursory decline to Georgia, I packed my bags and moved to Milwaukee—sight unseen.

Having grown up Catholic and having cheered ruthlessly for every Catholic school's team on the planet, I was over the top with excitement at the incredible opportunity to go to college at THE Marquette University. I had no idea about anything about Milwaukee or Wisconsin, and I didn't even care.

Being a member of the athletic community at Marquette certainly made my first days easier. I immediately became part of a group—I had connection. In the late '70s, tennis was mostly a "white sport." I had grown up with that just being what tennis life—and all life in small town Virginia—was. Yet, what did I find at Marquette? A living, breathing Black female tennis coach, Sharon Randolph. In hindsight, I think Sharon and I both felt pressure although we NEVER said it out loud. Hers to not appear to be partial, mine to prove I earned every bit of the #1 spot I held for three years without favoritism from her.

My college career representing Marquette University on the tennis courts was more than I could have hoped for. My experience was enriched by being one of only three freshmen on the team, and I landed Linda Raymonds as my doubles partner. Linda was the daughter of Hank Raymonds, who was assistant men's basketball coach. Linda and I were partners on court and partners in being the lone freshmen to take the required right of passage "mentoring" from our upper classmen teammates. We forged a friendship that lasted well beyond our Marquette days. Because my home was so far away and my family was unable to always afford plane fare home, I spent Thanksgivings with the Raymonds, always feeling welcomed and wanted.

Being part of a mostly white athletic team with scheduled practices and study halls pretty much kept me away from Black student social circles. It was not intentional, it was just how things played out. I had to report for school earlier because tennis was a fall sport. As a consequence, my first friends were my white teammates. So, we ate meals together, we studied together and their friends became mine. I was not an EOP student. I of course saw, met and knew other Black students. But even then, many of them were also female athletes or fellow J-school students. It would be my sophomore year before I began to broaden my world, previously opting to remain in the safe cocoon that athletics often provides.

In that cocoon of athletics, sometimes, the real world is far, far away. Race and culture matter less than your ability to score a win for your team. But the outside world, even at Marquette, creeps in. Looking back, for me, those intrusions taught me so much and have shaped my perspective on so many things since.

One of the things I loved about being at Marquette was being able to learn more about my Catholic faith because I wanted to and not because I was forced to as in grade school. I was excited to learn the hows and whys of my faith. And then one day, in a class on the history of Catholicism, I was suddenly thrust back to the whispers of the Jim Crow South that I knew too well as a child. In a class, in 1979, a fellow student confidently said, "Well it's the colored people who have all the children." All I heard was "colored." So, in an effort to bring him at least CLOSE to the enlightenment of 1979, I asked if he meant "Black people." NO ONE in the class even understood that in 1979, Black folks had come a long, long way from "colored." I realized that further protest was futile and chuckled that I had to travel all the way to the edge of the world to still be called "colored."

One of the biggest takeaways that I learned in my associations at Marquette was to be careful on judging people too quickly and to not label folks too quickly. That discovery, years ago, is a cornerstone of the cultural understanding and inclusion sessions I facilitate today. One of my good friends and my next-door neighbor freshman year was from Beaver Dam, Wisconsin. Even though we were friendly, she often stared at me as if she were memorizing my face and every move I made. One day, I just asked her about it. Without hesitation, she replied "Because I have never seen a Black person before." I laughed, and said, "No, really, why?" And then the look on her face made me wish I had not asked again. She had never seen a Black before "except on the *Jeffersons*." Still not believing it, I asked to see her high school yearbook where I thought surely the cook, janitor, crossing guard, SOMEBODY looked like me. Nope. Not a one. How is there a town with NO Black folks? How on earth do you become any kind of functional person only seeing people who look, think and act like you? I became more patient and I learned not to discount people for their lack of experiences or exposure and to give them welcoming space when they want to learn more.

My whole Marquette experience changed when I pledged Delta Sigma Theta Sorority. My mother was a Delta—making me a legacy. But unlike many proud sorority moms, mine did not provide me with much insight other than to know my mother was a Delta. Encouraged by Francine King, one of the very few non-athlete Black people I knew, I found myself online and suddenly in the midst of a whole Black student world I never even knew existed. There were parties at the Black student gathering building. There were "step parties" at the Union. I came to understand that although I was Black, as an athlete I enjoyed a bit of privilege that other Black students may not have. I did not know or understand some of the challenges Black students spoke of. I learned to juggle life in two very different, sometimes very complicated worlds. But, I loved Marquette even more.

Today, I treasure having gone to Marquette University. Indeed, placing Marquette University on my resume has earned me credibility. I count it as one of my proudest achievements—not just because I was an award-winning athlete or because I managed to get a degree—but because of the lasting friendships, coming to better understand my faith and my place in it and because Marquette and Milwaukee have always felt like home. I am forever grateful to that unknown student who called me years ago and started me on a wonderful journey. WE ARE MARQUETTE!

Greg Eagles

Class of 1983

My name is Greg Eagles. I am a writer, actor and producer currently residing in Los Angeles. And a Marquette University graduate class of '83. Even as I write this, it doesn't seem like it could've possibly been well over 30 years since I navigated a college campus. I don't really feel that much older, but I am a lot more assured. I am also a Milwaukee native and the first in my family to receive a college degree.

I decided to go to college a few years after I'd graduated from Washington High School. My parents, like a lot of parents of my generation, migrated from the South to the northern cities in search of better job opportunities during the '40s and '50s. My parents are both Louisiana natives who chose Milwaukee as their particular destination. My father worked as a laborer at a company called Milwaukee Malleable and Grey Iron Works located on the South Side. After I'd been rather languorously contemplating my future while on the couch, my father suggested (insisted) I go apply for a job there. I did. I got hired. And the first day on the job I saw Black men pour melting hot iron that looked like liquid fire into the holes of little moldings composed of condensed coal so it would congeal to make auto parts. God forbid the fire should miss its target and splatter. One could easily suffer third degree burns and be scarred for life. Some of the men even showed evidence of this. And I guess it was at that moment that the "fire" got lit under my ass (metaphorically speaking) to change my occupation and further my education. I wasn't sure what I wanted to do but I knew I couldn't do this type of labor, not because I was lazy or weak. But because I knew I had options. I respect my father immensely for doing what he did for many years to take care of his family. Did he like getting up a 5 a.m. to work every day, sometimes in the dead of winter in freezing temperatures? No. But he did it. And whenever I'm feeling exceptionally lazy I remember that and it inspires me.

After a few months on the job I decided to go back to school. Wasn't sure what I wanted to pursue. I just knew I'd rather be in front of a book than a big urn full of liquid fire. As fate would have it while reading a local Black newspaper, I saw a notice about the EOP Program at Marquette University and how they were accepting applicants. To be eligible you had to have a high school diploma and fall within a certain economic bracket. What did I have to lose? It was Marquette. I wasn't Catholic, but I was a big fan of the basketball teams. So I gave it a shot.

I had an interview with a very nice gentleman, Mr. Mayberry as I recall. He gave me some forms to fill out and we talked about my goals. But I think to this day, what sealed the deal for me was an essay I wrote as to why I wanted to further my education. I included my experiences at the Foundry, as it was called, and how it appeared to me to be nothing more than compensated slavery.

The EOP staff was great and supportive. They even had a summer program designed to acclimate one to life on a college campus. They had college "prep" programs as well to ease one back into academia, which being a few years out of high school I definitely benefitted from. I liked the fact that for the first time in my life I was living someplace else other than my parent's home. It gave me a sense of independence. I was finally becoming an adult. Now the EOP consisted of a lot of African American and Latino youth who, much like myself, could never have afforded an opportunity to go to a university of Marquette's caliber, or any university for that matter. So we were alerted to the potential culture shock of being in a predominantly white environment and the racism that would inevitably come with it. I remember one Black student counselor saying there was racism on campus but it was "subtle." I have no idea what he meant by "subtle." Racism is racism.

I do recall one incident very vividly however. There was this white guy who lived on the same floor of my dorm. He seemed nice enough. Somehow we got into a discussion of names. Family names. I explained to him my name, Eagles, was part of my Native American heritage, my father being of Native American and African American lineage. As if to one-up me he went on and on about HIS last name and how he was so proud of it and his European heritage and the significance of it. His name? LYNCH. At the time I didn't think to impress upon him the horrific connotations that word had on my race. Was he even remotely aware of the bizarre irony of bragging about a name like that to a Black person?

I honestly think, in hindsight, he didn't have a clue. But I should've let him know, and I regret to this day that I didn't. It could've been a teachable moment. But I've come to learn that some people prefer to stay in the dark, with their own delusions. And this nice white kid had no idea that his name symbolized barbaric inhumane persecutions to hundreds of Black people. He just prattled on and on about how "great" and "noble" it was. Talk about ironic!

I recall another incident where a big stink arose on campus when as part of a concert series the Black students lobbied for the group Sister Sledge to come to Marquette and perform. This caused much umbrage among the white students who associated them with "disco." This was the '80s. And this big disco backlash had occurred. There was a "disco record burning" ceremony at Kominsky Field in Chicago. There were taunts among Midwestern hillbilly types that disco was basically for "gays" and "Blacks" and therefore unacceptable. The Sister Sledge concert went on under this stupidity. There was a picket line composed of white male students outside the Varsity Theater on campus. I saw this, and walked right in the middle of it. My own form of counter protest. They surrounded me, chanting all kinds of nonsensical gibberish. But they didn't dare lay a hand on me, fortunately for them. Not too "subtle" there.

But despite the racism that came with the territory, Marquette opened me up to experiences that have come to enrich my life as well as people I never dreamed I'd meet. Dick Gregory, the great comic/activist came on campus to speak about the Iranian Conflict that was in full throttle at the time. I was asked to escort him and host a Q&A with him and the local press of Milwaukee by the Journalism Department of Marquette. That was one of the highlights of my college experiences. Just meeting him and talking with him was phenomenal. I was exposed to great speakers, inspiring pioneers like Alex Haley, Wilma Rudolph, Cicely Tyson, Coretta Scott King, just to name a few. I also attended the annual Communications Conference held at the HBCU Howard University in Washington, DC, again, at the behest of Marquette. Other than trips to visit my grandparents in Louisiana as a child, I'd never left Milwaukee until that point. It was my first time on a plane, and it was an unforgettable experience. I was going to our nation's capitol! And I truly experienced a culture shock of sorts being on a college campus comprised of basically an entirely Black student body. I thought that was amazing, and it was enlightening to see that one could receive a quality education and gain agency in this world without the white man's approval as to your worthiness. It was truly an eye-opening experience.

After I received my communications degree in '83, I immediately set out for Los Angeles, California. Fortunately for me I had an aunt, my father's sister, who had migrated there from Louisiana and had lived there many years with her family who consisted of my cousins, some of whom I'd never even met. So spring break of my senior year I decided to fly out for a week to pay them a visit. But it was really to get the lay of the land, so to speak. Who wouldn't want to live in California? I'd already made up my mind I wanted to take a stab at a position in the film industry, even though at this point I had no idea in what capacity. But just the thought of leaving Milwaukee to spend a week in LA filled me with anticipation. Plus I had a friend who enrolled at Marquette in the EOP program the same time as I who had transferred to USC. So an added incentive was that perhaps he could show me around since I was thinking about applying to the USC Film School for graduate studies (never happened).

Suffice it to say, my maiden voyage to California was everything I anticipated and more. My aunt even lived minutes away from the USC campus! But what sealed the deal for me to return was the moment the plane touched down back in Milwaukee. This was March of '83, before global warming, right in the middle of one of the biggest snow storms of that year! It was literally fighting a blizzard to get from the airport back to my dorm. I had just left a part of the country where it had rained one day while I was there and the rest of the time seemed like perpetual summer to come back to a blizzard! Talk about a sign.

So in the fall of '83, after I received my BA, I headed back to LA. This time for good. When I got back I hit the ground running. Within the first year I managed to get hired at CBS. It was a basic entry level job as a page. Being a page was as "entry level" as you could get. We were basically production assistants. But even for that you had to have a college degree just to be considered. The job consisted of handling audience members for the live tapings of the numerous game shows that were being produced at the studio during that era. Again, this was the '80s. Daytime television consisted mostly of soap operas and game shows. As a page I was exposed to both. I got to see the behind the scene details of how this type of television was actually produced. I honed my people skills by being an audience handler for eager tourists vying to be contestants on game shows like *The Price Is Right*, and I got to watch actors rehearse and directors direct the soap operas. The latter had the biggest influence because it was the first time I seriously contemplated becoming an actor myself. Soap actors are a photogenic lot, but a great many are lousy actors, to put it bluntly. Even with cue cards in their faces a lot of them blew lines and gave wooden, stiff performances. I figured I couldn't possibly be any worse.

While at CBS I had my share of celebrity encounters. There were always shows being taped and stars wandering about. One of the most memorable was when I saw this little Black lady wandering around the halls outside the soundstages. What caught my attention was the way she walked. Her "boss lady" swagger. It didn't take me long to figure out who she was. I followed her into the commissary. I tentatively approached her and told her how much I admired her work. I had just bought the album recording of her one woman show on Broadway. Despite her bold front, she was very warm and gracious. And I'll never forget how inspiring it was to meet her as I was just delving into stand-up comedy myself. Whoopi Goldberg was fresh off her Oscar-nominated performance in *The Color Purple* and was at CBS taping a comedy special with Carole Burnett and Robin Williams. Every now and then I would sneak up and peek through the glass door in the rehearsal halls and watch as she and Carole went through their routines.

By the time I left CBS I'd made up my mind to give acting a shot. To test the waters rather than pursue taking classes, I did something far more ballsy. I decided to try stand-up comedy. On a dare to myself I went out for an open mike audition at the Comedy Store in Hollywood. The first time I got on stage I was well received. The audience loved my impressions and I was asked to come back. After a while Mitzi Shore, the imperious owner of the club anointed me and made me a paid regular. I was performing alongside some of the best in the business. Arsenio Hall had just gotten his talk show and featured me on a segment. Eddie Murphy would come in and work out material. I know people who would go on to become household names before anyone knew who they were, Jim Carey, Martin Lawrence and Dave Chapelle just to name a few. One of the first "road gigs" I ever did for the Comedy Store I shared a condo with Chris Rock before anybody knew who he was. It was a very heady time.

I was managing a living as a stand up. There were ups and downs. But my life changed when I signed with an agency just as they were starting their voice over division. I've always excelled at altering my voice and have been blessed with the ability to sound like anyone I focused on. An asset for any actor. The first time I auditioned for a VO commercial with the agency I booked it. And I was off. I've since done tons of video games. *Metal Gear Solid*, *Mortal Kombat 10*, *Crash Bandicoot*, *Grand Theft Auto*, just to name a few. But what I enjoy doing the most is animated series.

I hit pay dirt when I booked a lead role in the first series produced by Dreamworks Animation called *Invasion America*. None other than Steven Spielberg was the executive producer. My character was a rarity in animation. A strong Black professional Special Forces Agent named Phillip Stark, dedicated to stopping an impending alien invasion. One of the first "dramatic" animated series to air in prime time on what was then the UPN network. I got to work with actors I never dreamed I'd work with. One such actor was a gentleman I grew up watching and was an avid fan of. I walked into the recording studio only to find that that particular day they were recording a scene with just the two of us. So I somehow managed to stay in my professional zone and get through it. It wasn't until after that I basked in the fact that I'd just gone toe to toe with the legendary Leonard Nimoy. Spock himself!

I've voiced many characters in animated series, but the one I'm most known for is the voice of the "Grim Reaper" in the Cartoon Network series *The Grim Adventures Of Billy And Mandy*, which has become a Cartoon Network classic. It aired during the period commonly referred to as the Golden Age of CN. It is still popular today, as it airs in syndication and is about to be acquired by HBO to continue to air. As a result of the success of this cartoon I put the stand-up grind on the back burner and concentrated on acting and creating my own projects. I created and produced and voiced an animated short for Nickelodeon called "Teapot" about an 11-year-old African American boy who dreams of becoming a rap star only he has no clue how awful he is. I'm very proud of how this project evolved. And I'm currently, despite some setbacks, diligently working on making it a regular series. I think there's a dearth of African American presence in mainstream animation. I'm doing all I can to rectify that.

I've been very fortunate that in addition to a thriving career as a VO actor, I've also worked as an actor in front of the camera. I've had guest starring roles on shows like *The Shield* (where I worked opposite the great Glenn Close), *NYPD Blue*, a recurring role on *A Pair Of Kings* for Disney, and I even returned to my old stomping ground CBS to guest star on the soaps *The Bold And The Beautiful* and *The Young And The Restless*. Talk about full circle! My most recent credits include the third season of *Narcos Mexico* for Netflix, *S.W.A.T.* again for CBS, and the great FX series *Snowfall* created by the late John Singleton, who I got to meet while filming. I can also be seen in the upcoming feature film *Sylvie's Love* starring Tessa Thompson and Nnamdi Asomugha. It was well received at the 2020 Sundance Film Festival and was purchased by Amazon for distribution.

I've had a pretty good ride so far. There are many things I've yet to do that I want to in my career. But I live by the credo "If it is to be, it's up to me." Nowhere is that more apt than show business. I might have wound up an "artist" whether I received a college degree or not. I think that is an undeniable compulsion, along with being blessed with talent. But I know that getting that degree gave me the courage to leave Milwaukee and actually venture to a part of the world where I could actively pursue it for all it's worth. For that I feel very fortunate as I diligently work on the next chapter.

Levester Johnson

Class of 1984

"Opportunity" This word most accurately describes my life experience. Growing up in the '60s and '70s in what was considered then and remains the inner city of Milwaukee, there were many challenges for me to even consider attending college. Socioeconomic, cultural, racial and gender challenges were just a few. Although I had excelled in high school and was extremely active in cocurricular activities, I never thought about attending college. My experience did not include family members attending college, I had not stepped foot on a college campus and was not exposed to any African American males who were attending college or had achieved a higher education degree. Had it not been for a conversation my high school senior year with my best friend's mother after cross country practice, I would not have had the opportunity to attend college and have my life forever changed. The conversation went something like this:

Friend's Mom: Levester, have you begun to look at colleges and started the application process?

Me: No, Ma'am.

Friend's Mom: Why not? You are in the top 20 of your graduating class along with my sons and extremely involved at school.

Me: I'll tell you what my mom told me ... "Not sure how you're going to college with no college money!"

Well, that conversation led to my friend's mom (Maxine Smallish, Marquette University Native American Counselor) assisting me in completing an application for the Marquette University Educational Opportunity Program (EOP). She was also smart enough to not describe what would be my "interview" for the program and simply shared that I would meet with an Art Mayberry on the fifth floor of

Marquette Hall and he would ask me questions for about 30–45 minutes. Then she gave me 50 cents ... a quarter to ride the bus to the Marquette campus and a quarter to get home. I reached that fifth floor destination (yes, I took the stairs as very few people knew about the one elevator in the back of the building at the time), met with Mr. Mayberry, answered all his questions and was oblivious as he shook my hand and exclaimed "Welcome to Marquette University!" The entire ride home I pondered, "Did that just happen?" "Did I hear him correctly?" Yet three days later, I received official notification of my acceptance into the EOP!

It was at that moment that I realized that "Opportunity" means that one must have prepared themselves and accomplished a firm foundation of competencies from which to build upon, possess the willingness to take advantage of the chance being placed before them, value the wisdom of role models/guidance angels who recognize their potential and believe in them and one must embrace to the fullest the new path that awaits. And what an exciting and enriching experience it turned out to be! My first year at Marquette I picked up where I left off in high school engaging in whatever activities I was introduced to during my first fall semester: track, Black Student Union, gospel choir, Marquette choirs, and pledging into my fraternity. Noticed what's missing? Yes, "academics"! I quickly found out that there are priorities within the collegiate environment, and first and foremost must be maintaining your grades! The EOP turned out to be a saving grace, providing the structure and support to get me back on track after a spring semester of study hall in room 300 of Marquette Hall (and I know some of you joined me there or had your own time within the space). From that point on, my collegiate experience was a snapshot of engagement. I was an active student leader and student athlete serving in Associated Students of Marquette University (ASMU), President of the Nu Xi chapter of Alpha Phi Alpha Fraternity, member of the Black Student Union, a group discussion leader (GDL) for new student orientation, served on the New Student Orientation Steering Board and being a middle distance runner on the men's track team. One of my proudest moments was being honored with the Outstanding Minority Student Leader Award my senior year (not to slight being selected as a Sweetheart of Alpha Kappa Alpha as well!).

I owe much to Marquette University and the personal, professional and academic development that took place during my five years (yup ... did the five-year plan) as an undergraduate. Back then I fully embraced the institutional mission which promoted "Excellence, Faith, Leadership and Service" and remain committed to these tenets, which shape my very being. I am thankful for the rigor offered through the academic coursework such as my most memorable course, an ethics class taught by the brilliant Daniel Maguire. Equally impactful were these strong roles models: Maxine Smallish, Sande Robinson, Art Mayberry, Dr. Howard Fuller, Dr. Arnold Mitchem, Dr. Toby Peters, Coach Jim Allen, Mark McCarthy, James Scott, Jim Moore, Linda Kuk, my parents Reverend Nathaniel Johnson Sr. and Rosie Mae Johnson and my siblings who guided and supported me along a successful path to degree completion and becoming the best Levester Johnson I could possibly become. To this day, I can hear their voices echoing from Marquette Hall, the Mug Rack in the Brooks Memorial Union (BMU) and the Armory with words of wisdom, challenges to excel, inspiration to make a difference and encouragement that all will be ok.

But for me, the most impactful component to my ultra-positive experience at Marquette University were the relationships and bonding times with my classmates and roommates. I cannot express how important it was to learn the unwritten rules to successfully navigating a predominantly white campus from upper-class students of color. The lessons learned along the way from peers who were outstanding roommates in Schroeder Hall freshman year through living in "The Mansion" (next to the row houses) with 12 other outstanding student leaders my senior year! The development of a drive to excel was nurtured through internal competition and camaraderie between my track teammates and a sense of brotherhood from the fraternal bond developed with the men of Alpha Phi Alpha. Finally, the leadership competencies fostered and fined tuned through the hands-on experiences with my peers as a GDL, ASMU and building supervisor at the BMU. It was these shared good and challenging times, the support we offered each other and the fun we had while thinking creatively and doing our part to contribute back to a vibrant campus community that I will remember the most. These friendships remain to this day. Whether returning to campus for Alumni Weekend and National Marquette Day, attending home and tournament basketball games or engaging in class Facebook pages or chat rooms, the bonds developed from our undergraduate experience continue and remain for a lifetime.

So, what were the outcomes of the Marquette University experience? No surprise for me as it entailed a pursuit of my passion and love for higher education and engaging in work where I could give back by nurturing our future leaders navigating our collegiate campuses! Upon graduating from Marquette with a Bachelor of Arts in broadcast communication, I entered the higher education administration master's program at Southern Illinois University at Carbondale

(SIUC). Upon graduation with a Master of Science in college student personnel from SIUC, I was hired at SIUC as a hall director and then later promoted to an area coordinator position.

After eight years at SIUC, the next step within my career path landed me in Indianapolis, Indiana, serving as Assistant Dean of Students and Director of Residence Education at Butler University. While at Butler University, I was blessed time and time again by being recognized by the university community and colleagues throughout the nation for my contributions to the Butler campus and the higher education profession. I was promoted three times while at Butler, rising to the position of Vice President for Student Affairs, serving in this last role for 20 years. In assuming this position, I became the first person of color and of African American descent to serve in this role in that institution's history. Somehow along the way, I also managed to complete my doctorate in higher education administration at Indiana University and help raise a family! Over the years, I've held numerous leadership positions within national professional organizations including NASPA–Student Affairs Administrators in Higher Education where I served as Chair of the Board of Directors and was recognized as a Pillar of the Profession. I've also been recognized throughout higher education for my innovative and effective use of social media in engaging campus communities. My current role as Vice President for Student Affairs at Illinois State University continues to provide me the opportunity to encourage and inspire our future leaders by engaging with them on a daily basis assisting them in their personal development and providing those same types of "opportunities" that were provided me at Marquette and have been so influential in my development.

As one can see, I have nothing but love, affection and gratitude for what Marquette University did in transforming my life and the lives of my family members. While certain elements of the MU environment remain the same and will continue to contribute to the development of more graduates to come, I am encouraged watching the institution strive to become even better to meet today's societal challenges of microaggressions, racism, equity and inclusion. As alumni we play a part in promoting, creating and fostering a positive, impactful and transformative Marquette experience by giving back and I pledge to continue doing so: "Time, Talent and Treasure!"

"We Are Marquette!"

Herbert Lowe

Journalism, Class of 1984

It wasn't until applying to graduate school at Marquette University in 2010 that I realized just how poorly I had done academically as an undergraduate there.

My transcript showed that only one of the 16 students graduating in December 1984 with a major in radio/television—from what was then the College of Journalism—had a lower GPA.

After two decades as a reporter at five daily newspapers along the East Coast and having served significant roles with national nonprofits that advocate for African Americans, I began earning a master's degree in communications a semester after returning to MU as journalist in residence.

A faculty colleague, James Scotton, was the college's dean back then. His recollection of me as a student in Johnston Hall: One always standing against a wall, seemingly afraid to talk to anyone.

That changed during my junior year. The catalyst was meeting Rose Richard, who had become an assistant dean. She was confident. She was beautiful. She was African American. She helped Black students in the college to better find their way in an environment dominated by white ones.

I was also a student in the Educational Opportunity Program (EOP). The program helped students like me to survive and succeed at MU. No question that this child of welfare could only stay at the university thanks to the additional financial aid EOP provided. And its staff—including, most especially, Sande Robinson—looked after and challenged me to do better.

But Rose was different. She all but demanded that I do better. She was in Johnston every day, which made her hard to escape as I went to my journalism classes. Once, she inspired the new student chapter of the National Association of

Black Journalists to attend a college job fair at Howard University in Washington, DC. Another chapter member and I let Rose see our handwritten scholarship applications a few hours before the postmark deadline.

"Journalists type!" Rose declared. She made us sit in her third-floor office right then and there and use her typewriter to redo our applications to her satisfaction. Her insistence paid off. We were the only two among our chapter to not have to pay registration for the job fair.

Serving as the chapter's president during senior year was my most primary leadership role as an undergraduate. Rose also helped me get a couple of internships—one at what is now MU's Office of Marketing and Communication, the other at the WISN radio station down the street.

What if had I met Rose as a freshman? What if her big-sister inspiration and accept-no-excuses commitment to Black student success had greeted me when I arrived as an aspiring network television anchorman? These questions motivate me every day now as a journalism educator.

A Last Minute Decision

Enrolling at Marquette was not in my plans as a high school junior in Camden, New Jersey.

After deciding to skip the 12th grade and pursue early college admission, my preferred choices were Temple University and Syracuse University. At the last minute, I found a MU undergraduate catalogue in my bedroom nightstand. A guidance counselor had let me take it home as a ninth grader, soon after MU won the NCAA men's basketball championship in 1977.

I had not otherwise heard of Marquette. I attended Catholic schools from the fifth through ninth grades, but religion wasn't a factor in my decision-making. I didn't want to go to a HBCU or be a commuter student. Being in a strong journalism undergraduate program was important. I didn't want to major in English. Marquette's acceptance letter preceded those from Syracuse and Temple. Syracuse was too expensive, and my mother forbade me from being on Temple's main campus—in a Philadelphia neighborhood she deemed too hardcore for a 17-year-old.

Her letting me go 854 miles away—sight unseen to Wisconsin instead of a 30-minute drive from our home—remains one of the great parental mysteries of my life. In any case, she and my seven-year-old sister rode with me via Amtrak from Philadelphia to Milwaukee. My belongings were in cheap luggage and a barebones trunk bought the morning we left.

Before leaving me outside McCormick Hall at the end of orientation weekend, my mother gave three admonitions: Remember who you are and whose you are (she pointed up to God). Don't worry about letting anyone else down; don't let myself down. "And leave the white girls alone."

Months earlier, a high school teacher had said I might do well academically at Marquette, but was not yet mature enough to be on my own at college. It was reverse. It was amazing how many students seemed to lose their mind because of their newfound freedom. I didn't drink alcohol and valued every dollar too much to waste it or get wasted at the bars on Wells Street.

Black students who came to MU not liking white people could find plenty of reasons to justify their thinking. But if you were open to dealing with people of any kind, there could be just as many causes to enjoy the experience. No doubt, there were far too few Black students on campus. Then again, every day or week it seemed, I saw one who I had not met before. My four years working in the cafeteria at McCormick had me thinking that I was among the ten most known students on campus—Black or white—who were not on the men's basketball team.

The Black fraternity and sorority parties each weekend in the Brooks Memorial Union fed my soul and helped gird me for the week ahead. And that was before I finally crossed the sands into Alpha Phi Alpha. The countless hours playing basketball at the Helfaer Recreation Center—both pickup games and intramurals—may have helped to doom me academically. But they also surely went a long way toward building my confidence in ways far beyond just athletically.

I enjoyed going to see Glenn "Doc" Rivers and the Marquette Warriors battle against the likes of Notre Dame, Syracuse and DePaul at the Mecca. Why did I choose to attend a university without a Division I football team or 80,000-seat stadium? Why did I pick a city where the temperature actually reached minus-26 degrees—or where it snowed big-time on April 15 freshman year?

An Early Lesson About Diversity

My first college roommate was white and from Minnesota. Putting it nicely, our worldviews were far apart. Before we escaped one another midway during our first semester—him to room instead with a white friend, me with a Black one—we learned an important lesson in diversity.

He and his pal came into our room crying one night. What's wrong, I asked. John Lennon had just died. "What floor was on he on?" I asked, thinking someone had just jumped from a McCormick window. They were aghast that I didn't know the names of the Beatles. Still needing to learn about empathy, I shot back: "Hey, can you name every one of the Jackson Five?"

There were just four or five Black males in my freshman class in the College of Journalism. I reported a story for *The Marquette Tribune* that first semester. A student editor praised it and urged me to submit more articles. Strangely, I didn't like it that a white peer had the authority to evaluate my work, so I didn't go back. It was one of the dumbest decisions of my life.

I remember the names of only two of my college professors: Daisy Tucker, who gave me my first A, on my first journalism class assignment; and Arthur Olszyk, a pioneer in Milwaukee television news, who beseeched me to practice my craft. I really enjoyed producing 20-minute newscasts for WMUR-AM. Who knows, though, if only I had listened more to Professor Olszyk, and worked harder, might I actually have become a network television news anchorman?

Most people say I have done OK. I became a reporter for two major metropolitan newspapers: *The Philadelphia Inquirer* and *Newsday* in New York. I am a past president of the National Association of Black Journalists and a former communications director of the Congressional Black Caucus Foundation. One of my proudest professional achievements occurred just months after graduating from MU, when I found a job at the *Milwaukee Community Journal*, the city's largest Black newspaper. A freelance photographer remarked that I was the first MU alumnus who he liked. Every other one, he said, acted as if they were too good for other Black people. It was then that I first understood that most Black Milwaukeeans found it impossible to attend MU.

My engagement with my alma mater from the late '80s through 2008 consisted mostly of returning to campus for EOP's anniversary every five years. (It was a major honor to serve as keynote speaker during the 2004 fete.) My wife and I moving to Chicago soon after Barack Obama's presidential election and the Marquette alumni association tapping me as its communicator of the year in 2009—both helped to better reunite me with my college friends.

I taught journalism classes for seven years at the Diederich College of Communication and served during the last three also as founding director of its O'Brien Fellowship in Public Service Journalism. Since 2017, I have taught multimedia reporting and a course on race, sports and culture as well as direct a high school journalism program at the University of Florida.

I am among far too few Black male professors at predominately white institutions nationally. As a MU faculty member, I have African American students from across campus come to my office to discuss their struggles as well as their aspirations. They were in college as the Trump presidency and #BlackLivesMatter movement converged. I keep thinking about hearing a Black female student tell her peers that she worried that her boyfriend might encounter police, and that she wished that white female students wouldn't all but clutch their bookbags when she passed by.

I love getting to #BeTheDifference every day for one student or another. It's a great privilege and opportunity to interact with and serve so many amazing young people. I particularly value my role in helping to teach white students about inclusion, diversity and equity, realizing that what they learn in college will govern how they lead and manage others forever more.

Beyond that, my hope is that any number of them will look back years from now, and say I mattered to them as much as Rose Richard did to me when we were in Johnston Hall.

Lisa Osborne Ross

Journalism, Class of 1984

My Southern raised, HBCU-educated parents believed in the beauty of being Black, living Catholicism through service and the power and purpose of education. These principles gave them a good life and a confident lens through which to raise their four children. It was not enough, however, to prevent them having the "the talk," keeping my brothers psychologically safe and healthy or to protect any of us from being called the N-word or monkey.

We grew up when DC was Chocolate City, the epicenter of Black Excellence. My father worked for his frat brother, Walter Washington, the city's first elected mayor under home rule. My mother was the "Hidden Figures" of HHS, co-leading the agency's transition from a manual to automated payroll system. We lived on a street reminiscent of a Black Mayberry. While my siblings and I attended all-white, private Catholic schools, the public schools were brimming with future Black scientists, litigators, advocates and change agents. Though I was one of six Black girls in a class of 100, the feminist nuns reinforced in school the sense of self-worth and confidence I got at home.

My two oldest brothers loved and hated their experiences as young Black men attending Saint Louis University in the early and mid-seventies. As my third brother was matriculating at Marquette, I made a choice to attend Boston University to break the Jesuit mold and make my own mark. But my parents had other ideas: they refused to let me attend BU, citing racial unrest following desegregation of the school. And they sent me to Marquette instead.

As a young adult, it became my joy and pleasure to reveal—and then constantly remind them—that Milwaukee was the most segregated, racist city I had ever been to. Twenty-five years later, when my daughter attended Marquette, I found that despite the facelift, the city by and large was the same. That said—borrowing from our First Lady, Michelle Obama—I *became* at Marquette. It was there I found the life lessons I've lived by and taught throughout my life and career.

135

Faith Matters

I had a blast in college. I was that girl who loved everything about the college experience—dorm then apartment life, basketball games, step shows, the library, even the food, but like any meaningful experience there were times when I struggled. Two months into my freshman year, my favorite uncle died. My sophomore year I pledged my beloved Alpha Kappa Alpha Sorority, thought I fell in love for the first time, and definitely fell out of friendship with my soul mate. I started my junior year learning my father was dying from cancer while my best friend (aforementioned third brother) left Marquette and moved to San Diego. My senior year, despite good grades, I only had one real job offer and it was with a newspaper in Pittsburgh, far before Pittsburgh was named a most livable city. If Gesu and Joan of Arc had not been by my side and across the street, I'm not sure that my heart and soul would have remained intact.

At Marquette, I began practicing my faith in a way that was relevant to me, not necessarily how I was raised. It has been a staple in my life and for that I will always be grateful.

Privilege, Power and Protection are Root of Racism and Anti-Racism

Having grown up in a fairly sheltered, almost isolated environment as it related to racial tension, I came to college naïve. I hadn't really seen poor white people until I moved to the Midwest. People who were Latinx didn't really identify as such. I had met gay men, but we really didn't talk about that either. They were just my really kind uncles. My dad had some Jewish co-workers but again, we had no real conversations about faith outside of our Catholic community.

In one of the few classes Marquette offered on racial equity, I noted to the instructor that many of my Black friends didn't like white people and asked: Isn't that racism? To this day, I can see the face, but can't recall the name of, the Black male professor who patiently—kindly, yet firmly—responded with a definition of the impact of systemic racism that I hold and teach to this day. Without judgment or resentment, he explained that because white people are in positions of power, their negative feelings toward others manifest themselves in dangerous and material ways.

A racist admissions counselor can prevent me from attaining the education I choose. A racist loan officer can keep me from buying the house I've selected. A racist job recruiter can prevent me from securing a position I am qualified for. When power and protection are in the wrong hands, the outcomes are real and tangible. If privilege, power and protection can't be for all they shouldn't be for any.

Failure Is an Option and Very Often, a Good One

We are raised to win, to be right, to overcome all obstacles. Black children in particular are told that we have to be the best, better than everyone else. We are told to follow the path, carefully. We are told to make money in order to live a good life and create the pipeline of wealth that has eluded us for centuries. What we are rarely told is to have fun, relax and color outside the lines.

What we don't learn until much later—something I learned at Marquette—is that winning isn't everything. Very often you will make the wrong choice or choose the wrong path. You can still come out on top. Very often you can do something silly or stupid and still succeed.

I also learned at Marquette that just because someone looks like you, they are not always about you (a prominent Black alum reneged on a job offer two days before my graduation!). Conversely, though my Black professor WOKE me up, an old white professor (LBJ's former Press Secretary George Reedy) reminded me of the importance of civil service through communications.

The mistakes I made, the wrong paths I took, may have hurt me at the time but they also made me stronger. Embracing those lessons has empowered me to be more bold in my thinking and my actions. Being wrong has allowed me to grow and learn and teach with authenticity. In forgiving myself, I am better at forgiving others. My ability to accept what's been done and move forward has given me an advantage throughout my life and career.

I left DC a wide-eyed child sure of myself and everything around me. At Marquette I became a young woman prepared to embrace and thrive in a world that could quietly and blatantly misunderstand, fear or ignore me. I left Milwaukee, a young woman stronger, more prepared to **Be the Difference** to my race, my faith and the world around me. I am ... Lisa Osborne Ross, US Chief Operating Officer–President, Washington, DC, at Edelman.

Bishop Walter Harvey

Bachelor in Arts, Class of 1985

The Awakening

"Jesus was probably darker skinned than you." Those were the words spoken to me by a Jewish rabbi and associate professor, the late Francis Barry Silberg, as I sat in the front row of his theology class as a Marquette University freshman in 1980. His words and the point of his finger directly at me, pierced my wounded soul.

I was 19 years old when I began attending Marquette. I was a first member of my family to attend college and had experienced a spiritual rebirth as a follower of Jesus Christ, just a few months prior to enrolling as a student. My prior exposure to Christianity or religion was filled with Eurocentric images of Jesus and other characters of the Bible. Until that day, I was missing a relevant ethnic connection to the God and people of the Bible.

My first emotion to his bold statement was embarrassment. In fact, I wished I had someone to hide behind or a row that I could slide underneath, but there was none. I was already seated in the front row. My presence was obvious to everyone in the class. I was one of two Black students in the entire class and the only Black male. The other Black student was Nichelle Mitchum, the daughter of the founding director of Marquette University's EOP Program, legacy leader, Dr. Arnold Mitchum.

My feelings of embarrassment soon turned to curiosity. My curiosity then turned to pride, and the pride turned to confidence. Rabbi Silberg had awakened a sleeping giant within me. He ignited a quest for me to discover the Black person's presence in the Bible. I am certain he was mandated by and on assignment from God to affirm my human dignity as one created in the image of God, and he solidified my Christian faith.

That was a day of awakening. Marquette University, like every educational institution fulfilled the true purpose of a university as described by Rev. Dr. Martin Luther King, Jr., when he said, "The function of education is to teach one to think intensively and to think critically. Intelligence plus character—that is the goal of true education."

My "Blackness" had become a source of pride for me and other like-minded people, but it is also a stumbling block for some in the greater society. Not just for me, but for many other Blacks, our skin color is a badge that some people erroneously believe marks us for inequity and mistreatment. More on this in a moment.

My ethnic, educational and cultural awakening at Marquette University continued under the influence of another EOP pioneer, Dr. Howard Fuller.

In the fall of 1981, Earnest Lacy, a 22-year-old Black male was killed while in police custody. This tragedy is all too familiar in Black and Brown communities. Lacy had been arrested under the suspicion of committing a rape. Another man was later identified as the rapist. It was estimated by the Milwaukee medical examiner that Lacy could have died from complications from a police officer who put his knee in Lacy's back while trying to handcuff him during a struggle, which might have been a factor in his suffocation. Lacy also had cracked ribs.

He died in a police van near the Marquette University campus at 24th and Wisconsin Avenue. Needless to say, Lacy's death inflamed racial riots and protests, and Dr. Fuller was at the helm of the demonstrations.

I and other Marquette students spilled out on the streets of Wisconsin Avenue to march in protest. 1981 is not unlike the year 2020. The year of 2020 will be known as the year of COVID-19, but it will also go down in history as a year of a multi-ethnic people standing up against racial injustice and standing with Black people who all too often die in the hands of law enforcement officers and are incarcerated in disproportionate rates higher than whites. My education at Marquette caused me to realize that "I am my brothers' keeper." I am Earnest Lacy. I am Ahmaud Arbery. I am George Floyd. I am Breonna Taylor. I am Jamar Clark. I am Philando Castile. I am Michael Brown.

I am a proud and educated graduate from Marquette University, but that degree does not exempt me from being presumed guilty until proven innocent nor from being profiled as DWB (driving while Black) or JWB (jogging while Black) or BWB (birdwatching while Black) or SWB (shopping while Black). I and other individuals are judged not by the content of our character, but instead by the color of our skin. We live every waking day of our lives with a fear of being targeted, brutalized, falsely arrested and possibly killed for no other reason than the amount of pigment that we have in our skin. We are chastised by the media for claiming that our lives matter while daily we view video on social media that underscores the fact that we don't. However, my Marquette University experience has awakened me to these realities and inequities within society and have also given me the tools to resist the wrong and rebuild for the good. I embraced the calling that God, my experience and my education have equipped me for.

I completed my Bachelors in Arts degree in 1985 (majoring in psychology). Immediately, I began pursuing a vocation in Christian ministry. I had been youth minister at a church on the northside of Milwaukee 1985–1992 and the lead pastor of Parklawn Assembly of God Church in Milwaukee's Sherman Park neighborhood, 1992–2020.

History repeats itself again and again. In the summer of 2016, Sylville Smith, a 23-year-old Black male, was shot and killed by a Milwaukee police officer in Sherman Park. This tragedy occurred just three blocks south of my church's campus. What followed were multiple nights of protests and social unrest that mirrored 1968 when Dr. King was assassinated and 1981 when Earnest Lacy was killed by police.

This was now my time to step into the mold that Marquette University, Dr. Mitchum, Dr. Fuller, my parents and so many others had prepared me for. I knew that I had to either "lead, follow or get out of the way." I chose to lead and to lead others—pastors, church members, community stakeholders and elected officials—in efforts to bring about justice and a peaceful end to the unrest. Our neighborhood was greatly spared from the level of tragedy that other communities often experience in the wake of injustice and related protests. Sherman Park is not a perfect place, but it is once again a relatively peaceful place.

Our city and our nation are moving towards two societies, one Black, one white—separate and unequal. Dr. King taught that "we are caught in an inescapable network of mutuality, tied in a single garment of destiny. Whatever affects one directly, affects all indirectly."

This lesson was reiterated in another Marquette theology classroom, Fr. William Kurz's class on Pauline Epistles and the study of First Corinthians. Fr. Kurz embraced the Pentecostal values and works of the Holy Spirit and saw them as congruent with the Catholic Church. That was also affirming for me as a Pentecostal student. The apostle Paul writes in 1 Corinthians 12:26–27, "If one part suffers, all the parts suffer with it, and if one part is honored, all the parts are glad. All of you together are Christ's body, and each of you is a part of it." In other words, Paul and Dr. King are saying the destiny of one is indirectly tied up in the other. What happens to Black Americans impacts Anglo Americans.

I am so grateful to have experienced an awakening at Marquette University. May I never become complacent with my purpose and calling.

Kevin Ingram

Class of 1985

Allow me to start my story with the fact that I was born out of wedlock. Therefore, according to Webster's Dictionary, I came into this world on June 13, 1961, as a bastard child. 1. *"A person born of parents not married to each other; illegitimate child."* I may have entered the world illegitimately. But, thanks to my EOP and Marquette University family, I will leave this world as a legitimate person. Because on February 15, 2019, I received the *Milwaukee Times Newspaper—Black Excellence Award for Community Leadership*. Pretty good accomplish for an illegitimate child!

Prior to attending Marquette University in 1979, I was 1 of 10 million African American children *Under the Age of 18* living in the United States. I was 1 of 6.8 million African American children *Born out of Wedlock*. I was 1 of 2.8 million African American children who lived in a *Single Parent Home*. At the age of six, I became a motherless child when my mother died. I was 1 of 5.7 million African American children who lived in a *Low-Income Household*. I was 1 of 3 million African American children *Living in Poverty*. I was 1 of 1.3 million African American children who *Received Free/Reduced Lunch*. Last but not least, I once was 1 of 1 million African American children *Raised by a Grandparent* (grandmother). Thanks to my having the opportunity to enroll and graduate from Marquette University, I no longer *Live in Poverty* nor *Live in a Low-Income Household*. The statistics that I mentioned, came from an NAACP *The Crisis Magazine* in 2003.

My journey to Marquette started when my high school counselor, Mrs. Carolyn Bolton, directed me to contact Mr. Arthur Mayberry, recruiter for the Marquette University's Educational Opportunity Program (EOP). After interviewing with Mr. Mayberry, he pointed out that I would be living on campus and living in McCormick Hall (nickname: *The Zoo*).

I did not choose Marquette because it was a Catholic Jesuit institution. I didn't know what religious affiliation Marquette was connected too. I also applied to

UW-Madison and UCLA. I had only three career goals in mind. Become a basketball player, a lawyer or an actor. Marquette offered me admission to attend the Summer EOP Bridge Program, and I accepted. UW-Madison and UCLA never came back into view for me. I suppose that was because I didn't want to be away from my grandmother, who raised me starting at the age of six.

As I mention, I didn't know what religious affiliation Marquette was connected too. What I did know was that Marquette had won the 1977 NCAA Basketball Tournament Championship. Butch Lee and some other MU players from the team came over to our neighbor playground that summer, Columbia Playground, on 14th and Columbia Street. That left an impression on me. I was not recruited to Marquette to play basketball. That was because I rode the bench on the John Marshall High School basketball team my junior year, and I was cut from the team in my senior year. But, I was able to convince Coach Oliver to give me a private workout. But Coach Hank Raymond said I was too short to make his team. So, I took my skills to the Rec Center and played on the Intramural Basketball Team. What I had were good grades (i.e., mathematics) that allowed me to enroll into the College of Business Administration.

The Summer EOP Bridge Program provided me with a head start. I learned my way around campus and learned where all my classes would take place. But most importantly, I knew the location of the Recreation Center. My EOP and Marquette experience nurtured, guided and taught me how to be a human being. I was not among the best students academically during my undergraduate experience. I graduated with a 2.1 GPA. This didn't bother me. That's because I came to learn that there were also quite a few white students that were C average students too. The issues of Marquette being a predominately white and racist institution never bothered me. This is because, I had the EOP counselors to vent my frustrations to (my outlet). My EOP counselors kept me on the straight and narrow focus on earning my degree first. I could battle with racism down the road, because racism wasn't going away.

However, that did not keep me from participating in campus rallies/protests, demanding Marquette offer us (Black students) a more ethnically diverse curriculum, giving speeches and storming into Dr. David Buckhold's small philosophy office, demanding that he listen to our cries and needs. Neither did it stop me from marching down Wisconsin Avenue in protest for justice for Ernie Lacy, while wearing a T-shirt with the EOP label. In contrast, I also marched down Wisconsin

Avenue in celebration of the Milwaukee Brewers winning the American League Baseball Pennant. Those were *Good Times!*

Because of my *"Eyes on the Prize"* type focus, I never pledged or joined a fraternity. However, I did win second place on the Delta Sigma Theta Sweetheart Court. Only to lose to my good friend and golf buddy, Bishop Walter Harvey of Parklawn Assembly of God Church. I also was selected and was on the Sigma Gamma Rho Sweetheart Court.

My goal was to stay focused because I was a C-average student, and I didn't want to flunk out of school. So in order to immerse myself into the entire college experience, I sought out employment opportunities on campus. My first job was cleaning the men's and women's locker rooms at the Rec Center. My second job was becoming an EOP Upward Bound summer tutor counselor (TC), tutoring and counseling 9th–12th grade high school students. My TC job defined my purpose and launched my eventual professional career in the field of education. My third job on campus was being a Brooks Memorial Union building supervisor. I was a TC during the summer months and a building supervisor during the academic year. Not bad for a kid that grew up on welfare and the occasional dose of government cheese.

These five jobs or internships launched my professional career that has spanned four decades: (1) Marquette's EOP Upward Bound counselor (2) EOP Upward Bound assistant director (3) EOP pre-college director and (4) state director for the Wisconsin Educational Opportunities Programs and the Office of Urban Education for the State of Wisconsin Department of Public Instruction. Now, I am currently serving as (5) an education consultant with the Teacher Education and Professional Development and Licensing for State of Wisconsin Department of Public Instruction.

When I graduated from Marquette University, I made a promise to myself, "To never let the negative issues that continue to exist in our society destroy the relationships that I have built with the friends I have met and made along my journey, regardless of their cultural/ethnic background, their gender or sexual orientation." This to me is the true meaning of the Ignatian spirituality: *Curu Personalis* ("care for the [individual] person").

In closing, I leave you with the words of a great motivational speaker, the late Bishop Tyrone Crider of Chicago, Illinois, whom I met in 1989 while serving as a co-chair for a ten State Regional Student Leadership Conference, held in Fontana, Wisconsin, his version of the ABC's of Life:

A. With an A, Accept the challenges put forth to you
B. With a B, Believe in yourself
C. With a C, Combine your words with action
D. With a D, Dedicate your life to your dreams
E. With an E, Expect some hard times
F. But with an F, Be faithful, fight on and finish your courses
G. With a G, Get good grades
H. With an H, Have a made up mind
I. With an I, Inspire yourself to be the best you can be
J. With a J, Begin your journey with the first step
K. With a K, Keep on keeping on
L. And with an L, Let love be the light to show you the way
M. With an M, Make every minute count
N. With an N, Never say I can't
O. Take that O, and Overcome your obstacles
P. With a P, Put your best foot forward
Q. With a Q, Quit quitting
R. With an R, Run the race with patience
S. And with an S, Stand strong
T. With a T, Trust in the Lord
U. With a U, Use your talents positively
V. With a V, value you your time
W. With a W, Work until your work is done
X. With an X, X-ray your own life
Y. With a Y, Yearn to achieve all the dreams you seek
Z. And with a Z, Zealously strive to reach your peak

"When you do your Best, God will do the Rest!"

Brian Distance

Class of 1987

Despite my Presbyterian baptism, I received my entire academic and hence religious training in Catholic schools. My earliest memory of traditional Catholic parochial schooling was experiencing the business end of a wooden ruler because I proceeded to write left-handed. This healthy appreciation of nuns was further cultivated during my secondary school experiences at a military school run by these saintly figures. Four years later, I graduated from Loyola High School–Blakefield in Baltimore, Maryland. By the time Marquette University accepted me into its School of Engineering, I was steeped, sufficiently, in so-called Catholic guilt as well as in the excellence of Catholic academics and Jesuit scholastic and community-minded endeavors.

In effect, Marquette University became the natural continuation of my lifelong pursuit for scholarly knowledge and connectivity to others. I started Marquette University at McCormick Hall (the "Beer Can") at the corner of 16th and Wisconsin. My freshman year revolved around acclimating myself to Marquette social life, entrenching myself into my academic studies, learning the nuances associated with surviving a Wisconsin winter and playing lacrosse (a sport at which I excelled from an early age). Growing up in Baltimore, lacrosse was a statewide passion, the unofficial sport of the State of Maryland and as such a religion, my second religion. In my freshman year, I haunted the neighborhood culinary and drinking establishments (The Gym, The Avalanche Bar, O'Donohues, Wales on Wells, Mr. G's, Real Chili and Miller Brewery) while maintaining a respectable academic average and pledging my dream fraternity, Kappa Alpha Psi Fraternity.

Kappa Alpha Psi Fraternity, a long time stalwart of the African American community, became my safe harbor at Marquette. Founded in 1911 during the height of the Jim Crow era, Kappa Alpha Psi Fraternity is one of the oldest Black fraternities with chapters throughout the world. The dual missions of Kappa Alpha Psi Fraternity have always been personal holistic growth (spiritually, socially and professionally) and community service. The fathers of several of my high school friends were members of this fraternity so I was exposed to Kappa Alpha Psi Fraternity at a very young age. The Baltimore chapter of Kappa Alpha Psi Fraternity always hosted various community events from blood drives to car washes, to baked goods sales, to discos for the high school students (of which I and a large contingent of the high school-aged children always attended). When I learned that Marquette had a chapter of Kappa Alpha Psi, the Delta Kappa Chapter, and that one of my childhood friends was the polemarch (President) of that chapter, I knew immediately that I had to join. In those days, the pledging process was all encompassing: it was physically, mentally and academically grueling. However, the process was immensely rewarding in that it taught responsibility to yourself, responsibility to your fraternal brothers and ultimately responsibility to your community. These responsibilities or maxims meshed perfectly with my Catholic and Jesuit teachings and influenced my life at Marquette and everyday thereafter.

My father told me that my college years would be "the best years of my life." To that end, I embraced enthusiastically that axiom and thereby sought to savor and experience all that Marquette life had to offer. I attended Marquette basketball games; drank beers/sang songs at the Mug Rack (I think my personalized mug may still be enshrined there, lol); commiserated with, nursed hangovers with, and planned future escapades with friends at the Brooks Memorial Union; and at the end of the day, attended numerous Masses at the Church of the Gesu and sought solace and moments of reflection at the St. Joan of Arc Chapel. In essence, Marquette offered spectacular and ecumenical experiences and I gratefully accepted and fully availed myself of them. Milwaukee offered all of the experiences of a sinner, but Marquette redeemed you with the salvation and forgiveness worthy of a saint.

My experiences at Marquette University and my Jesuit/Catholic basis shepherded and guided my life steps thereafter. I graduated Marquette University with a B.S. in Mechanical/Industrial Engineering. I worked a full year as a public health engineer for the State of Maryland. Feeling the desire to expand my knowledge and serve others in a greater capacity, I enrolled at Tulane University in New Orleans, Louisiana, to study law. Despite the vagaries, open debauchery and contradictory Catholic underpinnings that exemplify New Orleans, I graduated, miraculously, from Tulane University with a Juris Doctor degree with an emphasis in maritime and civil law. Thereafter, I passed the California and Louisiana Bars and practiced political law in New Orleans for close to a decade while managing the campaigns for several local, state and federal political officials. During this time, I never lost a race and during those tumultuous and exhilarating years prior to Hurricane Katrina, I followed the teachings of St. Ignatius of Loyola (the warrior saint) by attending Masses at the St. Louis Cathedral in the French Quarter and volunteering countless hours at the Ronald McDonald House (New Orleans). When my time in New Orleans came to an end, God uprooted me and moved me to New York City.

Specifically, my experiences at Marquette University and my Catholic teachings, generally, prepared me for the events of September 11th. Just a year before, I arrived in New York City, as a Wall Street finance attorney working for a major international investment bank. That day started like any other September "Indian summer" day in New York City, sunny, brisk, and full of the sounds of a city that was beginning to transition from the carefree malaise of summer doldrums to the fall machinations of business. Unfortunately, that day ended with the downing of the Twin Towers; the smells of asbestos, burning concrete and death; nuanced shades of grey; and the irreverent silence of shock, disbelief and anger. During my long walk home from Wall Street to Piermont, New York, (all of the bridges and various modes of mass transport into and out of the city were shut down), I realized that I was merely existing. I was earning a paycheck, paying bills but not contributing to society. Somehow, in the pursuit of the trappings and riches of Wall Street, I lost my way. I lost my way, the way of St. Ignatius of Loyola and the teachings instilled by Marquette University, Loyola High School, Mt. Washington School for Boys and St Cecilia's Roman Catholic School. In essence, I was living a life in contravention to my Catholic upbringing.

Marquette University, and by extension all of my Jesuit and Catholic teachings, taught me the value and sanctity of the human experience. As such, I vowed to truly experience life and pursue my true passion, acting. Thereafter, I enrolled in and graduated from one of the 25 best acting programs in the world, the William Esper Studio in NYC. Since 2001, I have played in over 50 television network and cable programs, feature films and off-Broadway plays. Most notably, I was a cast member in the multiple Oscar winning movie *Green Book*, a recurring cast member in the CBS drama series *NCIS: New Orleans*, and had appearances in *Lincoln Rhymes: Hunt for the Bone Collector* (NBC), *Nos4A2* (AMC), *Billions* (Showtime), *Bull* (CBS), *Blindspot* (NBC), *Daredevil* (ABC), *The Mysteries of Laura* (NBC), *Gotham* (Fox), and

Under the Dome (CBS), as well as the movies *Tower Heist, Law Abiding Citizen, Ace the Case, Side Effects, Rob the Mob* and numerous others.

In many respects, my college years at Marquette University were some of the best years of my life. My experiences at Marquette University were neither specifically Black experiences nor white experiences, neither specifically male experiences nor female experiences. In sum, my times at Marquette University were my experiences, the experiences of Brian Distance, a Roman Catholic, a member of this imperfectly perfect yet deeply fulfilling human experience that is life. We are Marquette.

Karma Rodgers Butler

Law, Class of 1989

My Marquette experience began after leaving another institution of higher learning in the deep South. Shortly after arriving in Milwaukee, I attended a career college thinking it was a shortcut to higher learning and a lasting career. While attending the career college I worked part-time at a nearby retail store. There, older clerks bragged about their children going to this "great university" called Marquette. I wanted my parents to brag about me. So, I applied for and was accepted at the great university. I could not afford to attend Marquette without some serious financial assistance. I also applied for and got a job at Marquette's Educational Placement Center counseling students on how to package their resumes, intro letters and transcripts to get a job after graduation.

In addition to wanting my parents to brag about my attending Marquette because it was a great university, I knew they would like the fact that it was a religious affiliated school. My parents are very religious people and lived (still do) in the South. Although I had an aunt and uncle living in Milwaukee at the time, my parents were concerned that I was so far from home at a young age. They thought a religious school was a great choice especially since my aunt and uncle as well as other Milwaukeeans had such high praise for Marquette. Although the school's reputation was important— frankly—I did not think about its demographics. Since I did not personally know anyone who had attended Marquette, I had no one to ask about the impact a Jesuit university would have on my career or life.

After receiving a bachelor's degree, I worked for a telecommunication company where I met my husband. A short time later and with my husband's support, I returned to Marquette as a law student. I was a commuter student during both my undergraduate and law school days. Therefore, I did not have an opportunity to meet many of my fellow students or form study groups except with a few other commuter students. As commuter students, we primarily met at each other's homes since parking was an issue on campus. It was by choice that most, but not all, of my study group partners were African Americans who lived near my apartment. In short, study groups evolved into commuter student groups. Being a commuter student also made it difficult to participate in sports, student government and other school activities. One notable exception: I would occasionally attend basketball games and eagerly participated in the NCAA championship game celebration on Wisconsin Avenue.

The professors were mostly concerned and caring. Frankly, I have never thought of my experience as a Black Marquette experience. I only had one experience that I thought was racially biased. It was during an office visit with an undergraduate professor. When he said something to the effect of "you're the other one." I responded by asking "the other what." He had pulled my paper to discuss my grade but pulled another student's paper instead. He pulled her paper thinking I was that student. There were only two African Americans in the class so that meant I was the other African American student, and he had simply confused me for her. I met Dr. Robert Neuman when reporting "the other one" exchange to Marquette's administration. Dr. Neuman was friendly and professional. He ultimately facilitated my transfer to another course, alleviating my concerns that the professor in question might retaliate because I reported the incident. Although there may have been one or two other professors or administrators who appeared to be indifferent or maybe somewhat hostile, I do not remember their names or other incidents. Perhaps, because I choose to focus on the positive. My law school professors Phoebe Weaver Williams, Christine Wiseman and Edward McBain were kind, friendly and helpful with respect to advice about study habits, getting real world experience and future job opportunities. They always seemed happy to see me and gave practical, helpful and sage advice.

My one disappointment was being denied funding via EOP. Because of that denial, I had to pay my way through both undergraduate and law school. I graduated with loans that took almost five years to repay. Although I was disappointed that EOP did not accept my application, I got over it after graduation. Further, I realized that there were students who may have needed the financial assistance more.

My Marquette experience has been an overwhelming advantage professionally and personally. Other Marquette attorneys and judges are always willing to assist a fellow Marquette attorney with advice and counsel. My favorite classes were related to employment law and trial practice. They influenced my decision to initially concentrate in the labor and employment area.

My most memorable Marquette experience is meeting Felicia Mabuza, Kevin Kelly, Agnes Johnson, Ricky Amos, Patricia McGowan, Joseph Kromholz, Annette Kingsland Ziegler and others. Today, I am still in contact with several of them. If I had it to do over again, I would choose Marquette hands down. Marquette was the launching pad for my education, meeting my husband of almost thirty years, two daughters, and making my parents proud to have a Marquette attorney in the family. It is also the primary reason I became an equity partner in a law firm of one hundred plus attorneys with offices in six states.

Gina Eanes

Communication, Class of 1989

As a young person growing up in Kansas City, Missouri, in the mid 1980s I aspired to leave the confines of my neighborhood, not that my neighborhood was filled with violence and poverty, it was quite the opposite, it was a neighborhood filled with people from all walks of life who believed in hard work and home ownership. Conversations were often centered around where you were going to college, not "if you go." I wanted to expand my wings to experience something different from where my friends were going. As a kid I often visited relatives in Milwaukee during the summer, which was great, Summerfest, the lake and cooler summer temperatures (a stark contrast to Kansas City's hot, sweltering summers). As I began to seriously think about college and majors during my junior and senior years in high school, my focus became laser sharp on Marquette. At that time, I wanted to be an accountant, and Marquette's accounting program was top notch. My older sister, Gwendolyn Sides, graduated from Marquette in 1974 and was well established in her career so I felt confident that I would have similar results. Little did I know what was in store for me.

I grew up in a neighborhood in which everyone looked like me, including the doctors, pharmacists, lawyers and grocery store owners. Arriving on campus for the EOP pre-collegiate summer program was somewhat eye opening with respect to classes and overall student population, but the real eye opener was the fall session when school was in full operation. I was not prepared for the lack of African American students on campus, nor was I prepared for how homesick I would become. I spent my freshman year really wanting to transfer; I did not think that I fit in. Fortunately, I was convinced by my family to give Marquette another chance and to spend my sophomore year getting involved and enjoying campus.

One would say that the beginning of my sophomore year started off on an interesting note. I lived in West Hall, a co-ed dorm composed of freshman and sophomore students on 26th and Wisconsin Avenue. I moved into my room prior to my roommate arriving; we had not met nor spoke over the summer months therefore I was excited to meet her. When my roommate arrived in our room, she was SHOCKED to see me, and not in a good way. She was so shocked that she rarely stayed in our room the first week she was on campus and by Labor Day requested that she transfer out of the room. While I felt that my roommate's desire to move out because I was Black was initially disheartening, it did not make me feel inferior. My resident advisor and friends on my floor were very encouraging and reassuring, which made me confident of my decision to return to Marquette. Their actions showed me that while we were different, we were still on a mission for the same goal, to graduate from Marquette University. I eventually did get another roommate that was open and caring, and we got along fabulously.

At the beginning of the semester West Hall hosted "Screw Your Roommate," which was a social event to fix your roommate(s) up on a blind date. Since I did not have a roommate at the time, my resident advisor and a couple of other friends that lived in the dorm decided to sign me up for "Screw Your Roommate." The guy they selected for me lived on the floor below me and had transferred from another university to Marquette. I figured I had nothing to lose, besides this was the year I was going to become more involved. We attended the event, which was held in the ballroom of the dorm. It didn't take us long to figure out that we wanted to leave the "party" and walk to try and get to know each other a little better; that first walk 35 years ago was the beginning of many of more to come. My Marquette experience was beginning to take on a more positive light, I worked on campus, began to meet more people that shared similar dreams and goals and became involved with extracurricular activities; it also didn't hurt that I was dating someone that not only had ambition but also believed in community service. By the end of my sophomore year transferring was off the table; I was enjoying myself both in class and outside of class.

As I continued my studies, I explored different majors. College was the place to try and figure out what you want to do with your life. I changed my major three times, which caused a delay in graduating, hence I was on the "five year plan." Although it took me longer than expected to graduate because I could not figure out exactly what I wanted to major in, I credit Sande Robinson and the EOP staff for ensuring that I stayed on course to finish the task at hand. I recall Sande calling me into her office to discuss my grades and to tell me that I should "spend a little more time studying instead of socializing with Mr. Eanes." Sande also told me that a degree from Marquette University would open many doors and an employer would train me in whatever specific job I was applying for. Sande encouraged and challenged me to improve my grades, which I did, and I am thankful that she pushed me. Professor Lynne Turner, Dean Mike Price and Dean Sharon Murphy also encouraged me and pushed me to excel. All of my professors did not want to see me succeed. I had one professor who did not want to pass me for any reason; it seemed as if I could not get anything right, or at least not in his view. My relationship with the professor reached the point in which I had to speak with the dean of my college about the professor's behavior, which I felt was biased. Throughout my college career I experienced professors that made me think and explain my position, which gave me the confidence to challenge the professor I felt treated me unfairly. After speaking with the dean about the issues I was having with my professor, Dean Price looked into the situation and later advised me that I would not have any further problems with professor, and I would in fact pass the class.

While at Marquette not only did I learn the technical matter that was needed to receive my degree, but I also learned the importance of merging a successful career with community service and social justice and the art of entertaining. To this day all those things still matter immensely to me, hard work, knowing the details of my craft and helping others.

As I reflect on my time at Marquette, I realize that it was a special place for me, I made friends that have endured past college. Raullo Eanes, my "blind date" from "Screw Your Roommate" and I dated throughout our time together at Marquette, have been married 31 years and we have two adult children. Marquette was so special to us that we encouraged both of our children to attend. Our daughter Marlena graduated from Marquette in 2014. Our son Alexander decided to defect, and he graduated from St. Louis University in 2016.

Raullo Eanes

Communication, Class of 1989

We Are Marquette. I never thought I would actually say and know the meaning of that phrase in my own family. I can only say that God has a way of working miracles and weaving them through the tapestry of life. Our family, Gina's (formerly Banks, Comm '89) and mine, has the great distinction of being the first Black Legacy Family at Marquette. Our family journey begins with the enrollment of my sister-in-law Gwendolyn Sides in 1970 and her graduation from what was then known as the College of Speech in 1974. This legacy ends with the graduation of our daughter Marlena Eanes, Ed '14. Between 1970 and 2014 our siblings, nephew and cousins all attended and graduated from Marquette. So, we have a great family tradition to be proud of.

I come from a hard-working blue-collar traditional working-class family. My father worked in a transmission factory as a machinist, and my mother was a homemaker. I am the eldest son of four siblings. Our dearest and baby boy Christopher was what today is known as "special needs" but growing up was "mentally retarded." He never spoke a day in his life. My upbringing led the way for the work ethic I have today and that I instilled in my children.

My proudest accomplishment is graduating after life reshaped itself around me. Graduation was also a tough one, as my immediate family was not there to see me graduate. My father passed away my second year at Marquette, my mother had suffered a massive stroke my senior year and was incapacitated, my sister was recovering from a horrific accident that left her incapacitated and my brothers were just too young.

Spring of 1984 I was determined to go to college and as I told my parents, "be my own man." I was accepted at several schools including Marquette, but at that time I was 17 years old, thought I could play baseball in the majors and wanted nothing more to do with Racine, Wisconsin. My junior and senior years of high school, my parents would tell me, "you need to apply to Marquette so you can go to school with your sister, Marcie." She graduated Journalism December 1984. She and I were always close and later, she and Sodie Rivera and a host of her other good friends showed me a great time on Marquette's campus, but I was determined to just do me.

Late June 1985 changed our lives dramatically as Marcie was injured permanently in a near fatal car accident. The accident, impairment of her writing career and physical and mental damages would challenge her until her death in 2015. Despite dying, coming back to life, initial paralysis, brain surgeries and constant pain, she would continue to write and leave her mark at Marquette and the world around her. She would publish several articles and books as well as live independently.

In fall of 1984 I headed off to Indiana State University (not my parents' choice) to accomplish my dream of independence. After my play and partying was stopped by an injury in the spring of 1985, my mother made it clear that I would be transferring to Marquette. She arrived in Terre Haute, Indiana, with all of the transfer papers completed for me to sign. That is exactly what I did, and it turned out to be the best choice of my life. In October of 1985, I would meet a young lady who lived in my dorm, West Hall, whom I would date my entire time there. We married three months after graduation, had two children and celebrated our 30th wedding anniversary July of 2019.

Fall of 1985 marked my second year in college. It also marked the time where life would deal me monumental changes and decisions. I was 19 years old, started out as an accounting major, met some great friends like Sandy Harrison, Ronnie Watson, Morrice Blackwell (soon to be best man at my wedding), Tara Doughty, Joe Gold, Dave Schneider and a host of others. Making friends would not be an issue. I spent so much time with the Kappa brothers (Tighe Bronaugh, Darryl Day and Rob Drain) that most thought I was a Kappa—not, just good friends and great guys.

My years at Marquette were enjoyable, difficult and life changing. Given the circumstances, I went from my father paying tuition and me not working to meeting the bursar and understanding immediately what it meant to pay/earn your way through school. I always remember that day. After coming back from burying my father and taking on the role of head of the house, I quickly learned to grow up. The bursar said, "Raullo, your dad owes $6,500 for this semester." My response was, "Wow, he's gone so I don't know how you're going to get that?" He reared back in his chair and offered me three choices: 1. Pay $6,500 and you can stay in school, 2. Pay $6,500 and you can transfer to another school with our glowing recommendation, or 3. Pay $6,500 and you can go home and find a full-time job. The answer was clear—pay $6,500 of which I had no means or clue to get unless I went to work, and I did. My education was extremely important, and I had promised my father I would graduate from Marquette.

Faith and prayer were key. For the first time, I was able to see God's hand in my life. Through my girlfriend and Sande Robinson, as well as Fran Gipson and "Crazy" Joe, I saw God move those to keep me in school rather than to start life's journey differently. This was the beginning of my journey with the Educational Opportunity Program (EOP). EOP, Sande Robinson literally saved my academic life. I tell that to anyone I meet when I discuss any post academic success. Sande arranged for EOP to support me, the university awarded me a breadwinners scholarship, Mrs. Gipson arranged for another campus job, Crazy Joe ensured I was fed, Gina provided me emotional support, balance and discipline and I took on a job at Colortyme TV Rentals and later Rent-A-Center selling TVs, electronics, furniture and appliances. I would go on to become the top sales and collector.

These events as well as the kindness and direction of professors like Steve Mauer, Dr. John Cotton (He would help shape my thinking and direction of my final major), Dr. Bob Shuter, Dr. Lynn Turner, Dean Sharon Murphy, Fr. John Raynor and a host of others in the offices of EOP, the College of Communications and Business Administrations. In 1989, I graduated SP '89, and would soon take on my first real job as a financial analyst at J.I. Case (n/k/a CNH). Subsequently, I would work in finance my entire career, from managing multi-million dollar budgets in billion dollar companies, commercial banking, starting a bank, buying a manufacturing company and eventually consulting numerous companies and turning them around to profitability. Today I advise, consult, restructure and source capital for middle market and small companies.

I tell people all of the time that it really worked. A working class kid who went from 19 to 45 overnight, made it through a tough school, got married, raised two wonderful college-educated kids (both have their masters degrees), moved from working class to upper middle class, contributed economically and through volunteerism, gave back, traveled extensively and most importantly revered God above all. If my parents could only have seen all that I accomplished based on their sacrifice. I made it and it works. You can "Be The Difference" through prayer, hard work and perseverance. My experience at Marquette helped me pivot and shape my life. Why go, because this precious time in your life will make the biggest difference in your life. No matter what, stay focused and hang in there.

Dr. Syb Brown

Communication, Class of 1990

"**L**ord, where are we?" It should have only taken 45 minutes from my home in Northern Illinois to Milwaukee. My Dad told us to take the 94 West Bypass. We did. And we passed the Marquette exit too. Oops! We made a mistake, that's all, and we were half way to Madison, Wisconsin, before we realized it. I was riding with classmates from then Carmel High School for Girls in Mundelein, Illinois. At Carmel, we were educated and encouraged to earn our bachelor's degrees from colleges like Loras, Notre Dame, Bradley, Loyola, DePaul and Marquette. We missed the full tour that day, but it didn't stop me from becoming a freshman at Marquette University in the fall of 1986.

While in high school, I played volleyball for four years, capping off my tenure as captain of the team. I thought I would play for Marquette too. That was not a card I had been dealt. I tried to try out but I was not in shape. I was so unprepared I had to be assisted back to my room in O'Donnell Hall in excruciating pain. It was embarrassing. Fortunately, I suffered my shame in silence. Grateful to my roommate Lesley LaRou Stuart (Mallory Keaton from *Family Ties* look-alike) for not sharing my secret agony. One of the best parts of my freshman year was looking down the hall and seeing another Black female. She had on a tank top, daisy dukes and a straw hat. I thought, "Who is this country creation?" And I'm sure she thought, "Who is this chick wearing a Jheri curl?" We've been friends 34 years. Thank you for my sister, Mrs. Elserita Burton Crosby. Oh, the trips to the Grand Mall for a baked potato with three cheeses and chocolate chip cookie. Or the early afternoon runs to Kentucky Fried Chicken when the original recipe was original. We won't discuss the trips to go dancing to the Interns East, Sonny's on Broadway and Victors. Most of my Marquette memories include Elsa and she'll take many of them to the grave.

I also gained many more sisters during my time at Marquette. Pledging the Alpha Kappa Alpha Sorority in the spring of 1990 blessed me with many sorority sisters. It wasn't easy attempting to pledge carrying 18 credits, being a resident advisor, working in the McCormick Hall store and at the *Milwaukee Journal Sentinel*. But eventually I did it. I count my line sister Mrs. Marquita Teasley Davis among my closest friends today. Shout out to my other line sisters Tomika Culpepper Ransaw and Kathy Lanier. I'm also grateful to Sorors Kim Alexander Brooks, Alicia Pugh Stingley, Hosanna Farr Mahaley, Vanessa Batchelor, Sharisse Scineaux and in loving memory of Tiffany Neal. Other dear friends from my Marquette days include: Thomas Kelly, Trina Finley, Colleen McGowan Ezzeddine, Wanda Liddell and the entire Hudson family.

One of my first duties as a freshman was restoring the gospel choir. It only had a handful of members, so I literally walked up to students asking if they could sing and inviting them to join the choir. We often rehearsed on Friday nights. Oh, and many of us pulled double duty singing in the Unity in the Community choir too. For four years we labored to compete in the National Baptist Convention Collegiate Choir competition. Some years we didn't have enough members to participate. Another year we just weren't good enough. Yet my senior year we competed once again as choir number 5. Under the direction of Barry Ward, we sang a tailored version of Handel's Messiah. We practiced until we were hoarse. Yet when the lights went on, our voices went up and our arms did too. It was a powerful performance punctuated with movement to emphasize every note. When the winners were being announced we were stunned when we did not secure second or third place. We were competing against the likes of Prairie View A & M, so we figured we just didn't place … again. When we heard, "The first-place winner is choir number 5," it didn't register at first. When the victory finally sank in, several underclassmen literally tackled me to the floor. This is still one of the top memories in my life. We did that!

I'll never forget Father Naus or the smell of the breweries or the stench of beer in the residence halls after some students went on a 25-cent bar crawl. It's probably the reason I don't drink beer to this day. Wales on Wells, the IHOP on Wisconsin Avenue and the Johnston Hall will all be remembered as well. The architectural design of Lalumiere and McCormick Halls will forever be etched in my memory. Having history classes with Fr. James Donnelly in the Varsity Theatre so large, teaching assistants including Dr. Timothy McMahon had to take attendance. And I'll never forget trying to play water polo (not being able to swim) and falling into the water trying to keep up with my buddy Steve "Duck" Danner.

Academically, two professors will always rise to the top of my best memories at Marquette—Dr. Michael Havice and Pauli Taylor Boyd. Dr. Havice is still one of my mentors today. He was an exceptional teacher because of his humanity. As a Black student on a predominantly white campus, we must look for encouragers. He didn't take my excuses. He knew when and how hard to push. I learned a great deal about teaching from him. Pauli Taylor Boyd taught Black social thought, a pivotal class for this Black student educated in a predominately white school system. Professor Taylor Boyd introduced me to W.E.B. Dubois, Ida B. Wells and more. It was the education I needed the most at that age. I was also immersed in the culture on the gospel choir trips to places including Baton Rouge, Louisiana, and Atlanta, Georgia. A separate trip through the Black Student Alliance took us to Howard University where we heard Minister Louis Farrakhan speak. On campus we hosted Juan Williams, author of *Eyes on the Prize: America's Civil Rights Years, 1954–1965*. We also welcomed a living legend in poetry, Nikki Giovanni, and a master historian, the late Dr. John Hope Franklin.

My academic advisor took a job at Northwestern University after my freshman year. I don't recall being assigned another advisor. Back then the course catalog was like the Bible. And, a classmate named Katy became my Moses. Whatever Katy did, I did. Katy interned at WISN-Radio. I interned at WISN-Radio. Katy became a paid assignment desk trainee at WISN-TV; I followed suit. Katy secured an internship at WLS-TV, ABC in Chicago, and the next summer I was there too. That was the summer 1989. The *Oprah Winfrey Show* was being filmed in the ABC studios. I walked into the future legend and attended her show several times. But the most memorable experience that summer was using a crisscross book of names, addresses and phone numbers to contact family members of those aboard United Airlines flight 232 that crashed in Sioux City, Iowa, killing 111 people.

After graduation, Katy found employment as a producer in northern Wisconsin. That was the first time I was unable to follow. I secured a position as an associate producer at WISN-TV, where I answered a now infamous call. A witness told me she saw a half-naked Asian man running down the street. The call was so strange I was too afraid to hang up; so, I handed it off to a reporter. The man was the one who escaped serial killer Jeffrey Dahmer in the summer of 1991. After living in O'Donnell and serving as a resident adviser in Schroeder and Cobeen, I lived off campus my senior year not far from where the Dahmer victims were found.

As a member of the Black Student Alliance I rose to the rank of President. I was able to represent the Black student point of view to the Vice President Dr. James Scott and Dean of Students Dr. James Moore. It wasn't always an easy position. I worked closely with then Dr. Lisa Jones, Director of the Multi-Cultural Center who became a trusted big sister. To protest the lack of diverse faculty, staff, students and administrators, Stephen (Woody) Simon and I led a televised rally. My efforts were acknowledged with several university awards throughout my years at Marquette and the Marquette Senior Award in 1990.

In 2018 the Marquette University Diederich College of Communication recognized me with the By-Line Award. The By-Line Award honors an alumnus/a for distinction in journalism and related fields. It was a huge honor right up there with winning the national choir competition. One that I will cherish forever. I love Marquette dearly. I laughed, lived, loved and learned and yes, I would definitely do it again! Thanks Mom, Mrs. Rosa Brown, for investing in such an invaluable education. It still pays dividends. This is Dr. Syb, two-time Emmy award winning journalist, author, *Innovate: Lessons from the Underground Railroad* and full professor of journalism at Belmont University and I approve this message.

Ingrid P. Jagers

Bachelor of Arts, Class of 1992

When I think about my years at Marquette University, there are three things I believe played a part in my personal and professional growth: the Educational Opportunity Program (EOP), the Marquette University Gospel Choir and the Criminology program.

I transferred to Marquette University my sophomore year of college, after being accepted into the Educational Opportunity Program. I was so excited to be back home in Milwaukee and on Marquette's campus, I lost track of my main goal, which was to receive a quality education and degree. Well, after receiving my first semester grades and realizing they were not acceptable to me, my parents or the staff at EOP, I buckled down and regrouped and never went below a 3.0 GPA during the remainder of my college career. Sande Robinson, who I will always consider the face of EOP, was instrumental in pushing me to excel. I can remember many days sitting in her office discussing which classes I should take, my plans to attend law school after college and of course financial aid.

My first year on campus I also joined the Marquette University Gospel Choir. We would practice every Friday night under the guidance of Reverend Barry Ward. Our choir practices would often turn into impromptu church services. I remember traveling to Ohio, Tennessee and Texas to fellowship with other churches and choirs and compete in various gospel choir competitions. We traveled by bus and spent time on the road listening to and sharing our testimonies. It provided a bonding opportunity that still resonates today.

In between practicing, performing and traveling with the gospel choir, I went to my classes, studied and studied some more. I had always been fascinated with the law and justice system and decided early on I wanted to become a defense attorney. While at Marquette, I majored in criminology and was able to study very interesting subjects including white-collar crime and juvenile justice. I once wrote a research paper on the origination of gangs in Detroit, Michigan, and spent hours at the downtown Milwaukee County Library gathering resources for the paper. During the last semester of my senior year, I interned at a local agency that provided services for people who had committed minor crimes. My responsibilities included ensuring clients performed their court ordered actions timely and accurately. One day, I was assigned to go to the Milwaukee County jail to interview a young lady who had been arrested on a trespassing charge. She was still sitting in jail because her mother would not pay the bail that amounted to $50 for her to be released. Prior to our interview, I spoke to her mother, and I recall her saying her daughter needed to sit in jail for a while to learn a lesson. When the young lady was brought in for the interview, I was taken aback by how young she looked. The interview evolved into what would appear to anyone looking at us like a casual conversation between two young African American women. At one point, she said "I could be on the other side of the table where you are sitting." I agreed she could definitely be sitting/standing in my shoes. After speaking with her that day, I left the jail feeling dejected and questioning what I had always thought would be my career path. I did not want to see people who looked like me sitting in jail with shackles on (they literally had leg shackles on her) because of a trespassing charge and a $50 bail. Instantly, I decided I did not want to be a defense attorney, but I had already taken the LSAT and been accepted into law school ... at that moment I didn't have a Plan B. Friends on campus helped me come to the realization I could focus on another area of law while still helping my community in other ways.

After graduating from Marquette, I went on to the University of Wisconsin-Madison Law School and graduated with my Juris Doctor. A career in criminal law did not pan out, but I have enjoyed a career in healthcare compliance for over 20 years. In order to balance my career with serving the community, I volunteer for several organizations that serve the youth. I also serve on the Marquette University Black Alumni Association's board of directors, so I am still active on campus. I want the students coming behind me to realize they have a place at Marquette University and they do belong on that campus.

From the support I received from EOP, to fellowshipping with the gospel choir, and the quality education, I consider transferring to Marquette University one of the best decisions I ever made. EOP and the gospel choir also introduced me to other African American students, who along with my college roommate, became lifelong friends who are truly like family to me.

Bridgette Richmond Balwin

Class of 1993

I was born and raised in Milwaukee, Wisconsin. I belong to the Pentecostal faith, and my family was very religious. Marquette University (MU) had never really appeared on my radar. I was not really familiar with Catholicism and even less with the Jesuit tradition. It was my senior year, and many students were excited about the opportunity to go to college. Most of my friends were going to UW-Whitewater or UW-Milwaukee. I had come from a low-income family, which had no experience with college selections, and although I attended Rufus King High School for the college bound, I really had no idea of what I was looking for in selecting a school. Before entering MU, the racial demographics did not play a major factor in my decision. My pre-existing educational experience in high school had introduced me to a multi-racial atmosphere. And every school on my list was a predominately white institution.

A counselor in the Education Opportunity Program (EOP) at MU came to speak at my high school. I was initially attracted to MU because of the financial aid opportunity that EOP offered me on top of any existing scholarship and grants for first-generation college students. The ability to pay for a college education was a huge obstacle in my life. Although I had obtained a few scholarships, the expense reached beyond anything my family was able to contribute. I was also attracted to MU because of EOP's commitment to help me navigate the college experience through academic counseling, mentoring and guidance. I was welcomed into a tradition of excellence rooted not only in the legacy of EOP but also with MU. All of these variables were quite attractive to me and moved MU to the number one spot on my college list.

When I think about my particular affiliations on campus—the Multi-Cultural Center (MCC), Delta Sigma Theta Sorority, EOP and other affinity groups—I always felt comfortable and connected at MU. However, the security of these networks often prevented me from seeing how very isolated I was as a woman of color. There were many social networks that I did not see. At the center of MU livelihood were levers of power and influence to which I had no access. Therefore, my specific campus life both secured me and blinded me to seeing how MU actually worked.

Outside of the classroom experience, I spent most of my time with Black students. I now realize that it was a result of both choice and necessity. My networks were a product of shared values, interest and culture. But at the same time, there were many white students on campus and a white culture on campus that attempted to push Black students to the margins. I was confronted with a different kind of white culture at MU. In high school, whether Black, white or other, we were all from Milwaukee. While there might have been some degrees of separation, we listened to the same music, went to the same parties and we all knew what it meant to be from the city. At MU, the campus brought together white students from progressive and conservative standpoints, rural and urban demographics, and wealthy and modest economic backgrounds. In short, I was confronted with a whole segment of white students that had never come into contact with a dynamic Black/Latino urban experience and were hostile to our very presence on campus.

But I also came of age at MU during a time of heightened activism from students of color. We were speaking out and organizing against the Eurocentrism of the curriculum, racial biases of student services and policing, and the reality of sometimes being accosted with racial epithets. Therefore, the realities of choice and necessity are conditions I had to navigate on a constant basis.

My first three years, I lived in Cobeen, Schroeder and Mashuda Halls. I truly enjoyed my dorm life experience. It combined the challenges of independence with the security of institutional supervision. I was forced to slowly grow up while still in a controlled environment. I went to class, interacted with my friends, and engaged in campus activities. And all of this had to be managed by me; no one was there to tell me what to do. At the same time, if I did run into problems or if I felt like I was losing my way, there were resources all around that could help me figure things out.

When assessing learning experience at MU, my teachers veered from indifferent to neglectful. Most didn't go out of their way to connect with me on an individual level, and some were culturally and racially insensitive in their teaching of general subject matters. While there were a couple of notable professors, I was most struck by the diversity of classroom experiences. I had never had a white person teach me African American history. When LGBT issues were still controversial, an openly gay professor made philosophy more accessible, understandable and appealing. And, in theology I was forced to hear very different interpretations of religious scripture while reading from the same Bible. But as I began to excel in certain courses, my instructors also invited me to clubs and the honor society when there were very few people who looked like me in its numbers. I did not have a favorite class. But what I remember most is going to MU Gospel Choir (MUGC) rehearsals. It was there that I began my week and ended my week in prayer. This gave me a level of religious stability and a confirmation of my faith that set the tone for all of my other campus experiences.

I cannot say that there was any student activity that I participated in that I did not enjoy. Student activities allowed me to confirm my own sense of purpose while also branching out into the broader campus community. The MUGC allowed me to confirm and celebrate my faith. Working at MCC exposed me to new layers of university administration and power. My sorority strengthened my bonds with other women of color. Student clubs celebrated my academic achievements. And various affinity groups offered a safe space for me while living in what was, many times, an alien environment.

One of my most memorable experiences at MU was winning the extremely competitive choir competition at the national level in four consecutive years. We were competing against primarily Historically Black Colleges and Universities (HBCU) with a much longer history of gospel choir excellence. Our ability to go down South, into the hotbed of gospel music tradition, and win, was a memorable feat.

Additionally, EOP made the difference. I could walk up the four flights of stairs of Marquette Hall and enter a world of understanding and care but also a place that demanded high standards. EOP served as both a sword and a shield. It protected me from a campus that did not always want to understand who I was while also pushing me to take advantage of every opportunity the school had to offer.

I have returned to campus for multiple alumni events. It was always a pleasure to reconnect with friends and come back to campus for speaking events with my husband, Dr. Davarian Baldwin, who I met at MU. We were both members of EOP and active in campus events. Speaking at MU was an important act of service to help the next generation learn from our challenges and accomplishments and think more clearly about their own paths going forward. We were also able to bring our oldest son back to MU for a soccer showcase. This experience sort of rounded the circle from our initial contact with MU to delivering it as an opportunity for our own children.

Out of many achievements, my greatest personal success has been my children. Most people say they eventually want to have children at some point in their life. But it is quite something else to perform the labors of nurturance, care and guidance. You can have the greatest intentions, but you cannot guarantee the outcome. I am happy to say my children are healthy, brilliant and model citizens in our community.

My greatest professional achievement has been my transition from practicing the law to educating the new generation of legal professionals. It was MU that served as a bridge between my undergraduate experience and my law school career. Leaving MU on my way to law school I knew that I wanted to be a soldier for justice. And I was able to do that as a criminal defense attorney in NYC. I had no idea that I would teach law. But here I now stand as a law professor for nearly 20 years.

The Golden Eagle Years

1994–Current

Torrey A. Adams, PhD

Chemistry, Class of 1994

My MU experience began in the summer of 1986 with Upward Bound (EOP). At the time, I was just participating in a summer program that I learned about through some neighbors that grew up with me. Little did I know that this experience would start a lifelong journey with the MU family where I would have exposure to amazing times and meet friends that I am still very close to date ...

As my high school years progressed along with the UB years, I had fully entrenched myself in the MU experience as much as I could and enjoyed being a part of that. I felt very proud of the fact that I was considered one who could claim MU as my own. However, as I approached the decision to choose a college, I can admit that MU was not my first choice—only because I wanted to go away to school being a Milwaukee native.

I was never pressured from any of the UB counselors or staff to choose MU, but I was constantly reminded of how well this family had my best interest at heart so I knew that if I did choose MU, I would be looked after and supported to the fullest. Thankfully, I did, and I was. I did choose MU (EOP), and I have never regretted it at any time. I was supported, I was encouraged, I was treated like family. Even with the lack of diversity at MU, I had my EOP family who understood and provided a place of comfort to shoulder me through any uncertain times as would be commonplace for any student—let alone as one of the members of the small group of Black students. I will say, however, to the credit of MU, that I never felt like an outcast or like I didn't belong. I was given the opportunity to be myself and not having to conform to any ideologies that did not line up with my own beliefs. I was heard, I was protected and I was included.

I have been a part of the MU family for over 30 years and I grew up at MU and was prepared to go out into the world with excellent tools to excel from EOP to professors and counselors—I had support. I joined student and fraternal organizations and developed leadership skills that helped me to go on to graduate school through the McNair Program and then on to a career.

In all, my experiences at MU were first rate and very fruitful. Deciding to attend was one of the best decisions that I have ever made! Yes, I am a very proud Marquette University alum, I am even more proud to be a member of my EOP (TRIO) family. If MU calls, I'll be there ...

Derek Baxter

Engineering, Class of 1997

When I reflect back on my Marquette experience, I think about the thought processes I used to make the decision to come to Marquette and my experience. The first factor in choosing Marquette was the major that I was pursuing, which was mechanical engineering. When I was researching schools, I knew Marquette was one of the top and best schools for engineering. One of the other points of consideration was the class size, so you had the opportunity to get that one-on-one attention when needed. Overall, I had good experience with my professors, and I learned a lot. You were challenged, but it was a good experience because it was a way of unleashing your potential.

The second factor was the financial aid package. The financial assistance Marquette provided was beneficial in that I was able to use the financial aid as a tool to pay for my education.

The third factor was community. What I mean by that is, that once I walked the campus and began connecting with peers, friends, and faculty and got a sense of some comfort, I felt Marquette was the right fit and place for me to be. I am appreciative of the Marquette experiences. They allowed me to grow, and I was able to apply those experiences to my personal and professional life. I believe being involved in organizations also allowed me to assimilate well. While in college, I was a member of National Society of Black Engineers (NSBE). I believe getting involved on campus and integrating into the community was a great tool that I used to get involved. I was also involved in programs and organizations off campus as well. For example, I was a member of Inroads, which is an organization that works with business and industry to place diverse talent and prepare them for corporate and community leadership. Through this program, I was able to intern with a local company throughout my college years. This was a way to gain work experience and use the classroom lessons and apply those tools. These were experiences that helped me personally and professionally.

One of the experiences that I was able to gain exposure to while at Marquette was learning and working with individuals with different & diverse backgrounds from my own. For example, in most of my engineering classes during my college time, I was one of three or four other African American students. The overall experience was good, and it prepared me for what my experiences would be like when I would be in the professional environment. The Marquette experience opens your eyes to new things and opportunities as well as how to navigate the waters.

One of the most significant experiences at Marquette was making the Dean's list. This experience gave me drive and focus to work that much harder toward my goals that I had I set for myself. If I could offer some advice for future students: make your goals before you sit in your first class. This will give you focus and purpose, in my opinion, and the drive to never stop or give up despite obstacles that may arise through your time.

In thinking more about my Marquette days, I would like to speak to the dorm experience. I met some of my lifelong friends in the dorm. I enjoyed time in the dorm, East Hall. This was the old downtown YMCA. I was able to experience living on my own, and everyone had their own room. It was nice having my own space and a good way to meet other classmates. I can remember the late nights of studying and hanging out. If there were any minuses from the East Hall dorm experience, it would be the dorm was not directly on campus and was across the bridge on 11th & Wisconsin. If you had late night classes, then you were probably going to be late for the dining hall. Living on campus overall allowed great opportunities to make lasting college memories and networking.

Marquette's education has led to good personal and professional achievements. Personally, I am still connected with Marquette—being an active alum with Ethnic Alumni Association and the Black Alumni Association. I have my engineering and MBA degrees on professional achievements. I am a lead mechanical engineer for my profession. I am appreciative and blessed with the opportunities that I have been able to obtain. Marquette gave me a drive to go after and achieve my goals. I use my experiences to give back and help where I can. I set my foundation by putting God first and having the confidence that all things are possible when you set your mind to it.

If I had to make the choice of colleges all over again, I would choose Marquette. It gave me a well-rounded experience that contributed to my growth personally and professionally.

James Austin, Jr.

Arts, Class of 1998

Marquette University: Where I Became Myself

I attended one of Chicago's premier Jesuit high schools, St. Ignatius College Prep. My parents were strong believers in the value of Jesuit education. When I was accepted into Marquette University, it seemed like an ideal fit. On one hand, I knew I wanted to go away from home and have a legitimate college campus experience. On the other hand, it was important to my family that I not be too far away. Marquette offered the right balance, an excellent Jesuit education that was within a two-hour drive from home. In hindsight, I'm very happy with the choice we made. My Marquette experience really catapulted me into becoming who I am.

My academic experience at Marquette helped me develop the work ethic necessary to excel professionally. Before Marquette, I was coasting academically with just a moderate amount of effort. However, in my first year at Marquette, I learned that a moderate effort would not cut it. After earning mediocre grades in my first year, I was challenged by my academic advisor, Dr. Virginia Chappell, to become a disciplined and focused student. Dr. Chappell, affectionately called "Dr. C" by her students, saw great potential in me. She encouraged me to enroll in her writing course as a sophomore, and she made certain that I didn't get away with cutting any corners. I remember one occasion where I attempted to make an excuse for a poor effort on an assignment, and she looked me in the eyes and said, "I don't know what you do in your other classes, but you are going to do my work!" I am very thankful for the role Dr. C played in helping me to become refocused on my academics.

Beginning in my sophomore year, my academic performance improved dramatically. By my junior and senior years I was performing at a very high level each academic semester. I attribute this in large part to the prodding Dr. C gave me at a time when I needed a kick in the rear. My Marquette experience also fueled my intellectual curiosity and helped sharpen my critical thinking skills. I enjoyed courses in theology, history, social and racial justice, philosophy, and cross-cultural and intercultural communications. I was fortunate to have a few professors who, like Dr. C, saw potential in me and really encouraged me in my scholarly pursuits. Dr. Robert Shuter, with whom I took two courses addressing cross-cultural and intercultural communications, and Dr. Shawn Copeland, with whom I studied critical race theory, are two professors who were particularly important mentors and nurturers of my intellectual development.

In addition to classroom learning, I benefited from a variety of real world learning opportunities that Marquette offered. One of the more impactful opportunities was my work with Marquette's Service Learning program, which integrated community service as part of the curricular learning experience. Although working with community organizations and facilitating service learning opportunities was meaningful in itself, the friendships and community shared by the program staff were just as meaningful. I also gained valuable work experience working as a student tour guide for the admissions office, as well as working with the special events department of the Alumni Memorial Union.

Beyond my academic and work experiences, Marquette provided me a wide variety of extracurricular and campus life activities. For a period of time, I was a pianist for the gospel choir, and I played the euphonium in the symphonic and pep bands. I spent a lot of time socializing in the Multi-Cultural Center of the Union, mostly playing cards, listening to music, and talking about sports and culture. The highlight of my extracurricular life, however, was pledging the Omega Psi Phi Fraternity near the end of my first year. Our chapter at Marquette had been inactive for some time and it was exciting for me, and for Black Greek life on campus, to bring the Ques back "on the yard." I also benefitted tremendously from the cultural and arts resources available in the city of Milwaukee, including concerts, festivals, museums, films and other similar activities. Most notably, I participated in a several month long residency of renowned jazz pianist Dr. Barry Harris that was sponsored by the Wisconsin Conservatory of Music. Meeting Dr. Harris literally changed the course of my life, as he became one of the most influential persons in my inner circle.

After Marquette, I pursued dual professional careers in music and law. I graduated from the University of Wisconsin Law School three years after graduating from Marquette. Immediately after law school I pursued graduate study in music performance at the Royal Conservatory in The Hague, Netherlands. Thereafter, I returned to my hometown and commenced practicing corporate law by day, while gigging on the jazz, R&B and gospel music scenes by night. A few years later, I participated in the prestigious Thelonious Monk International Jazz Piano Competition and was a semifinalist in that competition. This experience motivated me to relocate to New York City, the epicenter of the jazz world, to pursue opportunities to collaborate with and learn from the living legends of the music.

Since moving to New York City, I have had continued success in both careers as a business transactions attorney and as a jazz musician. A recent accomplishment that I am particularly proud of is the release of my debut recording of *Songs in the Key of Wonder*, a collection of my jazz arrangements of songs composed by the great Stevie Wonder. Many of the skills and competencies that have fueled my success are attributable to my Marquette experience. My work ethic, intellectual curiosity, interpersonal skills, business acumen and social confidence were either developed or greatly enhanced during my four years at Marquette. Indeed, I think it is fair to say that I became myself at Marquette.

Shellisa Multrie

Class of 2000, 2004

Marquette University was my first and only choice. I graduated from high school a year early and felt like Marquette was familiar. I had fallen in love with Marquette's campus while in competing high school programs like Young Lawyers in Milwaukee. I remember someone mentioning getting a "double M," which I understood to mean getting both of your degrees from Marquette. I wanted to be a lawyer, so this was going to be the perfect plan.

I remember freshman orientation in the summer of 1996. There was so much to see and experience. I remember someone reading Dr. Seuss' *Oh the Places You'll Go* to us in our assembly. I made a few friends during that time. I think we were all excited to find someone else who looked like us quite frankly because there were not many Black students at orientation. There were five of us ... Charles, Leslie, Kyeshia and LaShonda ... only two of us were from Milwaukee. We hit it off, and by the time we officially arrived on campus ready for school to begin, we had all started navigating our own paths. I was a commuter student while everyone else lived on campus. Thinking back, this is something I would have done differently because I found that once I was on campus, I rarely wanted to leave. I stumbled upon the Multi-Cultural Center or the "MCC" in the Alumni Memorial Union. You could get lost in the nearly 17,000 students roaming Wisconsin Avenue, but when I found the MCC, I found my sense of community. This first floor space right next to the Office of Student Life was where many students of color came to hang out in between classes, watch *Days of Our Lives* every day for lunch, play Spades, and do life together. This space provided an outlet for social justice conversations and was where many came for solace. It was everything for me because it gave me a place to connect. As a commuter student, the MCC was my home base on campus.

My early friends at Marquette got me involved in Black Student Council and a few other fun activities that helped me acclimate. What was puzzling to me, almost immediately, was how it seemed like most of the Black students on campus that I met already knew it each other. They were already family. I found out about Marquette's Educational Opportunity Program or EOP and learned that students in that program spent the summer prior to freshman year in a pre-college program together on campus. My mom and I made an appointment to learn more, and shortly thereafter I was admitted to the program. To describe this program as a blessing is an understatement because all of a sudden, I had a family replete with aunts and uncles who were there to help me navigate through school academically and financially. This was the start of something for me that I really believe helped me make it through Marquette. By the spring of 1997, I felt like I belonged, and I was busy learning how I could make a difference on campus.

I became Black Student Council president in 1997 and I was excited to serve and help make an impact on campus. I also became a member of Zeta Phi Beta Sorority. I loved every minute of being on campus and loved my close-knit community in the MCC. I also learned that loving the social side too much could put your academics in jeopardy. Marquette was so different from my high school experience. School, up until college, had always come easy to me. I was always involved in student leadership, academic, dance and sports activities. I was always able to keep things balanced and be a star student. College was very different. I struggled in class trying to find a rhythm or recipe for success. My success as a student required me to attend study groups, extra help sessions and many, many late hours in the computer lab. I finally figured things out the summer after sophomore year and found my balance between being involved in student activities and academics. I went on to serve as president of my undergraduate chapter for my sorority as well as president of the African-American Greek Alliance. My favorite memory would be the creation of the Brew City Stomp Down, which at one point, for many years was the largest step show in the state of Wisconsin, and it made this student organization extremely profitable and able to give scholarships and other donations.

One of the best things about my experience at Marquette was the exposure to community service and working on campus. I have a heart to serve today, and I believe it was really born out of all of the opportunities to serve others. As a student transportation manager for the Community Service office, I saw all of the places our students served in Milwaukee. I also worked at the information desk in the union as a student manager. I was able to see so much and really become an ambassador for my school. I worked at the Writing Center my junior and senior year, and this helped me develop a passion for writing and helping others.

A few of my favorite professors were Dr. Heather Hathaway and Dr. Sean Copeland during undergrad and Dr. Terry Burant in graduate school. They were each very different but very passionate about what they do. I believe Dr. Copeland was the only African American professor I had during my years at Marquette, and she was outstanding. This did not seem odd, as I was normally the only Black student or one of a very small group in nearly every class. The longer that I was at Marquette, the more I saw that there may have been 500 Black students total, and that included the international students. Not all of those students associated with other Black students but for the most part, we were supportive of each other. There were some times that I do remember class discussions becoming quite spirited and it was always rough to be the only Black student or in a very stark minority. It was something that you got used to and learned to move past.

I came to Marquette to become an attorney. I graduated from Marquette in May 2000 with a degree in writing intensive English, returning two years later for graduate school. I did get my "double M," just not quite in the way that I planned to do it. I received my masters in educational policy & leadership in May 2004. I remember several of the Black arts & science graduates sitting together at graduation so that our parents would have a better chance of finding us in the crowd. I also had the honor of singing the national anthem at my graduation, which was very special. I loved my time at Marquette, and I am very proud of my alma mater.

As an alumna, I will admit that I have not really felt connected to Marquette. Beyond calls for donations and the occasional invite to Ethnic Alumni events, I have not really felt compelled to reconnect. In 2019, I received an invite to celebrate an important milestone of the EOP program. I also realized that my 20th anniversary was upon me. I attended the EOP anniversary program in the fall of 2019, and it was very apparent that it was time for me to get active. I remember the speakers impressing upon us that we are alumni too. We need to be more vocal and get involved to ensure that we hold the school accountable for keeping opportunities like EOP and others for students of color alive and well. I also reconnected with Black Student Council leaders and found that they too needed our help, our voice to speak for them and push from the alumni side for more support for Black students. I love my school, and I want them to reconnect to the familiar refrain from my time there, "We are Marquette!" To me, this meant all of us; everyone was valuable and had a role to play in the success of our university. I left Marquette happy and whole. Fully prepared to interact in any circle and perform with the best of people. I want to make sure that I reach back and do my part to ensure that more Black students have that chance.

Today, I serve as human resource executive in learning & leadership development at a large financial services firm. I have continued to serve in the community with my sorority in several leadership roles as well with the YMCA. I am a proud board member for the historic McCrorey YMCA in Charlotte, North Carolina. I also serve in the Junior League of Charlotte. I am a wife and mother of two awesome children.

Belton Flournoy

Class of 2003

G rowing up in Texas, I was frequently the only person of color in the room. I primarily attended Catholic schools, which shielded me from experiencing racism from others as a child. As a result, I grew up feeling that we have moved beyond race as a society. My belief was that if someone works hard enough, they will be recognised and be successful, looking at my parents for evidence of this. I saw the world as open to people of all colors, genders and orientations. What has influenced this view more in recent years is what I have come to witness from so many over the years, both on television and from personal friends.

I still recall the moment I realized I was different. I was nine years old and was at the Laity Lodge summer camp in Texas. A friend of mine ran up to me and asked, "Belton, how does it feel to be the only Black person here ..." I looked around and suddenly realized I was. It took someone else to call it out. It took someone else to notice. It took someone to look at me and say, "You are different to us." None of us are born feeling different. We feel this way as a result of a thousand little interactions we have with those around us.

My parents had such large role in my personal perception, mainly due to the fact that their upbringings caused them to want to raise me different to them.

My father was raised in La Jolla, California, by a single Black mother of three. His mother had to work twice as hard raising three children, so she took to cleaning houses and made sure her children focused on their studies. My father ended up receiving a college scholarship and became a first-generation college student, opening the doors to my future.

My mother, on the other hand, was born in Venezuela and raised in Trinidad. As a child her parents could not afford to take care of her, so she was raised in a convent with nuns. It was there she learned the Lord's way. After she turned 18, she started working for an American who invited her to return to the States with them when they moved back. A few years after her arrival, she received her green card and then met my father. When she had me, she vowed to give her son a better childhood than she had endured, with college being a requirement in her mind, further setting me on this path.

I made the decision to attend Marquette University with the support of my high school guidance counselor. I attended Strake Jesuit College Preparatory, where they spent a great deal of time supporting students though the college decision making process. Being from Texas, the climate in Milwaukee was not what I would have ideally chosen (especially after spending my first winter there), but I wanted to continue my Jesuit education, and I recall reading about an event called Summerfest (some of you may have heard about it). I did not know anyone who had attended Marquette before, but when I was invited to attend and join the Freshman Frontier Program (FFP), I jumped at the opportunity.

When I first arrived at Marquette, I was excited to be away from home. I had an over-protective mother, so the freedom that came with living in the dorms felt good—maybe too good as you will soon hear. During the summer of 1999, I made a strong group of friends in my FFP group, as there was a limited number of us and we lived in the dorms together. I found my initial experience to be one that was extremely welcoming; however, I did notice I started to swap my chain wallet for an Abercrombie top in order to "fit in."

When the semester finally started, I felt like I was a step ahead of my peers, as I already had a good group of friends from my summer program.

My first dorm was O'Donnell Hall, which happened to be co-ed that year. It was there I met some of my lifelong friends, including Kate Judd, Amanda Spaulding, Erick Koczab, Jeffrey Tincher, Christina Beck, Justin O'Shea, Christopher Swan and many others. It's been nearly 15 years, and I have been to all of their weddings, and once I find a partner, I hope they can all make it to mine.

As I mentioned before, my parents had invested heavily in my education, which caused me to not take it as seriously as I should have. This newfound freedom, combined with so many new friends, soon had me feeling like I was the "man of the campus." I recall thinking how lucky I was to be Black while attending Marquette. After many a night of walking around campus going from party to party, I woke the next day with a new set of friends—many of whom I did not remember, and not for the reasons you might think. I stood out. There were not many people who looked like me, so when I went to a party and met people, they tended to remember me. Like someone with red hair, or a significant height, my race made me memorable, and therefore, I frequently had people saying hi to me around campus, when I could not even remember meeting them due to the sheer number of people I had met. I know if I had looked like everyone else, I would not have been as memorable.

As I entered my sophomore year, my lack of focus started to catch up with me. My GPA was falling, and I cared more about hanging out with the new friends I had, as opposed to my schoolwork. The first person at Marquette who would change my life for the better was my FFP counselor, Amy Chisnell Rowe. She saw past my excuses and told me to focus. She would not know until much later how much her words would change me.

It was shortly after this discussion when I received word from Marquette that my loan for the following semester was denied. I did not know at the time that my parents were going through financial struggles, and this event unexpectedly turned my normal safe world upside down. The loan denial resulted in me being forced out of Marquette. As I started to see my friends graduate around me, my carefree attitude fizzled away. I no longer had it all; I was a Black man who had been forced out of university. I started to feel like those statistics I heard about, and that little voice in my head told me people would look at me and assume it was typical for a person who looked like me.

I refused to listen to that voice.

I made the decision to stay in Milwaukee and was able to get a job at a local high-end restaurant, The Social. I worked there until I turned 25 and was able to apply for financial aid as an adult. This time, I researched future incomes and made the decision I wanted to move from majoring in public relations to marketing. With the help of the Marquette loan officer, Michael Tindall, I was able to secure funding to re-attend, on the requirement I was re-accepted.

I excitedly made an appointment with the Assistant Dean of the Business school to discuss my re-admission. I walked into his office on a sunny the summer of 2015 and told him my story. He seemed engaged, went to the screen, took one look at my grades (1.7 at the time), and then made the comment, "I am sorry, but there is no way you are coming back to this university with those grades, let alone transferring into this business school." This was the second time I was faced with a challenge.

I refused to take no for an answer.

I looked at him straight in the eye and said, "I did not come here to ask your permission, I want you to tell me what I need to do to return." I do not know where I got that courage from to challenge him, but I knew I was tired of doors closing in my face. He informed me I needed to revise two of my past grades and he would consider it. I took the summer classes, got an A and a B, asked both my teachers to write him letters for re-admission, as well as contacting one of my old teachers, Donna Shuster, to also write a letter for re-admission. When I came back to his office the next time, the first words this time were, "Please stop having people write me letters." I was admitted back into Marquette in 2005. Upon my return, I received A's in nearly all of my classes and received offers from three top global organizations upon graduation. My GPA was restored.

It was the second time I attended Marquette that I truly wanted it. I wanted to learn, and I appreciated every second of it. I made the commitment to sit in the front row of every class, and to ask at least one question per class—one of my good friends the second time around was Brett Smith. When he introduced me to his then girlfriend, Jenna Lara, her response was "Oh, that guy … he is the one always asking questions in my class." My marketing professor, Dennis Garrett, re-ignited my passion for learning by making it fun, and, during my intro to IT course, it was Dr. Monica Adya who made an offhanded comment that ended up having me pick up IT as a second major to marketing. The comment, "IT is not about technology. IT is about how we manage information using technology in innovative ways."

After interning for Johnson Controls during Marquette round two, I ended up turning down an offer there, as well as at Ernst & Young to join a young company called Protiviti in the technology consulting division. A friend had connected me to Terrance Ow, a professor in the IT department who had a reputation of making sure his students found jobs. I reached out and he took me under his wing, introducing me personally to a number of companies and speaking very highly of me. I will never forget the role he played in helping to start my career at the company I am still at.

After graduation I was also invited to join the MU National Alumni Board of Directors, representing the Young Alumni of Marquette. It was there I met another two inspirational ladies, Valerie Wilson Reed and Maureen Haggerty Warmuth. What these women did not realize is that without my family in Wisconsin, my social engagements were typically limited to my immediate peer group. While serving on the board with these powerful women, I was soon introduced to a variety of business leaders, including Val's husband, a Black audit partner of KPMG, a person who looked like me in a job I wanted to obtain—something that is unfortunately rarer than I would like.

Marquette has had a profound impact on my life. It was not just the University I went to. It was the University I **fought** to go to. I had so many people who impacted me, who supported me—from the moment of feeling accepted at the university, to the continued support of my teachers. I relocated to London less than two years after graduation and am now a director at Protiviti, the firm I joined from Marquette. While I had to step down from my role on the Alumni Board when I moved, I was able to establish the Marquette Club of London with two fellow alumni, Michael Peters and Marek Krawczyk, within months of my arrival. My personal background, combined with the community service-oriented Jesuit schools I attended, helped me to understand the importance that diversity plays in people's lives. In 2017 I worked to create Pride in the City, a London Mayor-backed initiative dedicated to creating more diverse workplaces, and in 2020 I was shortlisted as a Top-10 Inspirational Business Leader by the British LGBT+ awards.

My journey here has not been an easy one, but you see, it is these struggles that have me fighting for change today. Your unique lived experience makes you, you. Recognize it. Be proud of it. Think of the things that make you different or that you want to change about yourself, and realize that they are not inhibitors, they are an asset yet to be tapped.

Jim Milner

Class of 2003

"Experience: That most brutal of teachers
but you learn, my God, do you learn."
— C.S. Lewis

Thank you, Marquette University! Today I am the founder and managing director for a global consulting business and a nonprofit community development organization: Urban Strategies, Inc. and Sector Management Consulting Group, LLC. These achievements were made possible because of my journey through Marquette University where I earned a double major in leadership and organizational development and communications while discovering my favorite courses, such as human behavior, anthropology and finance.

Each subject I studied prepared me to grow to the highest levels in my field. Today I am an executive leadership and business management coach. I am one of 1,200 international master certified coaches sanctioned by International Coach Federation, a meta-coach graduate of Dr. Daniel Goleman Emotional Intelligence Program and I hold more than 20 assessment certifications in the coaching industry. My master's degree in business administration provides the foundation needed to assist in acquisition and mergers for startup businesses.

The university made the above possible; however, my plan was not to attend Marquette. I thought Marquette University was out of reach for a guy like me. In fact, my high school guidance counselor told me to work at a local factory at the time because that is where "all the Black men go" after high school. He said that would be a "better route" for me. While the factory life was not what I saw for myself, I did give it a try at the encouragement of my stepfather; he took me to his workplace, Crucible Steel.

I worked there for about a month, spending most of my break time hiding in the bathroom. I remember asking myself how anyone could work in a place that blows dirt and steel dust in the air until retirement. I had a dream, and it included leaving that steel mill as soon as I could to find something better. The truth is I was afraid, living in an unfair world without the privilege to know I could choose.

As time passed, I grew up and became excited by those individuals working in professional service worlds. I believed the professional world was for white men, synonymous to my thoughts of Marquette University. If I did want to be a professional, schoolteacher was the path. I was told there were very limited ways for an African American to land a professional job.

In the early '80s I got lucky. I found an opportunity with a local nonprofit, Lincoln Park Community Center of Milwaukee. My role was coaching career development strategies to young men transitioning out of the judicial system. My goal was to create a pathway to success for individuals that looked like me, without limitation.

I wanted the young men who entered the training center to see, perhaps, that what they saw in me they could also see in themselves. My purpose for living and giving of myself was my way of becoming the image of possibility in the minds of each young person that came to the program. I must admit, even though the road for success would not be easy, trust, care and support were the key ingredients to keeping the focus.

I was learning more about myself as I was coaching them toward achieving their careers. The process of sharing relevant information creates a burning desire to give these young people more, and in turn, I wanted more for myself. As fate would have it, I would soon learn that returning to school and working in leadership for community-based organizations, creating social enterprises, would be in my future.

My world started to change when I met this gentleman who was a business development counselor for Milwaukee Area Technical College. This man, Mr. Ben Johnson, eventually would become a longtime mentor, just as I had been a mentor for young men early in my life. Ben's primary responsibility as a business counselor was to support start-up minority businesses in the Milwaukee market.

I hung out in his office regularly, hoping to get a foot in the door for my own development. Attending Marquette University was not a consideration for me until Mr. Johnson told me that it was going to be the best career and life decision I ever made. As I mentioned earlier, I never considered Marquette because I truly did not believe that it was achievable for me to attend as an African American. I believed that I would not survive in what I saw as a well-respected, all-white institution.

Nevertheless, with Mr. Johnson's encouragement, I took on the challenge. I made my way to the admissions office, where I was asked to complete an essay and secure letters of endorsement from business leaders that knew me and my work. A couple months later I received a letter of acceptance. At age 44, and 26 years after graduating from North Division High School, I was finally going to college. However, as you can imagine, being an adult student at the university, living on campus and the exposure to sports had no real relevance for me; I was there for the education. Further, while I did not have any family members that had previously attended the university, I knew it was best that I take this journey alone.

My first challenge coming to Marquette University was getting comfortable and being familiar with the Catholic faith and the Jesuit educational structure. I found it all to be a lot more difficult to handle than I originally thought. I came to class feeling as though I had a secret. I grew up in a family of Pentecostals; my grandmother raised us to pray, to believe in God, to have faith in things unseen and to believe in the possibility of all things. The Catholic faith to me was order and protocols. I believed Jesuit education was about thinking deeply and studying your options.

In fact, I remember my first day of class, the dean of the college, Dr. Bob Deal, came in the classroom to introduce himself. He said, "Welcome to Marquette University. Because you have chosen to come to this college, you have made the choice to change your life. We are going to interrupt your current experience. No longer will you have to take at face value what someone else tells you. When you are done with this program, you will be able to research, study, determine your own truth and make your own decisions." After hearing him say that out loud, for all to hear, I remember thinking to myself, did he mean to give me, a Black man, that message, which I thought was a white man's secret?

Being one of the oldest students in the program, and usually the only African American man in my predominantly white and female dominated classes, I often felt like an outcast. Additionally, I felt as though I was significantly behind the learning curve. I had to work harder than anyone to maintain a persona that I belonged. Despite the challenges I faced, my mantra was to just keep moving and "stay the course." Looking back now, my inner struggles with the issue of belonging and acceptance probably made my experience more difficult than it needed to be, but I made it through.

My indirect experiences with various professors opened my eyes to the amount of influence we have with each other. My value to care was important to me, even when others showed little care, but it made me strong. In addition, I now know that some of the best instructors I had were the most difficult ones, but it allowed me to see that I was more than capable of being as successful as they were; it built a confidence in me that I do not think would exist without that experience.

I am thankful for the opportunities my Marquette education affords me. But as an African American, there are still challenges I face. After I graduated, I was viewed as not good enough for the white culture where top leadership positions were available and "too good," in some cases, for the Black culture because we are all competing for the same positions. But of course, when asked if I had to do it over again, would I still consider Marquette, my answer is absolutely, yes!

Despite the various challenges I faced, I truly believe my Marquette experience has shaped a large portion of who I am today. The work I do as an executive leadership and business management coach requires a high level of emotional intelligence. I credit Marquette for giving me the foundation for learning to do this work well.

As a Marquette University graduate '03, my greatest achievement thus far: "It is okay to be Black and not be afraid to run in the suburbs"!

Teon Austin

Class of 2004 and 2011

I am a part of the fellowship of Upward Bound. This statement carries serious weight for me. My most formative academic and transformative experiences at Marquette University came from my experiences in its federally funded TRIO Programs. From an early age, even before I knew exactly what college was, how to get there, what it took to be successful or how it would impact my life, I knew I was going to Marquette University. I knew I was going to college, and I hoped I could make it through. I also knew the students, faculty and staff would be very different from the people I learned with and from, the people I idolized and looked up to, and the people I felt and still feel were valuable and knowledgeable. My story is not different from a lot of the students I have served in my professional life as I work to remove barriers to higher education for students, especially the students of color.

Marquette's campus was drastically different from the environment I grew up in. Although I was used to seeing faculty and staff who looked nothing like me, with a few exceptions sprinkled here and there in my early education, I was always used to the student body sharing social, cultural, ethnic or at least economic profiles that were similar to mine. I knew Marquette students were different. I knew this from the stories my grandmother told me from her interactions with them as she cleaned their dorms, classrooms and gyms. My grandmother worked for Marquette for many years on the cleaning staff until the day she retired. She provided me with Marquette gear, interesting stories about the faculty and staff, and her firsthand account of students from all over the globe having fun, studying intensely and graduating. She was the first one to tell me I could go to college and promised to wear a dress at my graduation, something I had never seen.

The older I got the more I knew it would take more than me modeling my mother's work ethic and determination or my grandmother's well wishes and prayer to help me get to and through college, especially Marquette University. I have always loved learning, which was reflected in my grades in elementary and high school, but I had no idea if I was prepared for the rigor of college. Not ever having attended college, my family did not know exactly how to get me ready. They listened supportively to my dreams of college and desires to attend Marquette, instilled core values like dedication and hard work, and encouraged me not to give up on my dreams. I knew I needed to do everything possible to prepare for the challenge. This is when I met Steven Robertson.

Steven Robertson was a counselor for the Upward Bound Program at Marquette, a pre-college program for low income and first-generation college students, who came to my high school to recruit students. This program reiterated the values my mother taught me and in so many ways served as a surrogate parent as the staff helped me learn how to navigate higher education, develop healthy work habits and become more disciplined. In addition to learning how to "do the work" that would get me to and through college, the program provided me with social and cultural opportunities that helped broaden my horizons, aspirations, and motivated me to want to graduate from college and improve the quality of life for my family. Through this program I had many firsts: trips out of Wisconsin, college visits, airplane rides, professional sporting events, and supplemental education geared around college entrance exams and picking a major.

In addition to all the firsts I experienced, the Upward Bound program also helped me learn about programs, clubs and opportunities to look for in any college I was considering in order to make sure I had the support and resources I needed. One of which was the Educational Opportunity Program (EOP) called Student Support Services (SSS). I mentioned knowing how different the students, faculty and staff would be when I started college—and they were. I found the familiarity I needed on the fourth floor of Marquette Hall. I already knew Alexander Peete, Sande Robinson and Jackie Walker through my high school years on campus, so this made the hand-off between programs that much easier. As I started my freshman summer, I remember thinking for the first time how cool it was that the university would value the TRIO Programs so much that they would house them in their flagship building.

The EOP program, as Student Support Services (SSS) was often called, gave me a safe place from the culture shock, the overwhelming nature of being a first-generation college student and the occasional bias-driven incident. Even more important, the staff pushed me out of my comfort zone and encouraged me to get involved in events outside of the TRIO Program. As a result, I tried fencing with a fellow engineering classmate, joined the advertising club and developed friendships with many new people.

My years on Marquette's campus were very influential in helping me see how important it is to have the right people in positions to help young people not only make it to and through college but learn how to navigate life and define their journey. The impact the faculty and staff had, especially those in the TRIO Programs, is the reason why I have served my community and have served as a career counselor, youth worker, Marquette University Upward Bound counselor, college faculty, basketball coach, college access program director and assistant dean of students. These people represent Marquette to me, and they are the reason I saw my grandmother wear a dress—twice. I am looking forward to a third time as I finish writing my dissertation.

Shaun Hickombottom

Class of 2006

My Marquette experience was one that I did not initially want to partake in, but it ended up being one of the best decisions of my life. First and foremost, I want to thank my Mom and my Auntie Val for putting the idea (aka forcing me ☺) of applying to Marquette in my head. If it was fully up to me, my eyes were set on attending Eastern Illinois University with all my high school friends. I'm so glad I did not go that route.

Anyway, I grew up in Downers Grove, Illinois, and attended Montini Catholic High School in Lombard, Illinois. I was one of two African American students in my graduating class, and I never really had many Black friends growing up. Going into college that was one thing I really wanted to change. I wanted to be able to experience Marquette with students that looked like me and experience the same challenges and successes that might come my way while in college. Marquette gave me the platform to do that.

Going into my freshman year, I was enrolled in FFP (Freshman Frontier Program). This program allowed me to spend the summer semester before my first year on campus getting acclimated with college life. It also gave me an opportunity to meet a whole lot of new people. Out of that summer alone, I met four of my best friends still to this day. I also realized Marquette was definitely the place for me. I knew it was going to provide me with so many life options to help me grow as a young Black male. Things I knew I wanted in high school but didn't know where to look to get that fulfillment.

During my first two years, I met a lot of different people and was involved in numerous activities. I also chose a major; I decided to study advertising with a minor in marketing. I knew back then that I wanted to do something in the sports industry. By my sophomore year I had a great group of friends. Also, that year I pledged Alpha Phi Alpha Fraternity (Epsilon Tau Chapter) and my roommate pledged Omega Psi Phi Fraternity and we were both online at the same time. With both of us pledging, we were a great support system for one another. The experiences of pledging and being a member of a fraternity opened my eyes to a lot of things. The most important thing it showed me is that young Black males can come together and make a difference in the community along with growing a personal bond that will last forever.

My junior and senior years, I was the president of the Epsilon Tau Chapter of Alpha Phi Alpha Fraternity and also served as the Vice President of the Black Student Council. Serving both of these positions helped mold me into the man I am today. More importantly, serving as VP of the BSC also assisted me with meeting the love of my life, my wife, Courtney Ofosu.

Upon graduation, I knew I wanted to do something in sports, I just didn't know exactly what. Fortunately, my Auntie Val introduced me to another Marquette grad who worked for the Milwaukee Bucks. I had the opportunity to meet with her, and she helped me get an interview for an internship with them. Three months after graduating, I started an internship with the Milwaukee Bucks in their public relations department. I spent two years with the Bucks and in 2008 accepted a full-time position with the Chicago Bulls public relations department. Now, I'm entering my 13th season with the Bulls in the role of senior manager of player and team services.

Marquette University will always have a special place in my heart. The four years I spent there helped make me into the man, father, husband, son, brother, grandchild and friend I am today. It also gave me the necessary tools I needed to start a successful career. Although those four years went by extremely fast, Marquette lives in me every single day.

Thank you and Go Marquette!

Emanuel J. Wilder

Broadcasting, Class of 2006

In its complete totality, the hallmark of the Marquette experience, as I perceived it during my most formative years, and yet remains true until this day, is deeply rooted in service, purpose and the rigorous pursuit of academia. The "Marquette Experience," designed to motivate, guide and steer apt pupils towards channels of stewardship, temperance and self-discovery, has therefore uniquely positioned the university to consistently impact the lives of its graduates long after their tenures have ended. And it is indeed that impact which affords all of us contributing to this project a rare but necessary advantage as we continue to navigate the portals of our professional worlds.

While the more easily recognizable advantages of the MU alumni status include a vast professional network, esteemed camaraderie with notable peers and access to impressive resources, the more clandestine benefits may yield a more fruitful recompense. To be sure, our lives, professional and personal and otherwise, are deeply enriched from our time confined within the university's walls, but our spirits too have become stronger and hopefully more eager to serve, increasingly more aligned with the awareness of our individual purpose.

Nature has consistently proven that any species attempting to reap the bounty of their labors must first demonstrate a level of determination, dexterity, fortitude and resolve, and those laws of nature must be applied when attempting to understand the vast diversity of experiences we have shared at Marquette, whether we be Black, white, Asian or other. Fortune favors the ambitious, and MU has made sure that true ambition is rooted in service. But before purpose is fully understood and before the rigors of academia could have ever been applied to our selected trades, service is the mold to which MU has shaped my experience and the lens to which I have approached and embraced my chosen profession as educator.

Service—such volume, scope, dimension, diversity … so simple a word, and locked deep within that simplicity do we discover authenticity and goodness. As a professed Christian, I've found this truth unavoidable: that in every action, exploit, mission, pattern, thought, lies both the carnality of selfishness and the liberty of altruism. Marquette has been most advantageous in defining this truth, at least to me, and has helped me learn how to allow philanthropy to "win out" more often than not. Superficially speaking, the end of a collegiate education (gaining financial profit) is justified by the means (harsh studies) and those solely prescribing to the baseness of this formula may be productive but will lack depth of character. Marquette's key advantage at the time, in preparing me for a world beyond Wisconsin Ave, is that it constantly reinforced this proverb. There must be more to attain, beyond the degree and the profit, to make the experience worthwhile.

I can recall the redundancy of the slogan "Be the Difference" permeating through the very fabric of the campus landscape, and while it did not take root then, seeds were in fact sown that would later spring forth and guide my perspective (quite literally! More on that later). But it was through this new understanding of what a "difference maker" actually was that I was able to embrace the subtlest but most important values the campus had to offer beyond scholarship. To this discovery, the great Apostle Paul said, "Nay, much more those members of the body, which seem to be more feeble, are necessary," 1 Co 12:22. You see, it is here that Marquette played the active role in shifting the paradigm to which I understood "Greatness" and steered me towards paths ordained by the duties of service rather than those guided by the self-preservation of vainglory. So while some universities boast their strength of curriculum and their illustrious alumni and ceaseless endowment reserves to attract students, they are likened unto what Paul called the legs and mouth, and head and arms and chest and hands; those parts of the body receiving all of the attention and glory; those parts that we all admit perform the physical works, and provide mobility to accomplish all tasks. But what Marquette has preoccupied itself with is a focus on the more inward parts. Instead of relying solely on a strong portfolio of alumni and vain prestige, the university, in my opinion, has decided to promote service, character development and discovery of purpose above all else. Those things that we cannot see—virtue, service, teamwork, outreach, accountability and faith—are the very pinnacles that Paul and MU have deemed the most vital.

Collectively speaking, my peers, alumni mentors, professors and extended MU family have all been a tremendous help in helping me exhume the most necessary treasure one can discover, purpose. Only recently have I devised a formula to explain it, but my experiences at the university, both positive and negative, have played a major role in proving it: Composition + Production = Purpose (Service). Halfway through my junior year, and after exploring different clubs and activities the campus had to offer, I found myself as a guest on the set of a television show called *The College Perspective*. The MUTV show aired on the closed campus circuit, meaning only MU students were privy to the viewing, and the content was laid out in a talk show format. One host, two guests and a 30-minute discussion on the daily dealings and trends at MU from a current student's perspective. Even though the show was unscripted, I felt this scene in my life was ironically handwritten and ordained by God. Sitting on that haggardly couch, in front of three live cameras, lights glaring, mics live, made me feel alive. I had found more than a calling, but a purpose. A few episodes later, the producers of that show would ask me to host it full time, and for the next year and a half, I had begun to actualize purpose. Composition—the nature of my "ingredients," the way in which I was mixed and made, found serenity in the crucible of lights, chaos, frenzy and all things television. The production, the thing produced from my composition, was quite literally a unique perspective on the world around me, thoughtful, curious and humorous. Taken together (composition and production), I have found my purpose to be simple: to build the human spirit of my audience (any audience) and serve them by reinforcing their unique use and necessity in the great circle of life.

The second occasion in which the university helped me learn the true meaning of my collegiate experience and led me that much closer to the discovery of purpose came during the fall of 2004. The most inspiring professor that I've had the honor to sit under, Donna Decker Schuster (in memoriam), fell unexpectedly ill one particular class. Instead of cancelling the class or merely assigning work in her absence, she appointed me the class chairman. To be sure, I was responsible, engaged and dutiful, a fine choice for chairman (as brief of a stint as it would be), but two things left an impression on me that have built the cornerstone of my confidence. This professor, this Dr. Schuster, as renowned, accomplished, ambitious and as brilliant as she was, saw fit to designate me to this post in her absence. That she trusted me with such a responsibility was in itself unbelievable, but that I actually felt that same amount of peace and docility as I had while sitting on the couch during the *College Perspective* show, was astounding. That feeling returned! Let it be clear, purpose, true purpose, has nothing to do with our emotive response, or lack thereof. The true calling of destiny and purpose supersedes our mercurial emotions and neither calling nor destiny are governed by the goosebumps we feel. In spite of this stoic notion though, I still felt relieved, free, calm and useful and contrary to my previous stance, that feeling mattered. In that moment, in that email that she sent to the entire class naming me chairman, Dr. Schuster was able to agitate a sentiment that has stayed with me unto this day. She confirmed that my purpose, or at least part of it, was to, in some capacity, at some time, in some way, serve as an educator.

The prompt of this passage was simple: answer the question, "How has my Marquette Experience been advantageous for me in my professional world?" I now have the privilege to serve as the executive director for an organization called The Chicago Interview Institute, a program aimed at helping others articulate and communicate a clear, distinctive vision concerning their occupational futures. A role that allows me to fulfil purpose by serving others. Marquette taught me how to serve and most importantly, how and why I serve. MU did not neglect their duty of guidance, and without clarity of purpose, nothing else matters. I've been blessed to take this ideal into my professional world and share it with others. For it is divinely written, "Without vision, the people perish" (Pr 29:18), and I'd like to humbly add, "but without purpose they live in vain."

Shirley J. Knowles

Communications, Class of 2007

I tell people all of the time that attending Marquette has been the best decision I've ever made in my life. As an 18-year-old girl from Florida, I took a big risk leaving everything I knew—my family, my friends and my city—to attend a school I could barely pronounce correctly in Milwaukee, Wisconsin. Now that I think about it, I probably couldn't even identify Milwaukee on the map at that time. But that's a very different story now.

I almost didn't go to Marquette. I had been accepted to all of the schools I applied to in Florida, and going to school down there would have been easy. I had my choice of schools. But when I met the dean of Marquette's College of Communications and learned about the school, I fell in love with the school. But cost was a factor. I didn't want to add debt to my life, and I couldn't wrap my head around the logistics of moving to Wisconsin, so I withdrew my acceptance to Marquette. I was so bummed. It just didn't feel right. But right after I graduated from high school in late May, something came over me and told me I NEEDED to go to Marquette. That something great was waiting for me there. I had done the in-person school tour in October 2002, and felt so at peace on the campus. So why was I resisting what I wanted? I reached back out to the same dean, Bill Elliott, and let him know that I'd really like to attend Marquette if the offer was still on the table. Would I be able to get my scholarships back? Would I be able to live in the dorm I wanted? Was I still wanted? And the answer was yes to all of my questions. That's how my Marquette journey began.

I learned a lot about myself while attending Marquette from 2003 to 2007. It was the first time I lived on my own. The first time I had to do my own laundry, go grocery shopping or navigate my way through a new city—all things that seem so simple now. But it took me being on my own and starting a new chapter in my life that made me grow from a young girl from Tampa to an adult living at 16th and Wisconsin.

I am also grateful for my experience at Marquette because it allowed me to make new friends, something that wasn't easy for me initially. I'm naturally introverted—although some people would say that's not true since I normally take on various leadership roles—so walking up to new floormates and introducing myself was definitely off the table. I mean—I would walk around my floor with my head down just so I wouldn't have to meet and talk to new people! But being on my own "island" didn't last for long—the girls I lived with on 8-West in McCormick would not let me get away with being by myself. And, to this day, the relationships I formed on that floor during my freshman year are some of the strongest I have.

Marquette taught me to be independent. To discover who I am, and what made me happy. It's kind of difficult to do that when you're under your parents rule back home, but when you're on your own—it's a totally different ballgame. Marquette taught me it's OK to take classes that you weren't sure you'd like, but were curious about—I didn't know it initially, but I'd wind up loving all of my literature classes at Marquette, and would take as many as I could every semester. Marquette taught me the importance of diversity and inclusion, and how amazing it can be to meet and learn from young people from around the globe. I was a part of the inaugural CommUNITY program in McCormick, which brought young men and women from around the world together, and we took classes and lived with one another in an effort to learn more about each other's experiences. I am so grateful I had the opportunity to be a part of that program.

I didn't get too involved extracurricular activities at Marquette—everything I did revolved around working for the *Marquette Tribune*, and developing relationships with my teammates at the newspaper. I felt safe there. It was nice being around other introverts who were more focused with putting their words down on paper versus saying them aloud to others. During my time there, I was probably the only Black person on staff, but I was OK with that—most of my academic career, I've normally been the only Black person, so I never felt out of place or uncomfortable. The paper opened up the world of sports photojournalism to me, something I fell in love with right away. Shooting basketball, soccer, volleyball and lacrosse games felt second nature to me, and I became really good at it. I knew it was something I wanted to do professionally, but the "real world" made me go down a different world with my career.

Many people ask me from time to time if I'd go back to Marquette if I could do it all over again. It's a tough question to answer—going somewhere else would erase all of the fantastic relationships that I built with my friends. And those relationships (and experiences) helped to make me who I am today. I also don't think I'd be as comfortable with travel and being independent had I not gone to school out of state (very out of state for me). Marquette helped me to develop the "figure it out" mentality. I had to learn how to solve problems on my own, and not rely on others helping me achieve my goals. Even now, every job I've ever had has come from my hustling to get it. I've never had someone help me secure employment or an opportunity (although some folks did try). My drive to get what I want on a professional level all stems from my experience at Marquette—if I could make things happen on my own while I was there, I can make things happen anywhere!

And making things happen is just what I've done. After receiving my Bachelor of Arts in Communications from Marquette, I went on to earn my Master of Leadership (with a certificate in multicultural leadership) from North Central College; my Master of Science in Communications Management and a Master of Arts in Gender & Cultural Studies degrees from Simmons College; and I'm currently completing my dissertation tied to my Doctor of Organizational Leadership degree from Northeastern University. Professionally, I am the diversity, inclusion, and community investment officer for a large property and casualty insurance company headquartered in Boston, Massachusetts.

Evan Reed

Class of 2007

With a move to Milwaukee, Wisconsin, in 2001 and into my junior year of high school, I had not put much effort into where I would attend college as this was nothing no one spoke with me about. What I did know was that I would be attending college. New to Milwaukee, I quickly learned about the universities with rooted traditions in the state of Wisconsin. Atop the list of strong local schools was UW-Madison, where a senior trip quickly brought me into my reality. The large campus and 90-minute distance from Milwaukee showed me I had truly never been away from home and now was not the time to start. I desired to stay on campus, but also desired to be close to family in case they needed me or I needed them. Also, another top school in Marquette University with strong rooted traditions was in the heart of Milwaukee and only a 15-minute bus ride away from the place I had never been away from … home.

Marquette's profile was high due to its recent journey to the Final Four. The media attention caused me to research the school and with its proximity to home, MU was touted for its academic rigor while producing highly successful individuals throughout life with its focus on "Cura Personalis" or care for the whole person. Marquette felt like the right fit. I was accepted to Marquette and encouraged by a high school counselor to apply for the Educational Opportunity Program (EOP) into which I was also accepted. Naryan Leazer provided my interview for the program and saw my potential. To this day, I am grateful. I began at Marquette in the fall of '03 but have remained in contact with Mr. Leazer as he has become my certified financial advisor, attended my 2019 wedding, and professionally is a voting member of the Community Impact Committee at the Greater Milwaukee Foundation, where over $10 million in community grants are approved annually; I previously was a senior program officer at this foundation. Mr. Leazer's authenticity and commitment set a positive influence when entering Marquette that I have carried as a good way to live.

The 2003 summer was spent entering EOP at Marquette. The program gave some 40+ students the opportunity to attain the understanding of what the rigors of college would be like going into our first semester. This was truly a benefit as we were able to see that we could be successful with the coursework in a more patient environment. EOP allowed me to solidify relationships early on so that come fall, I was not a fish out of water. Many of those friendships nurtured in that first summer have lasted to this day with all my core friends (EOP and non-EOP) being from Marquette. Although 15 minutes from home, I did not want to be home. I stayed on campus with my first two years at O'Donnell Hall and the following at Campus Town East. I thoroughly enjoyed campus life. The primary highlight, which was not appreciated while in the moment, was having many of my friends living in this same space and time where we all enjoyed common moments, talks, events and life experiences together. As life has later taken its course many have moved overseas for work or live in different states, which in reflection made the time we were all in one place invaluable.

Although my EOP summer gave me hope of academic success, I feared a full course load entering the first semester still might weigh too much. I did not feel prepared by my high school education, and my socioeconomic status generated a false mental barrier that I was at a disadvantage. Learning in sociology the socioeconomic status many people are born into is the status they will likely be in all their lives did not help my confidence. In short, I feared I would not be successful. My focus was very intense during the first year at Marquette in order to do my best. Although many students were familiar with course work I was learning anew, the first year allowed me to realize we were all in the same courses together, and the work I put toward learning could alleviate the perceived disadvantage I thought I had. My first year was highly successful, giving me the confidence for my remaining tenure at Marquette without feeling unworthy academically. Although my feelings of disadvantages were more of my perception as it related to my academic ability, this statement does not equate to all people from disadvantageous backgrounds only having perceived barriers. For many of my colleagues, these barriers were real in academics, cultural climate and challenges associated with coming from poverty while seeking success in an environment where others were better resourced. I saw many classmates not return for a multitude of reasons of which a few bad choices on my end could have led to the same scenario.

Going into my sophomore year I had the pleasure of having the newly Robert B. Bell, Sr. Chair in Real Estate Professor Mark Eppli as my advisor. I entered the School of Business knowing a business career was in my future but had no guidance. A few advisory sessions with Professor Eppli where he showed a keen interest in my academic ability led to the pursuit of a double major in real estate and finance. This intention by Professor Eppli was the starting point to what has been an exciting career journey as an economic development professional and commercial real estate investor. Professionally, I began as a commercial real estate analyst, became a community lender at multiple community banks and organizations, led an economic development grant portfolio and impact investing program for the Greater Milwaukee Foundation, and currently am the regional director for Southeast Wisconsin for Forward Community Investments, Inc. My success to date is due to the support of EOP and Professor Eppli.

Finally, if I had to choose again, I would not change anything. As I previously stated, Marquette felt like the right fit and it was. Although feeling like I was entitled to my acceptance by the university at the time, looking in the rearview, the gift of a Marquette education is valued and appreciated. The education truly lives up to the values of shaping the whole person through the selection of courses, professors hired and the intentionality of critical thought woven into the academia. As I felt unprepared for the rigors of college coursework entering the university, I was ready to take on life upon graduation. Learning to follow my peace in decision making began at Marquette. My professional aptitude began at Marquette. My best friends are from Marquette. I began this narrative first as a reflection of my time at Marquette, but I finish as a THANK YOU, MARQUETTE.

Courtney Ofosu

Class of 2008

I graduated from Marquette nearly twelve years ago. Even so, pieces of the college will remain with me for decades to come.

At Marquette, I met some of my closest friends. I met my husband there. Indeed, it was the people at MU who most positively impacted my life. This is perhaps because "community" is a reverberating Marquette theme. But community did not organically happen for me. Unlike many of my classmates, I had to search for it, seek it out.

I began my freshman year in 2004 in the honors program. As an honors student, I lived in Straz Tower with a small, select group of freshmen with whom I would take core classes for the next four years. The honors program was right up my alley. We wrote and mused on the words of Homer, Brontë, Ralph Ellison and others. We tried to construct frameworks for ethics and social justice using Aristotle, Aquinas and Kant's teachings.

While the honors program kept me intellectually engaged, it was socially isolating. As far as I could tell, I was the only Black student in the program. I do not recall being asked to hang out with my freshman honors colleagues.

To remedy this isolation, I branched out and spent more time at McCormick Hall (may it rest in peace) adopting the friends of a friend. In due time, I met people who remain my closest friends today.

I also joined the Black Student Union (BSU) to foster community. It was energizing to see so many students who looked like me, who at times faced similar challenges as me and who included me.

Studying abroad in Madrid also gave me the opportunity to build on my community. For six months, my fellow Spanish students and I experienced being foreigners together. At the start, we bonded over our inability to accomplish simple tasks like ordering breakfast in Spanish at the local café in the rapid cadence Madrid demanded. Together we watched soccer matches, explored the seemingly endless avenues that boasted architecture older than America itself, and drank sangria in clandestine, smoke-filled bars. When our study abroad ended, we no longer felt foreign. The Spanish city became our collective second home, a place we were reluctant to leave. Marquette en Madrid was an experience that tied us together.

I carry the lessons I learned from Marquette with me. After graduating, I attended law school at the University of Illinois and forged community there by, among other things, serving on the Black Law Students Association board. After law school, I worked as a litigator at large law firms in Chicago. As a law firm lawyer, I recruited diverse law students and promoted inclusion to help ensure that law students and lawyers of color could experience "community" within a setting that has often lacked diversity.

Since Marquette, my life has evolved and expanded. I went from a wide-eyed college kid to a law student, lawyer, wife and mother. Throughout that transition, Marquette has remained with me. It manifests itself in the friends that I made there and kept all these years, in the man I married, in the lessons I learned about forging community in spaces and places that seemed closed off to me. Most poignantly, Marquette is now the place my niece will call home for four years. My hope is that MU students, faculty and others who came before her (myself included), have helped make community at Marquette more visible, inclusive and inviting. And I have every confidence that she too will embrace MU's mantra and be the difference for someone who comes after her.

Dr. George E. Koonce, Jr.

PhD, 2012

From the Locker Room to the Board Room

I, George Earl Koonce, Jr., came from a poor rural town in Eastern North Carolina. I worked hard and now my dreams had come true as I was now wearing a Super Bowl XXXI ring! I married my beautiful wife Tunisia, and we had two beautiful children. But I was getting older. My body had taken its toll. Although my mind was still there in the locker room and my body longed to be on the field, I didn't get the call to continue playing in the NFL. I must admit that was hard and a shock to my system. I lost it to a degree. It was all I knew. All I wanted to do. My wife Tunisia had faith in me and showed me that my life was just beginning, and I was much more than a football player.

Shortly after we found out Tunisia, who was only 35, had stage 4 breast cancer. I had a job offer at Marquette, and there was a cancer hospital there in Milwaukee that was one of the best in Wisconsin. We needed hope, we needed support. I prayed and God brought us to Marquette University.

Growing up in Eastern North Carolina, the Church was the fabric of our community. So religion was a vital part for me choosing Marquette University to work and to further my education. I knew I needed guidance, so I prayed and trusted the path that was provided to me, Marquette University.

My wife passed away during the middle of my PhD program. I was devastated but never alone. I was provided with such a wonderful, caring, support system that I desperately needed to complete my doctoral program. I will be forever indebted to Marquette University, Dr. John Cotton, Professor Martin Greenberg, Dr. Richard Jones and Dr. James Holstein and Marquette's alumna Mrs. Valerie Wilson Reed, who was my rock and taught me how to breathe again. So much gratitude to Mr. Greg Kliebhan for helping me to be the wind beneath my late wife's wings. Her service was in Eastern North Carolina, and seven representatives and alumni from Marquette were in attendance to support me through a very painful and difficult time.

How do you prepare to go from the locker room to the board room? How do you get there? I wanted to know! Well, let me tell you that one of the reasons I am where and who I am today is because of my time at Marquette University and Milwaukee, Wisconsin. Marquette University, the professors, students, many who became and still are friends. I felt at home. I was no longer a player for the Green Bay Packers or in the NFL. I must admit I thought I was experienced and knowledgeable, but I was not educated. I never imagined how much I would learn from Marquette that football and life couldn't teach me. Marquette trained me how to think.

I was a non-traditional student. I worked at Marquette University for seven years and was so inspired by those around me that I took classes in their PhD program during that time. My professors went above and beyond to get me into the program, and they worked even harder to see that I persisted through the rigors of their PhD program. It was all up to me, but I had a wonderful support system. Marquette provided me with an ecosystem of support. I graduated May 20th of 2012 with a Doctor of Philosophy.

Today I am Dr. George E. Koonce, Jr., proud husband to my beautiful, inspiring wife Gina. I have been blessed with a wonderful family. I serve as Senior Vice President for the Office of University Relations for Marian University.

I am honored to be a member of the Green Bay Packers Board of Directors and many other boards that help our community and youth. When we give back, we are the ones who receive the blessings.

I can honestly say that I'm not sure where or who I would be today without the guidance and family I found at Marquette University.

Toby Baker

Communications, Class of 2013

As a husband of one, son of two, father of three, and a brother of six, and now becoming one of 100 Black Americans, it's a blessing to be any one of these, let alone have the honor of being an alumnus of Marquette University. The school and its community have granted me access to some of the most life-altering experiences, enlightening conversations and has embedded skills that I use in my career. Here's my story ...

In 2008, I was a freshman attending the city's junior college, Milwaukee Area Technical College. Eager to make an impact, I started an organization teaching young men how to wear suits and tie their ties. At times, I would challenge them to articulate their thoughts, even through speeches. I too gave speeches to neighborhood schools. Then, I was invited to Marquette to speak to some of its students. I was blown away by the experience, the friendliness of people and the feeling of being on campus. I decided to jump off the deep end and apply for Marquette University.

I was denied!

There was no transfer program from MATC to Marquette at that time, so it was not the norm. Yet, I was determined to make it happen. I improved my grades and strategically selected courses based only on if they would transfer to Marquette. I also started to visit Marquette's campus events like the School of Communication's impromptu comedy club, which was only the tip of the iceberg of its student organization offerings. The school just received a significant contribution from an alumnus and began improving their resources, like the cameras for the campus' news station. I loved the environment and really wanted to come now. So in 2009 I applied again. Yet again ...

I was denied!

Frustrated at the results, I framed this denial letter and placed it on top of my television. Each and every time I pressed on the power button, I was forced to see this denial letter. Then it hit me, Press On! That TV's power button became my podium of motivation and above it was the resting place for a document that dared me to Push On! Denial was not going to get the best of me

I pondered how to proceed, prayed about it and consulted with others. I made the decision to fully engulf myself into the Marquette experience. By this time, I was on campus more than the school I attended! Making new friends, eating alongside students in the residence halls and becoming a member of multiple student organizations. I felt so much more confident around this time, and so I applied again. Yet, this time was different ...

I was accepted!

All my friends on campus were so thrilled that I was "official." It's one of those experiences that, even to this day, we still reminisce about. That summer remains one of my life's most memorable treasures because in that same year, I found my jewel.

While applying to Marquette, I was attending an on-campus comedy show. During intermission, I left to find a bite to eat near 16th & Wells and was accidentally introduced by a mutual friend to a beautiful young lady named Diamond, who was the student president of one of the campus's many faith-based organizations. Since the moment we met, I knew she was the one! Yet nothing I said or did that night could influence her to make eye contact with me. That short introduction ended with so-longs, and after finding out she was graduating that semester, it felt like goodbye forever …

Until I saw her that fall. A fellow student, who I'm still friends with today, invited me to an event a couple of blocks off of campus. On the way to that event, I had a flat tire and considered going back home. However, I decided to Press On. Upon arriving at the event, I was ecstatic to see the host for that evening's event … it was her! I most certainly didn't want her to get away again, and well, long story short, she didn't. We became friends, and two years later, we were married. And yes, we took the traditional Marquette alumni wedding photo with all the Marquette attendees! I credit the vibrant student body and their student-led events for helping me to find my beautiful bride of ten years and counting.

Though great in reputation, the small size of the campus makes it inevitable to meet new faces and reconnect with old acquaintances. The tight culture of Marquette's campus community extends beyond graduation. Whether it's interviewing an alumnus in the workforce, grabbing coffee or lunch with an old classmate or going over to greet the alum wearing Marquette apparel in a random airport, the desire to connect with a Golden Eagle or Warrior is ever present. It's so refreshing to be a part of a community where the year of graduation has little to no barrier on conversations that are had between so many. The feeling of being one united family never fades.

Self-directed learning is the same way. I was once told that once a mind has been expanded, it cannot return to its original state. I was challenged to teach myself how to learn at Marquette. A skill that has not faded. During one of the many late studying sessions, I hit a wall. I was sitting in Eckstein Hall, reading about the Socratic method, and the material wasn't sticking. After a short pause for prayer, I locked my gaze with a painting, hanging ten feet in front of me. It was Abraham Lincoln sitting and gazing in deep thought. In the bottom right-hand corner, there was an inscription. The gist of the message stated, "What takes a person months, years, or even a lifetime to put into a book, you can consume in a matter of hours." Then it hit me. I can extract years of implemented and refined knowledge of experts and do so at a much faster rate! I immediately started looking for books to start with and stumbled across a book by former Princeton professor Cornel West. Within it was a collection of essays, one of them being about "Black Intellectuals." At that time, I'd never seen, heard, or believed those two words could be in that sequence! After all, the peers from during my K–12 years made it clear that being brilliant is not cool and therefore it's something to remain hidden. From that day forward, I made sure to no longer hide it. That was an old belief that I outgrew, and so I decided to Press On. And that's cooler than keeping a lamp (of knowledge) under a bushel.

There were many individuals who walked me through, encouraged and helped me along the way. Professors, other alumni and even fellow students inspired me to press on regularly and aided my zeal to keep pressing on. That symbolic lesson that I captured from that old green TV was to Press On. While I still may catch a show or two from time to time, I now take more pleasure in growing my career, being a great father and loving husband, being a great supporter of my siblings and being about to read about the other honorable African American alums.

For those who are afraid to move forward, Press On.

For those who feel there's something holding you back, Press On.

If there's a door, go through it, and if not, create your own entrances, but always remember, there is power in pressing on.

Marissa Evans

Class of 2013

My first lesson on the reality of being a Black journalist happened at *The Marquette Tribune*.

It was spring 2012. I was applying to become editor-in-chief of the university's student newspaper. I had worked there for two years and was news editor at the time, had multiple newsroom internships under my belt—and, most important, was determined to make history. I wanted to be the first Black woman to lead in *The Tribune*'s nearly 100-year history, and for my face to be among the sea of white male editor faces in books and on the walls of Johnston Hall. The only other Black person to hold the title was Ron Smith. That was in 1989.

I had big plans for *The Tribune*. I wanted to bring in my newsroom recruiter contacts to help more MU students land internships. I wanted to recruit more students of color on staff, and to help commuter students balance getting the clips they needed and safely catching the last bus home at night. I wanted to see more students report from across Milwaukee. I dreamed about redesigning the paper and its website. I was eager to see *The Tribune* become on par with *The Daily Californian* at the University of California-Berkeley, *The Daily Northwestern* at Northwestern University or *The Daily Orange* at Syracuse University. I wanted our student journalism to matter and to see our paper be more competitive in national awards competitions.

But I didn't get the job. A board of faculty and student media leaders picked a younger, white male student lead. He had far less journalism experience, but he was more well-liked by our peers and wasn't seen as demanding or difficult—that all-too-common trope that limits the ascension of hypercompetent Black female leaders. I did not return to *The Tribune* my senior year. I did not want to take direction from someone less qualified for the job I knew I deserved.

I'm sure people around at the time will say my failed candidacy had "nothing to do with race." So many of my white peers had rarely interacted with Black people before we arrived on campus, never mind actually working or leading alongside them. Losing out on that job hardened me. I resolved to never apologize for wanting more for myself and for Black people.

It's a curious thing to always know you were denied a chance to make history. It's painful to have to bite your tongue and show grace in the face of that denial. Beyond that, there's the question of what might have been, and what it would have meant for future Black students to see my photo among the editors-in-chief on that third floor wall. How many more would have joined the newspaper because they saw someone who looked like them? But that is the reality of being Black and having the courage to try and lead. You always have to keep failure in mind.

My four years at Marquette were spent asking questions too many young Black women must ask: When will I be enough? Qualified enough? Smart enough? Kind enough? Pretty enough? Financially independent enough? Available enough? Non-emotional enough? The list goes on. Years after graduating and having success as a journalist, I'm still searching for those answers.

Marquette became rooted in my family when my oldest brother received a copy of its glossy admissions catalog in the mail while in high school in the early 2000s. We were a middle class family in suburban San Diego. My parents had always urged my two brothers and me to seek new adventures and opportunities. They were not the type to insist we stay close to home, especially if going far away would help us to make the most of ourselves.

I remember the hopefulness and excitement in my father's eyes when he handed me the gold envelope containing my MU acceptance letter. I still have that letter, and remain touched by the tinges of blue ink emphasizing how much my application impressed the admissions office. As I decided where to go to college, my father said repeatedly, "Go where you're wanted."

My time at Marquette was filled with endless classes, extracurriculars, working to make ends meet and career development opportunities. In addition to student media, I was a resident assistant for two years, restarted a student chapter of the National Association of Black Journalists, and always vied for my next reporting internship. I often felt like a ball of yarn, wrapped in strings of homework, clubs, family, friends, mentorship, financial concerns, all while developing my sense of self-worth, tempering my emotions and more. I couldn't afford to unravel. Too many people expected and or depended on me to keep my string together—no matter how much fuzz showed on the surface. Marquette taught me how to keep myself together.

One of my journalism professors in particular, Herbert Lowe, demanded my excellence—often during our 8 a.m. meetings in his office—whether I felt like rising to his expectations or not. As one of the two Black male teachers I ever had, he was trying to prepare me to be a leader. (My other Black male professor was also at Marquette—Father Bryan Massingale, for a theology class about the times and philosophies of the Rev. Martin Luther King and Malcolm X.) Mr. Lowe saw my potential and knew that tough love—though he would frown upon calling it love —was critical if I wanted to be a better journalist, leader and advocate for others.

Mr. Lowe was always there for me and countless other Black students who needed guidance, accountability, encouragement and personal clarity. He was there in 2010, when I held the medals on stage as six of the revered Little Rock Nine received the Père Marquette Discovery Award, the university's highest honor. He coached me when I was NABJ chapter president on how to pitch Lori Bergen, dean of the Diederich College of Communication, to pay for our student registrations and travel to a regional conference held at Northwestern.

We went over my talking points for pitching Dean Bergen to send the chapter to the 2013 NABJ conference in Orlando. He advised my campaign for the student representative's seat on the NABJ board of directors in 2011. My opponent and I tied, leading to the association's first election run-off. After I lost, Mr. Lowe was the first to call and to say he was proud I ran. He and his wife Mira Lowe were also the first to offer congratulations when NABJ named me its student journalist of the year in 2013. They were there when I introduced Dean Bergen at my college commencement. That weekend was the first time my family was able to visit me in Milwaukee.

Marquette also taught me to advocate for myself and ask for what I needed. But the resulting physical, emotional and mental toll often left me drained each weekend; often it meant staying in on Saturdays and Sundays to catch up on classwork and sleep. I regularly visited the financial aid office to ask if I was maximizing all that I was eligible for. Educational Opportunity Program Director Sande Robinson helped me to get into her program during my early years at Marquette.

Those funds helped me to stay in school. Another memorable moment: I was in DC for my internship at *The Washington Post* and short a few hundred dollars for my summer housing. I knew I could not ask my parents for help. Mr. Lowe suggested that I write an email to Dean Bergen about my situation. Without hesitation, she found a donor who gave me the money.

Over time, as was the case for many MU students hailing from states far from Wisconsin, Milwaukee became home. I was lucky to not be stuck in the "Marquette bubble." My best friend, Vanessa Harris, was from a Black middle class family in Milwaukee. We still laugh about how I had vowed, even before meeting her in person, that she would soon be my best friend. That was on the basis that she was Black, a journalism major, and in her Facebook photos looked like a kind person. There were many day trips on the bus around the city and—given I could not afford to go home to California for the holiday—special Thanksgiving weekends with her family.

Milwaukee was also my career launching pad. After graduation, I moved to DC for a health reporting fellowship with *Kaiser Health News*, then soon covered health policy and state legislatures for CQ Roll Call, the congressional news service. I then joined *The Texas Tribune*, an online news service based in Austin, and got to work on an award-winning project that held state lawmakers accountable for doing too little to prevent mothers from dying after childbirth.

I traveled to Poland through a Pulitzer Center on Crisis Reporting grant to write for *The Tribune* about what Texas could learn about preventing maternal mortality. That series won a 2018 Online News Association award for explanatory reporting. I'm also proud that my reporting about an ongoing mold problem forced the Texas Health and Human Services Commission to close one of its buildings and to relocate 127 state workers.

These days, I'm a reporter at the *Star Tribune* in Minneapolis, where I interned after my sophomore year in college. I'm writing about housing, race and other social issues in the Twin Cities, talking to tenants facing evictions and helping Minnesotans reckon with inequalities. I'm also one of several journalists of color penning our diversity demands to be delivered to our newsroom leaders in the aftermath of the George Floyd protests.

I am proud to say that my disappointment at not being named editor-in-chief at *The Marquette Tribune* did not deter me or my ambition. I marvel at how being in Milwaukee—including my time reporting for the Milwaukee Neighborhood News Service, an online operation that covered inner city communities—taught me about empathy, systemic issues and choosing compassion when it comes to understanding the complexities of others. Those lessons continue to affect how I approach stories about marginalized communities, and how society can tackle the most pressing issues of our time: racism, housing, homelessness, hunger, poverty and policing.

Milwaukee helped me to see that the world and its problems are so much bigger than me and my dreams. By choosing Marquette, by heeding my father's advice and going where I was wanted, even if it was 2,118 miles from home, I found myself and learned how to be part of the solution.

Arthur Jones

Communications, Class of 2017

When choosing Marquette, I was mainly looking at location, where I could have a school closer to home, and also looking for financial aid support, especially coming from two working class parents. I chose Marquette over California Lutheran University because of the financial support, the ability to be closer to home and the ability to be a part of a metropolitan city versus a college town.

I grew up with mainly Baptist roots, and my father's family was Catholic. I do think it aided my parents in trusting that I was having a balance between the real world and a spiritual world. For me personally, it was not a huge factor because I attended public school for my entire life. Marquette has a wonderful reputation for being a Jesuit institution and my parents felt comfortable about the positive influence it would have in my life.

The fact that the student body was overwhelmingly white was not particularly a part of my decision-making process in choosing Marquette. However, for my parents, this was a part of the "sell factor"; knowing I was going to a well-recognized university, in which I could assimilate. Unfortunately, race still comes up, especially in my career path.

I did not know anyone prior to attending Marquette. But the legendary alumni names of Ralph H. Metcalfe, Sr., Dwayne Wade, Doc Rivers and Rondell Sheridan were a big draw. I respected their careers, and they served as role models for me.

I was a non-EOP student. I am proud of my parents who were blue-collar, and both worked in private sector operations. My mother went back to school when I was in the third grade. So, I did not qualify as an EOP scholar. I would have liked the opportunity—just to have another support system to help guide me through the world of higher education. Also, this led to a lot of assumptions from my white counterparts because most of them thought I was an EOP scholar.

My first-year dorm experience was mixed. I lived in McCormick Hall; however, the guys on my floor were good about embracing me and welcoming me to dinners, going to the gym, studying, etc. Second year was a little different because I lived in Mashuda Hall, and it was further away from campus. During this time, I really learned more about the city and made friends with people off campus, which aided in me learning more about the city of Milwaukee. Years three and four were the times I felt like I "fit in." In those first two years, I did make a lot of strides, but they did not come to fruition until failure occurred, and in doing so, I rose over the occasion and came back better than ever. Then my professors took me more seriously, and appreciated my "hustler," I-can-do-anything sort of attitude.

There were a number of professors who were caring and concerned about my education and well-being. Timothy Cigelske always has seen me for EVERYTHING I am, and EVERYTHING I do. Linda Menck was always supportive, an ally and willing to give advice, even when I did not want it. Dr. Jodi Melamed was a great listener and advocate, who was willing to do anything to see her students become better lifelong learners and active citizens. Herb Lowe, my version of Mr. Mason in Cooley High. He always saved my hide, always kept it real and always reminded me to give 120%. The late Dr. John Pauly was another advocate who saw me for the potential I had, and did his best to keep an open door, open ear and heart. Dr. Gee Ekachai, though not super vocal, was in my corner and was supportive of my career path.

Several classes at Marquette that have influenced my life: African American literature (Jodi Melamed), Arabic literature (Enaya Otham), social media analytics/media writing (Tim Cigelske), theology—nonviolence and violence and mobile communication (Linda Menck). All of these courses allowed me to learn more about my passions, allowed me to become a more worldly thinker and allowed my creative spirit to continue to grow and develop.

There are three memorable experiences during my time at Marquette—the sad day I had to withdraw from classes for a semester because of poor academic performance, the great memory of the day I returned and the joyous day I graduated! I am a true example that if you have setbacks, you get back up, work harder and can succeed.

If I had to do my Marquette experience all over again from start to finish, I would. As a recent graduate, I have yet to crown my greatest achievement which is to become a VP of communications or brand manager; but just watch me soar!

Photographs

Mabel Watson
Raimey, one of
the earliest known
African American
Students, 1927

Ralph H. Metcalfe, Sr., circa 1935

Betty and Jon Washington at Marquette, 1953

Gloria Sylvester Bennett, 1953   Joy Bennett, 1977

Marquette University Cheerleaders, 1977. Courtney and Constance Bennett in front row on the right

Marquette University Cheerleaders in the old gymnasium, 1977-1978. Courtney Bennett is on Mike DiMino on the left, her twin sister Connie Bennett is on Terry Baker on the right, and Rondell Sheridan is the third man from the right

© Marquette University Raynor Memorial Libraries Special Collections and Archives

Maurice "Bo" Ellis poses for photograph on a vintage Mercedes-Benz at the Brooks Stevens Automotive Museum, 1977

© Marquette University Raynor Memorial Libraries Special Collections and Archives

Marquette men's basketball team, 1976-1977, at Brooks Stevens Automotive Museum. Pictured (from left): Jim Boylan, Bill Neary, Ulice Payne, Butch Lee, Jim Dudley, Gary Rosenberger, Bernard Toone, Jerome Whitehead, Craig Butrym, Robert Byrd, and Bo Ellis

Marquette Dorm Days, Carpenter Tower Hall, 1977

Marquette
Social Club,
circa 1979

Sharon Irving, 1980

Marquette President John P. Raynor, SJ, with Charlotte Broaden, 1985

MU Kappa Alpha Psi, circa 1986

James Austin and
parents at his Marquette
graduation, 1998

Founding members of the Ethnic Alumni Association (EAA), 2001: (kneeling
L - R) Henry Vasquez, Deshea Agee and Floyd Williams. (Standing L-R): Tim
Mahone, Douglas Kelley, Valerie Wilson Reed, Thomas Kelly, and Keith Reid

Shellisa Multrie,
graduation day,
2004

The Ethnic Alumni Association (EAA) 5th Reunion, 2006. Valerie Wilson Reed,
Cathy Stamps Covington, Yvonne Johnson, and Sheri Colas Gervais

Karma Rogers,
Agnes Johnson,
Felicia Mabuza-Suttle,
and Sande Robinson

Evan Reed,
Fallon Hollis,
and Shirley
Knowles

George Koonce
at his doctoral
degree conferment
ceremony, 2012

Valerie Wilson Reed (class of 1979) with her daughter, Francesca Reed Cianciolo, at Francesca's 2014 graduation ceremony

Raullo Eanes (class of 1989), Marlena Eanes (class of 2014), and Gina Eanes (class of 1989)

Valerie Wilson Reed and Rev. Robert A. Wild, SJ, at the Ethnic Alumni Association reunion, 2018

Syb Brown after receiving her College of Communications By-Line Award, 2018

Valerie Wilson Reed and Dr. Michael Lovell at the All University Service to Marquette Award dinner, 2018

Robert Simpson, Regina Dixon-Reeves, Douglas Kelley,
Valerie Wilson Reed, and Kevin Ingram, 2018

Rachelle Shurn, Valerie Wilson Reed, Janice Wilburn, Linda Hickombottom,
Ingrid Jagers, Moya Baylis, and Brittany Warren at the Big East Woman's
Basketball Tournament, Chicago, 2018

Kevin Walker, Minnie Williams, and George Lowery at the Educational Opportunity Program (EOP) Reunion, 2019

Dr. Gary Nunn, Dr. George Lowery, and Dr. Anthony Caceras, EOP Reunion, 2019

Robert Simpson, Sande Robinson, and Alderman Willie Hines at the EOP Reunion, 2019

William Coffer, Jr., Class of 1967 (circa 2020)

233